Illegal Markets and the Economics of Organized Crime

This book showcases recent advances in the theoretical and empirical understanding of the economic aspects of organized crime and illegal markets. It provides new insights into defining and quantifying the influence of organized crime by drawing on innovative approaches to studying criminal networks and organizations such as the Hells Angels. The book also includes analysis of the structure of illegal drug markets from international leaders in the field, both at the retail and at the wholesale level. Finally the book proposes two empirical case studies examining the organization of illegal wildlife trafficking.

This book was based on a special issue of *Global Crime*.

Martin Bouchard is an Assistant Professor at the School of Criminology, Simon Fraser University. He received his PhD from the Université de Montréal in 2006. His work specialises in the organization of illegal drug markets and on examining the role of social capital in criminal careers. Other areas of interest include social network analysis, street gang delinquency, and methodologies to estimate the size of criminal populations. Recent work on illegal drug markets appeared in *Contemporary Drug Problems*, *Global Crime*, *Journal of Quantitative Criminology*, *Journal of Drug Issues*, *Justice Quarterly*, and *International Journal of Drug Policy*.

Chris Wilkins is a senior researcher at the Centre for Social and Health Outcomes Research and Evaluation (SHORE), Massey University, Auckland, New Zealand. He has special expertise in illegal drug research with a particular interest in the economics of illegal drug markets and organized crime. Dr. Wilkins has published articles in *Addiction*, *Drug & Alcohol Review*, *De Economist*, *Contemporary Drug Problems* and the *International Journal of Drug Policy*.

I0891120

Illegal Markets and the Economics of Organized Crime

Edited by Martin Bouchard and Chris Wilkins

Routledge
Taylor & Francis Group
LONDON AND NEW YORK

First published 2010 by Routledge
2 Park Square, Milton Park, Abingdon, Oxon, OX14 4RN

Simultaneously published in the USA and Canada
by Routledge
711 Third Avenue, New York, NY 10017

Routledge is an imprint of the Taylor & Francis Group, an informa business

First issued in paperback 2012

Typeset in Times by Value Chain, India

British Library Cataloguing in Publication Data
A catalogue record for this book is available from the British Library

ISBN13: 978-0-415-63397-0

CONTENTS

Abstracts

INTRODUCTION: Illegal markets and the economics of organized crime

Martin Bouchard and Chris Wilkins

We highlight how the different studies included in this special issue contribute to our understanding of illegal markets and the economics of organized crime. A focus on the 'economics' of organized crime brings attention to the outcomes (costs and benefits), but also to the process leading to these outcomes, including analyses of the markets where criminal organizations are active.

What is a criminal organization and why does the law care?

Philip A. Curry and Steeve Mongrain

The Criminal Codes in both Canada and the United States allow for criminals to be penalized to a greater degree if they are a member of an organization. We draw on the economic theory of punishment, which states that expected penalty should be proportional to the social harm caused, to put a different perspective on such regulations. According to the economic theory, additional punishments are desirable if either: (1) the social harm from a criminal act is greater for a member of an organization than for an independent criminal; or (2) the probability of conviction is lower. We examine the extent to which both of these possibilities are true and use the findings to revisit the definition of a criminal organization.

The size and influence of a criminal organization: a criminal achievement perspective

Pierre Tremblay, Martin Bouchard and Sévrine Petit

It is difficult to measure the size, influence and growth patterns of criminal organizations embedded in illegal markets. In this paper, we argue that measuring the influence of a criminal organization by its size (in number of employees, or 'members') may under- or overestimate its sphere of influence in illegal markets. Self-report survey and size of population methodologies are combined to assess the regional economic influence of a criminal organization (Hells Angels) in three illegal drug markets (the cocaine trade, the cannabis trade and the cannabis cultivation industry) in the province of Québec. Findings suggest that a relatively small organization by conventional standards can nonetheless achieve a large influence on criminal markets. We then analyse how factors other than violence play a role in explaining differences in achieving economic influence across criminal organizations. Finally, we suggest that turning our attention to measuring economic influence provides some insights into the duration and intensity of the violent conflicts occurring in these markets.

Understanding optimal criminal networks

Stephen T. Easton and Alexander K. Karaivanov

We develop a theory of optimal networks in the context of criminal organizations. In this framework the criminals choose their network links with others according to a set of specified costs and benefits to participation. The optimal number and configuration of links within each network is solved for a set of 10,000 parameter simulations specifying the direct cost of links between agents, the benefit to connections, and the cost of being in the network with others. In addition, agents determine the size of the optimal network. This framework allows consideration of a variety of crime policy scenarios. In particular, removing the 'key player', the best strategy when the network is exogenous, may not be the optimal strategy in an environment in which the agents can change the size and structure of the network endogenously. More generally, optimal crime policy may be different if the criminals are aware of the policing strategy and can alter their network.

How illegal drugs enter an island country: insights from interviews with incarcerated smugglers

Jonathan P. Caulkins, Honora Burnett and Edward Leslie

A typology of drug smuggling 'technologies' is developed based on interviews with 110 inmates incarcerated in UK prisons for importing illegal drugs. Approximately three-quarters were involved in courier-based operations. The other 30 collectively accounted for substantially greater smuggling throughput capacity and fell into five groups: operations employing 'bent' lorry drivers; shipping drugs intermingled with legitimate commerce; transporting drugs on commercial airlines with assistance from corrupt officials; mailing drugs into the UK; and smuggling via boats landing between ports of entry. A Pareto Law seems to apply, with a minority of respondents being responsible for the majority of the smuggling. Most participated in smuggling to make money, but more than a few couriers reported being coerced and/or tricked into carrying drugs. Perhaps not coincidentally, rough calculations suggest that, when balancing profits against prison risk, crime does not pay for couriers but can for organizations employing bent lorry drivers.

Economic analysis of drug transaction 'cycles' described by incarcerated UK drug dealers

Jonathan P. Caulkins, Benjamin Gurga and Christopher Little

The fundamental activity of most drug dealers is buying drugs from a supplier and selling them on, usually in smaller lot sizes to multiple customers at a lower market level. Data on such 'cycles' of purchase and resale are derived from interviews with 65 dealers incarcerated in UK prisons. A power function relationship between price and transaction size is confirmed. Analyses reveal great consistency in proportional price markups across drugs and time, high cycle frequencies (typically weekly or more often) and importers who vertically integrate into the highest level of domestic distribution, so that an important share of their net revenues effectively derives from domestic distribution inside the UK, as opposed to importation *per se*.

The market for crystalline methamphetamine in Sydney, Australia

Rebecca McKetin, Jennifer McLaren, Erin Kelly and Jenny Chalmers

The market for domestically produced methamphetamine in Australia (sold as 'speed' and 'base') has been recently supplemented with imported crystalline methamphetamine ('ice' or 'crystal'), the supply of which is thought to involve different organized crime groups than those involved with domestic supply. The existence, or otherwise, of distinct retail markets for these different forms of methamphetamine has important implications for police and public health strategies. The aim of this study was to examine whether there was evidence of distinct retail markets for crystalline methamphetamine and domestically produced forms of the drug. A cross-sectional survey of regular methamphetamine users (n = 309) was undertaken in Sydney, Australia to assess the characteristics of the retail market (consumption, price, perceived purity, availability, purchase location and sale from dealers) for crystalline methamphetamine compared with domestically produced forms of the drug (i.e. speed and base). We did not find any clear evidence of a segregated retail market for crystalline methamphetamine. Only 3% of participants were exclusive crystalline methamphetamine users, and both crystalline methamphetamine and other domestically produced forms of the drug were readily available to consumers, being typically purchased from the same dealers, in the same location and at the same price.

The black market in China for tiger products

Brendan Moyle

Poaching of tigers is a major threat to the survival of the species. China is responsible for much of the demand for tiger parts. Poaching occurs because it is profitable and organizations able to procure transport and sell tiger products over thousands of miles and international borders also exist. Unfortunately there is little corresponding data on these organizations. It appears as if these organizations operate to minimize the most significant transaction cost along the supply chain. Tigers are a minority element in a portfolio of wildlife products assembled by smugglers in range states. Within China smugglers specialize in the skins and bones of tigers, and are most likely to operate in small, discrete groups. This is a function of the high coordination and evasion costs of operating in China. The demand for tiger parts has strong cultural and medicinal influences.

Exploring the organization of Russia Far East's illegal wildlife trade: two case studies of the illegal fur and illegal falcon trades

Tanya Wyatt

The Russian Federation is a source of wildlife and wildlife products that fuel the vast, and often overlooked, illegal wildlife trade that takes place around the globe. Out of the many illicit animal and plant trades, two of these black markets – the illegal fur trade and the illegal falcon trade – are used in this article to explore the organization of this illicit activity in Russia Far East. Using interviews from Russian and other wildlife trade experts, structural frameworks are established for each of these illegal wildlife markets.

Notes on Contributors

Martin Bouchard is an Assistant Professor at the School of Criminology, Simon Fraser University. He received his PhD from the Université de Montréal in 2006. His work specialises in the organization of illegal drug markets and on examining the role of social capital in criminal careers. Other areas of interest include social network analysis, street gang delinquency, and methodologies to estimate the size of criminal populations. Recent work on illegal drug markets appeared in *Contemporary Drug Problems*, *Global Crime*, *Journal of Quantitative Criminology*, *Journal of Drug Issues*, *Justice Quarterly*, and *International Journal of Drug Policy*.

Honora Q. Burnett, is an Associate at Deloitte & Touche Federal Practice, while finishing her Master of Science in Public Policy and Management from Carnegie Mellon University in Washington, DC. Burnett holds a Bachelor of Arts in History from Barnard College, Columbia University. Interests include the study of effective and efficient governing and fostering dialogue between community stakeholders and policy makers. Burnett participated in the Coro Fellowship in Pubic and Civic Affairs from 2006 to 2007.

Jonathan P. Caulkins, PhD, is Professor of Operations Research and Public Policy at Carnegie Mellon University's Qatar campus and Heinz School of Public Policy. Caulkins specializes in mathematical modelling and systems analysis with a focus on social policy systems pertaining to drugs, crime, terror, violence and prevention – work that won the David Kershaw Award from the Association of Public Policy Analysis and Management. Other interests include software quality, optimal control and personnel performance evaluation. At RAND he has been a consultant, visiting scientist, co-director of RAND's Drug Policy Research Center (1994–1996) and founding director of RAND's Pittsburgh office (1999–2001).

Dr Jenny Chalmers is a Senior Research Fellow in the Drug Policy Modelling Programme, University of New South Wales. She is currently researching the influence of drug prices on the patterns of drug consumption of methamphetamine users. She has a background in labour market economics and substantial experience in undertaking policy-relevant research in the fields of social policy and labour market disadvantage, the divide between good and bad jobs and the economics of gender.

Phil Curry is an Assistant Professor of Economics at Simon Fraser University. He received his PhD in economics from the University of Western Ontario in 2003. His research focuses on the economics of crime and microeconomic theory. He has published in such journals as the *Journal of Economics Theory*, the *Journal of Public Economics* and the *Canadian Journal of Economics*.

Stephen T. Easton received his PhD in Economics from the University of Chicago in 1978. While an economist he is also a part of the School for International Studies and is an Associate of the School of Criminology at Simon Fraser University. In addition to his work on networks and crime, he has also been involved in studying the marijuana industry in British Columbia and has written on matters describing the cost of crime, private prisons, legal aid and the state of the civil justice system in Canada. Outside of this work his publications have been in several areas including the economics of education, international trade and finance, and economic history.

Benjamin E. Gurga is a Data Analysis, Research and Evaluation Intern at the Allegheny County Department of Human Services in Pittsburgh, PA, while finishing his Master of Science in Public Policy and Management from Carnegie Mellon University in Pittsburgh, PA. Gurga holds a Bachelor of Arts in Political Studies from the School of Public Affairs and Administration, University of Illinois. Interests include operations research, particularly in the public sector, and application of computer science methods to public policy problems.

Alexander Karaivanov received his PhD in Economics from the University of Chicago in 2003. In addition to his work on networks and crime he works on problems of development economics, contract theory and applied microeconomics. Recent research involves solving, structurally estimating and testing competing theoretical models of financial market imperfections using data from Thailand. Other projects of his include learning in principal-agent models and the effect on inequality on public goods provision.

Erin Kelly is an Intern Clinical Psychologist and Research Officer at the National Drug and Alcohol Research Centre, University of New South Wales. Her previous research experience includes work on drug driving, the illicit methamphetamine market and a longitudinal study on methamphetamine treatment outcomes. She is now working as a psychologist on intervention trials, including a psychological intervention for methamphetamine dependence and comorbid depression.

Edward C. Leslie, is an Analyst in the Professional Development Program at the United States Government Accountability Office, currently evaluating efficacy of requirements for federal rulemaking on the Strategic Issues team. Leslie holds a Master of Science in Public Policy and Management from The Heinz School at Carnegie Mellon University and a Bachelor of Arts in Economics from Whittier College. Interests include the study and practice of managerial issues related to international development and healthcare. Leslie served in the Peace Corps in Western Honduras from 2003 to 2005 as an Economic Development Volunteer.

Christopher D. Little, is concurrently pursuing his Master of Science in Public Policy and Management at Carnegie Mellon University and his Juris Doctor at the School of Law at the University of Pittsburgh. Little holds a Bachelor of Arts in Business Economics from the University of California, Santa Barbara. Interests include drug policy, environmental policy, and international trade law.

Rebecca McKetin is a Senior Research Fellow at the National Drug and Alcohol Research Centre (NDARC), University of New South Wales, in Sydney, Australia. She runs a programme of research on methamphetamine use and related harms, which includes understanding the epidemiology of methamphetamine use, psychosis and violent behaviour among users and assessing treatment outcomes, and she has also undertaken research into Sydney's illicit methamphetamine market.

Jennifer McLaren is a Senior Research Officer at the National Drug and Alcohol Research Centre, University of New South Wales. She has conducted research on Sydney's illicit methamphetamine market, the potency and contamination of cannabis in Australia and cannabis and mental health, and was involved in the development of Australia's first National Cannabis Strategy. Prior to joining NDARC, Jennifer worked at The Smith Family in the Research and Social Policy Department.

Steeve Mongrain is an Associate Professor of Economics at Simon Fraser University and received his PhD from Queen's University in 1999. His research areas include public economics as well as the economics of crime. His publications include papers in the *International Economic Review*, the *Journal of Law, Economics & Organization*, the *Canadian Journal of Economics* and the *Scandinavian Journal of Economics*. Other areas of interest include the economics of morality laws and deterrence in tournament environments.

Brendan Moyle is a senior lecturer at Massey University, with joint qualifications in zoology and economics. He is a member of the IUCN-Sustainable Use Specialist Group and the IUCN-Crocodile Specialist Group. Since early 2007 he has been involved with tiger conservation in China.

Sévrine Petit is a doctoral student at the School of Criminology, Université de Montréal. Her research focuses on organized crime and criminal careers, with a special emphasis on outlaw bikers.

Pierre Tremblay is Professor at the School of Criminology, Université de Montréal. His current areas of interest include linking sub-cultural theories of crime and research on size of offender populations, and unifying anomie, social class and criminal achievement perspectives on criminal careers.

Dr Chris Wilkins is a senior researcher at the Centre for Social and Health Outcomes Research and Evaluation (SHORE), Massey University, Auckland, New Zealand. He has special expertise in illegal drug research with a particular interest in the economics of illegal drug markets and organized crime. In 2003 he was awarded a Fast-Start Marsden grant by the Royal Society of New Zealand to study organized crime in illegal drug markets in New Zealand.

Dr Tanya Wyatt completed her PhD at the University of Kent in Canterbury, England in November 2008. She is living in Washington, DC, interning at the Aspen Institute's Council of Women World Leaders and Wildlife Alliance, while beginning her job search. She hopes to find a position that will enable her to raise the profile of green criminology.

INTRODUCTION

Illegal markets and the economics of organized crime

Martin Bouchard[a] and Chris Wilkins[b]

[a]*School of Criminology, Simon Fraser University,* [b]*Centre for Social and Health Outcomes Research and Evaluation (SHORE), Massey University*

No matter how one defines 'organized crime', a recurring theme is to emphasize the economic motivations of offenders associated with criminal organizations. This of course serves to differentiate organized crime from (organized but) ideologically motivated crimes, like terrorism. However, for us it also calls attention to the central role played by material benefits in the pursuit of organized criminal interests. While money is a powerful motivational force for organized and disorganized criminals alike, the methods, the specific activities, the social context, and perhaps the relative success of organized criminals in securing significant amounts of money may differ from other offenders. A focus on the 'economics' of organized crime is thus likely to bring attention to the outcomes (costs and benefits), but also to the process leading to these outcomes, including analyses of the markets where criminal organizations are active.

It is not surprising that as a sub-field, the economics of organized crime has been developed mostly by economists. Economists became more seriously involved in studying organized crime during the late 1960s in response to political concerns about the influence of the Mafia in the United States. At this time, prosecutors and law enforcement agencies began describing groups such as the Mafia as the criminal equivalents of legal 'corporations', dominating the illegal markets for gambling, loan-sharking and illegal drugs. Economists were thus considered to be well placed to understand the 'business' structures and marketing strategies of these criminal corporations. That model faded away as a number of detailed empirical studies of Mafia families in the United States completed in the 1970s increasingly challenged the official view of the Mafia as espoused in the 1960s.[1] Of importance is the publication of economist Peter Reuter's (1983) *Disorganised Crime: The Economics of the Visible Hand*, which marked a significant development in the

---

1. See for example A. Anderson, *The Business of Organised Crime* (Stanford, CA: Hoover Institute Press, 1979); F. Ianni, *A Family Business: Kinship and Social Control in Organized Crime* (New York: Russell Sage Foundation, 1972).

understanding of organized crime.[2] Reuter drew on recent advances in the economic theory of industrial organization which used transaction costs and information costs as important determinants of market structure to investigate the size and scope of criminal organization. Reuter also set new standards in the empirical study of organized crime by examining seized records of illegal gambling and loan sharking and interviewing law enforcement officers and informants about Mafia activities, rather than merely accepting the official views and interpretations espoused by law enforcement agencies and prosecutors. He concluded that the failure of price fixing, freedom of entry and exit, level of competition and small size of operators suggested that these illegal markets were largely competitive rather than controlled by a single entity such as the Mafia.

Perhaps more than economists, however, it was criminologists and sociologists who pursued Reuter's research agenda on the organization of illegal markets. The original analytical strategy followed by Reuter certainly played a role in appealing to researchers in the social sciences. What Reuter found for the bookmaking, numbers and loansharking industries was also found for a variety of illegal drug markets, at all levels of the trade.[3] It was recognized that the vast array of determinants of the business of organized crime, both within and outside the organizations or markets in which they are active, makes their study an empirical enterprise to be undertaken by an equally diverse crowd of researchers. This book pursues this research tradition further, while providing an interesting snap-shot of the diversity of approaches possible to study illegal markets and the economics of organized crime. Ideally, we would have preferred to have the space to provide case studies on an even wider range of case markets and activities in which criminal organizations are involved (e.g. construction, prostitution, illegal gambling) than the ones presented here. We nonetheless hope that readers will conclude, just like we did, that the novel approaches and unique contributions provided by this collection of studies bring the sub-field to new territories.

It seems fitting to start this book with Curry and Mongrain, who make use of the economic theory of punishment to approach the thorny issue of what constitutes a criminal organization. The past two decades have shown that this long-lasting debate has not prevented research from going forward and contributing to our understanding of organized crime. The point of departure of the Curry and Mongrain paper is to remind us that the definitional issue is quite crucial for the criminal justice system – especially at the sentencing level where being a member of a structured organization is considered an aggravating factor. The results of their analysis suggest that defining organizations on the impact they have on illegal markets is more beneficial from a social harm perspective than definitions based on the structure of their network.

2. P. Reuter, *Disorganized Crime: The Economics of the Visible Hand* (Cambridge, MA: Hoover Institute Press, 1983).

3. See for example the studies of Adler (1993) and Desroches (2005) at the wholesale level: P. Adler, *Wheeling and Dealing: An Ethnography of an Upper-Level Drug Dealing and Smuggling Community*, 2nd edn (New York: Columbia University Press, 1993); Frederick J. Desroches, *The Crime That Pays: Drug Trafficking and Organized Crime In Canada* (Toronto: Canadian Scholars Press, 2005); and the studies of Eck and Gersh (2000) or Johnson et al. (2000) at the retail level: J. Eck and J. Gersh, 'Drug Trafficking as a Cottage Industry', in *Illegal Drug Markets: From Research to Prevention Policy*, ed. Mangai Natarajan and Mike Hough (Monsey, NY: Criminal Justice Press, 2000); B. D. Johnson, E. Dunlap and S. Tourigny, 'Crack Distribution and Abuse in New York', in *Illegal Drug Markets: From Research to Prevention Policy*, ed. Mangai Natarajan and Mike Hough (Monsey, NY: Criminal Justice Press, 2000).

Though very different in its approach, the paper by Tremblay, Bouchard and Petit is a natural extension of Curry and Mongrain's paper. They too propose to change the focus from the structure and size of an organization to consider the wider sphere of influence as an indicator of the importance of an organization in a market. Measuring the influence outside its immediate boundaries (affiliated members) represents an analytical challenge, especially in obtaining suitable and reliable data on the size of the markets and the dynamics of distribution in a variety of drug trades. Though necessarily bounded by many assumptions, Tremblay et al. propose an original analytical strategy to estimate the influence of one organization (Hells Angels) in three illegal drug markets (cannabis, cocaine and cannabis cultivation). They combine two pieces of information: (1) data on the size of offender populations supplying these three markets; and (2) self-report data on adult offenders reporting whether or not they or their associates were buying from or selling for the Hells Angels. The results show that a relatively small organization by conventional standards, like the Hells Angels, can nonetheless achieve significant influence over a large share of dealers and distributors. The authors interpret this result as evidence of criminal achievement at the organizational level.

The paper by Tremblay and colleagues argues that the organizational structure chosen by the Hells Angels contributed to the expansion of their economic influence without increasing the official number of 'members'. Not inadvertently, the paper that follows (by Easton and Karaivanov) provides a compelling demonstration on how offenders can choose network configurations and organizational size that will maximize benefits and minimize costs for the organization. Easton and Karaivanov's focus on network configuration contrasts with the usual approach of considering the structure to be fixed. Instead, the authors ask why a particular structure was chosen instead of a number of other possible ones. This particular analytical choice not only proves fruitful in illustrating the costs and benefits of a variety of configurations, but also from a crime combating policy perspective. One of the most salient contributions of the Easton and Karaivanov paper is to demonstrate how the strategy of removing the 'key player' – a perfectly reasonable strategy when the network is determined exogenously, may not be the optimal strategy in an environment in which the agents can change the size and structure of the network endogenously. More generally, optimal crime policy may be different if the criminals are aware of the policing strategy and can alter their network.

While the two preceding papers were mostly interested in the costs and benefits for organizations, the Caulkins, Burnett and Leslie paper examines the costs and benefits for both individual players and for drug-importing organizations using different importation methods. One of the finest case studies of the variety of importation schemes found in recent literature, the results of the Caulkins et al. paper show that a minority of participants are responsible for a majority of smuggling in the UK. Not only is this minority of participants successful at reaping interesting profits from larger importation loads, they are also generally more successful at avoiding detection. While researchers on the demand side have acknowledged the importance of such pareto-like distributions for a drug policy perspective, supply researchers (before Caulkins et al.) have been slower to recognize the existence of similar phenomena on the supply side, and their implications for policy.

Many of the previous papers focused on the material benefits for dealers and organizations active in a variety of contexts, but much less emphasis has been put on the nature of the transactions between buyers and suppliers, or on the 'cycles' of purchase and resale at different market levels. While much of the past work on cycles focused on retail dealing, the article by Caulkins, Gurga and Little offers a much-needed detailed description of these cycles at higher market levels, providing valuable information on the price mark-ups along the drug distribution chain for a variety of drugs. Among the many contributions of their paper, Caulkins et al. demonstrate how the price markup coefficients are very similar over drugs and time, suggesting that a very similar economic logic underlies the distribution of these drugs (despite different prices). Perhaps more importantly, the authors show that UK dealers derive most of their net revenues inside the UK, from domestic distribution, as opposed to importation *per se*.

The article by McKetin, McLaren, Kelly and Chalmers pursues the task of examining the organization of illegal markets, but now the focus is on the retail level, for a very specific drug (crystalline methamphetamine). The authors tackle an important question in the organization of illegal markets, namely on the evidence of market segregation for different forms of the same drug. The question is especially important for crystal methamphetamine in Australia, a drug for which availability has increased in recent years, and which can be found among at least two other forms of the drug, namely 'speed' and 'base meth'. Interviewing more than 300 users of the different forms of methamphetamine (including many dealers), the authors found a striking uniformity in the retail market for the different forms of drugs, including consumption and price levels paid by customers. These findings have, of course, implications for understanding the resilience of the market for crystal meth, and the likely substitution effects that would occur from reducing the supply of one form of the drug and not the other.

The last two papers bring the economics of organized crime to a new territory: the illegal wildlife trade. The first paper, by Brendan Moyle, draws on transaction-cost economics in providing a very informative case study on the black market for tiger products in China. The paper by Tanya Wyatt brings us to Russia, using a variety of sources (including interview data), to describe the organization of the falcon and fur trades in Russia. Despite the novelty of the illegal products being described in the literature on illegal markets, both authors show that the nature of the organizations active in these industries is subject to the same market forces as more traditional illegal markets, leading to a market populated by a diversity of relatively small organizations. However, the particularities of the products involved in illegal wildlife trade also emphasize some noteworthy differences. Moyle's analysis, for example, shows that the skills set required for hunting tigers is very specialized, creating barriers to entry that are simply not found in illegal drug markets. Of interest, Moyle shows how the market for tiger products is connected to other wildlife trades at the wholesale level but not at the retail level, suggesting a unique market structure that deserves attention in future studies. The paper by Wyatt also provides new insights. One of the important contributions of her study is to show how the existence of a parallel legal industry for a product greatly influences the kind of offenders who are involved and the organization of the trade. She found that the illegal fur trade is populated by individuals who are already involved in the legal fur trade, creating smuggling channels along already existing legitimate structures. The illegal falcon trade does not benefit from such a legitimate front, which increases the difficulty related to concealment, and may lead to the involvement of more sophisticated criminal organizations.

Acknowledgements

We would like to thank Federico Varese and Carlo Morselli of *Global Crime* for their guidance and for giving us the opportunity to act as Guest Editors of this special issue. We also would like to thank all the reviewers who provided time and energy in improving the quality of an already strong set of papers.

What is a criminal organization and why does the law care?

Philip A. Curry and Steeve Mongrain

Department of Economics, Simon Fraser University

Introduction

In the United States in 1967, a presidential report on organized crime was commissioned. In 1970, the Organized Crime Control Act was passed. A significant component of this act was the Racketeer Influenced and Corrupt Organizations Act (RICO). RICO was designed to target individuals or organizations engaged in a pattern of racketeering, defined as a minimum of two connected criminal acts within a ten-year period. It did so by allowing prosecutors to define a series of distinct crimes as a single offence, thereby avoiding many procedural, evidentiary and jurisdictional problems associated with prosecuting multiple offences together. RICO allows for rather severe penalties to be imposed. The maximum penalty for a single RICO conviction is twenty years imprisonment (which is increased to life imprisonment if any of the predicate charges permit it, such as murder) and a fine of $250,000 or twice the proceeds of the offence. In addition, RICO allows for the forfeiture of all the proceeds of crime.

The majority of states (45 at the time of writing) also have laws devoted to criminal organizations.[1] Of those 45, 25 have provisions to impose additional penalties for crimes committed by members of gangs.[2] Often, such provisions entail the automatic upgrading of the class of misdemeanor or felony.[3] A summary of the other types of legislation can be found in Appendix A.

The current legislation in Canada targeting criminal organizations was introduced in 1997 and revised in 2001. The Criminal Code of Canada defines a criminal organization as

1. The exceptions are Alabama, Maine, Nebraska, West Virginia and Wyoming.
2. Most state legislation is targeted at 'street gangs'.
3. Taken from http://www.iir.com/nygc/gang-legis/.

'a group, however organized, that (a) is composed of three or more persons in or outside Canada; and (b) has as one of its main purposes or main activities the facilitation or commission of one or more serious offences that, if committed, would likely result in the direct or indirect receipt of a material benefit, including a financial benefit, by the group or by any of the persons who constitute the group. It does not include a group of persons that forms randomly for the immediate commission of a single offence'.[4] The incremental penalty for being a member of a gang while committing a crime is no more than 14 years imprisonment.[5]

While prosecutors have had some success in convicting criminals under RICO, criticism of it is not hard to find. One particular criticism is that RICO is very vague in its definition of a criminal 'enterprise'.[6] In particular, legitimate organizations, such as corporations, labor unions and government offices come under the purview of RICO. While prosecutors have found this useful in combating white-collar crime, it is not obvious that RICO is the best tool for this venture.

RICO was influential in the design of Canadian legislation.[7] As is evident from the Canadian definition of a criminal organization above, Canada attempted to remove much of the vagueness found in RICO. One could argue that the Canadian definition has caused as many problems as it has solved, however. Currently, Canada has been unable to convict criminal members of the Hells Angels as members of a gang, primarily because they cannot prove that the commission of crimes is a primary reason for the group.[8]

How then, should the law define a criminal organization? It is perhaps not surprising that this has been a difficult issue to resolve given the many different types of criminal organizations that exist. Some are social institutions that also participate in crime, and may range in size from a small group of neighborhood youth to the Hells Angels. Some organizations are culture- or 'family'-based, which may be very loosely organized, or may exhibit many of the features of legitimate businesses, such as La Cosa Nostra or the Italian Mafia.[9] Should the law distinguish between these different types of organizations, perhaps punishing them differentially? Or should it take the stance that a criminal organization is a criminal organization, independent of its structure?

In order to answer these questions, we turn to the economic theory of punishment to establish why society would want to punish criminal organizations differently than independent criminals. We find that many of the reasons stem from the impact that criminal organizations have on markets (either illegal markets or metaphorical markets

4. Criminal Code of Canada, subsection 467.1.
5. Criminal Code of Canada, subsection 467.12.
6. See, for example, C. Morselli and L. Kazemian, 'Scrutinizing RICO', *Critical Criminology* 12 (2004): 351–69; M.G. Urbina and S. Kreitzer, 'The Practical Utility and Ramifications of RICO: Thirty-Two Years after its Implementation', *Criminal Justice Policy Review* 15 (2004): 294–323; R.K. Rassmussen, 'Introductory Remarks and a Comment on civil RICO's Remedial Provisions', *Vanderbilt Law Review* 43 (1990): 623–37; and J. Dombrink. and J. W. Meeker, 'Racketeering Prosecution – The Use and Abuse of RICO', *Rutgers Law Journal* 18 (1985): 633–54.
7. See Freedman, D. 'The New Law of Criminal Organizations in Canada', *Canadian Bar Review* 85 (2006): 171–219.
8. See 'Hells Angels Member not in "Criminal Organization"', http://www.ctv.ca/servlet/ArticleNews/story/CTVNews/20080327/hellsangelsguilty080327/20080327?hub=TopStories.
9. See F. Allum and J. Sands 'Explaining Organized Crime in Europe: Are Economists Always Right?', *Crime, Law & Social Change* 41 (2004): 133–60 for detailed descriptions of the types of criminal organizations around the world.

from crime) and from the use of violence. In other words, we feel that criminal organizations should be defined according to their presence in illegal markets and *not* according to the structure of their network. Interestingly, these findings are very reminiscent of Schelling's work that was influential in the design of RICO.[10]

Schelling's work has been criticized in the criminological literature as promoting a misconception of criminal organizations.[11] The source of this criticism is Schelling's assumption that criminal organizations must necessarily be large-scale, highly organized groups that form in order to achieve monopoly power in the markets in which they operate. While this criticism is correct in that criminal organizations clearly come in all forms and so are not all large-scale or structured like a business, we feel it is misguided in that there does not appear to be any reason to treat those organizations that do not achieve market power or use excessive violence any differently than independent criminals. In other words, whether a criminal organization should receive enhanced sentencing *should* hinge on the attainment of market power, no matter how structured the organization is, and even if that was not an initial goal of the group.

The rest of this paper is organized as follows. In the next section, we examine the economic theory of punishments and highlight the finding that punishment should depend on the social harm imposed and the probability of conviction. We then examine how criminal organizations may differ from independent criminals in these regards. In the final section, we consider how these differences can be used to construct a definition of a criminal organization and conclude.

Economic analysis of punishment

There exists a large literature within economics focusing on crime and deterrence.[12] In particular, much attention has been paid to the choice of punishment. To begin with, it is not socially optimal to have all punishments set at the maximum possible (such as the death penalty). If rape, say, were punished with the death penalty, then rapists would have incentive to kill their victims in order to reduce their chance of being caught. Further, if punishments were the same for all crimes, then criminals might have incentive to switch out of less serious crimes to more serious ones. This is known as the concept of marginal deterrence.[13] From this standpoint, and given that there are many possible crimes,

10. T.C. Schelling, 'Economic Analysis and Organized Crime', in The President's Commission on Law Enforcement and the Administration of Justice, *Task Force Report: Organized Crime* (Washington, DC: US Government Printing Office, 1967): 114–26.

11. See Morselli and Kazemian 'Scrutinizing RICO' and Allum and Sands 'Explaining Organized Crime in Europe'.

12. Early writings on the subject include C.-L. Montesquieu, *De l'esprit des lois*, ed. J.P. Mayer and A.P. Kerr (1748 [1793]); C. Bonesana, marquis Beccaria, *An Essay on Crimes and Punishments*, trans. from the Italian (Philadelphia, PA: William Young, 1767 [1793]); and J. Bentham, *Principles of Morals and Legislation* (Oxford: Clarendon Press, 1789). Specifically within the law and economics literature, G.S. Becker, 'Crime and Punishment: An Economic Approach', *Journal of Political Economy* 76 (1968): 169–217 is very influential.

13. See, for example, G.J. Stigler, 'The Optimum Enforcement of Laws', *Journal of Political Economy* 78 (1970): 526–36; D.D. Friedman and W. Sjostrom, 'Hanged For a Sheep – The Economics of Marginal Deterrence', *Journal of Legal Studies* 22 (1993): 345–66; or D. Mookherjee and I.P.L. Png, 'Marginal Deterrence in Enforcement of Law', *Journal of Political Economy* 102 (1994): 1039–106.

economic theory states that expected punishments[14] should be an increasing function of the social harm caused by the criminal act.

Further, there may be some crimes that enhance economic efficiency when committed. Polinsky and Shavell[15] consider a social welfare function that includes the benefits to criminals. In this case, efficiency requires that crimes be committed only when the criminal's benefit outweighs the social harm (which includes the cost of policing and punishment). They argue that optimal punishments entail setting the expected punishment exactly equal to the harm caused. When this is done, rational individuals choose to commit an illegal act if and only if their benefit outweighs the social harm.

Although the main focus of our analysis, deterrence should not be the only consideration in the design of punishments, particularly in the case of imprisonment. The incapacitation of likely offenders, their potential rehabilitation and retributive justice (or 'just desert') are three other important factors.[16] Interestingly, the inclusion of incapacitation concerns has little impact on our analysis. For example, offence severity has been shown to be a useful predictor of recidivism.[17] Consequently, offences that cause greater social harm should also be given longer sentences when incapacitation is the objective. Moreover, there exist many practical considerations over and above these 'idealistic concerns'. Laws are generally the outcome of very complex and messy political processes that can often lead to distortions away from what is socially optimal. While these factors are very important in the real world, we wish to abstract from them in order to consider the normative question of whether criminal organizations *should* receive greater penalties than individual criminals and under what circumstances.

To this end, consider the following simple model of optimal punishment, with deterrence as the objective.[18] First, denote by g the benefit to an individual (or to a group of individuals) from an illegal act. Let this benefit be randomly drawn (and be known to the potential criminal before the act is committed) from the probability density function $z(g)$ with associated cumulative density function $Z(g)$. Let the penalty associated with this illegal activity be denoted by s,[19] and let π denote the probability of detection and conviction. Let the cost of sanctioning be given by $c(s)$, where $c'(s) > 0$. While π is presumably a function of many things, most notably government expenditure on policing, we shall consider it to be exogenously fixed. This is not an unreasonable assumption if, for example, policing efforts are general in the sense that a large police force affects the probability of conviction for a multitude of different crimes simultaneously. Since our

14. Note that the expected punishment is the penalty times the probability of being caught.

15. See A.M. Polinsky and S. Shavell, 'The Economic Theory of Public Enforcement of Law', *Journal of Economic Literature* 38 (2000): 45–76.

16. While the economic literature on these other aspects is not large, it is growing. See, for example E.L. Glaeser and B. Sacerdote 'The Determinants of Punishment: Deterrence, Incapacitation and Vengeance', NBER Working Paper 7676 (2000); and I. Ehrlich, 'On the Usefulness of Controlling Individuals: An Economic Analysis of Rehabilitation, Incapacitation, and Deterrence', in *The Economics of Crime*, vol. 1. International Library of Critical Writings in Economics series, vol. 195. An Elgar Reference Collection (Cheltenham: Edward Elgar, 2006).

17. See M.R. Pogrebin, E.D. Poole and R.M. Regoli, 'Parole Decision Making in Colorado', *Journal of Criminal Justice* 14 (1986): 147–55.

18. For more a complete discussion, see Polinsky and Shavell 'The Economic Theory of Public Enforcement of Law'.

19. Given that our model focuses exclusively on deterrence, the swiftness of punishment can be thought of as a determinant of s. However, it is possible that this may not still be true if we were to include incapacitation objectives.

simple model considers only a single criminal act, and since the determination of the size of the police force should depend on consideration of all crimes, one can consider π as simply fixed.[20] However, we will later consider how the probability of conviction can be influenced by criminal organizations. Finally, h represents the social harm caused by a given offence.

If criminals are risk neutral, they will commit a crime when $g \geq \pi s$. The probability that this is the case is $1 - Z(\pi s)$. While the assumption of risk neutrality may seem extreme, it actually has little effect on our results. The introduction of either risk preference or risk aversion certainly affects the optimal *level* of punishment, but not the result that it is increasing in social harm. Interestingly, there appears to be evidence that criminals are on average less concerned with risk.[21] If social welfare does *not* include the benefits to criminal,[22] the social optimum is found by solving:

$$\max_{\{s\}} - [1 - z(\pi s)]h - c(s) \tag{1}$$

The solution thus entails setting the punishment $s*$ such that $\pi z(\pi s*)h = c'(s*)$. Punishment is used to the point that the marginal benefit of a reduction in criminal activity equals the marginal cost of punishment. Some illegal acts (those for which the criminal's gains are very high) are simply not worth deterring because it is too costly to do so. Further, as π decreases, one can see that the optimal punishment increases.

This simple model, as well as the above story of marginal deterrence, gives rise to two key results of the economic theory of punishment: criminal acts committed by an organized group *should* be penalized to a greater degree if either: (1) the social harm from the act is greater; or (2) the probability of conviction is lower. We now examine these two possibilities.

Social harm

We first examine the social harm stemming from criminal acts and consider if and when such harm may be greater when said acts are committed by criminal organizations rather than independent criminals. It is worth mentioning that this analysis holds such things as the act itself and criminal history constant. If members of criminal organizations committed different criminal acts from independent criminals, there should be no need for the law to impose additional penalties because that would already be incorporated into the punishment for those different acts themselves. For example, if only criminal organizations can commit extortion or smuggle large quantities of drugs across borders, then the penalties for those crimes would reflect the fact that they are being committed by a criminal organization. In addition, penalties are often increasing in the convicted party's criminal history, so there would be no need to penalize members of criminal organizations further because they tend to have committed more crimes in the past.[23] Under what

---

20. This assumption is consistent with the analysis in Polinsky and Shavell, 'The Economic Theory of Public Enforcement of Law'. It is worth mentioning that allowing for π to be a choice variable does not change our main result that punishments should be increasing in social harm.
21. For a physiological study examining individuals who engage in criminal activity, see M. Krakowski, 'Violence and Serotonin: Influence of Impulse Control, Affect Regulation, and Social Functioning', *Journal of Neuropsychiatry and Clinical Neuroscience* 15 (2003): 294–305.
22. Including the gains to criminals in the welfare function lowers the optimal *level* of punishment without changing the result that optimal punishments are increasing in social harm.
23. From the standpoint of incapacitation, there is similarly no need to have an additional penalty for

circumstances, then, would the criminal acts of members of criminal organizations cause more social harm than the same acts committed by independent criminals?

We first consider some specific criminal acts: those associated with illegal markets. This is a logical starting point since the provision of illegal goods and services (for example, drugs and prostitution) is a common association with criminal organizations. Criminal organizations of many different types, from as local street gangs to international criminal organizations such as the Triads, are involved in such markets. Let us first consider, however, what these markets would look like if the only players were independent, unorganized criminals. Such markets would presumably be quite competitive, with the marginal criminal earning zero economic profits (after accounting for the costs associated with risk). There would be little incentive for violence, as it is costly and the returns in a competitive market small. If a collection of criminals attempted to organize, however, the incentives for violence would increase as they attempted to attain market power and increased profits.

Many economists have argued that drug markets are somewhat non-competitive. For example, Fiorentini and Peltzman[24] argue that organized crime is more likely to flourish when there are economies of scale and monopolistic power. They also suggest that organized crime uses violence against other firms in the legal and illegal sectors. Gambetta and Reuter[25] also point out that criminal organizations can use violence to maintain their market power. Similarly, Levitt and Venkatesh[26] argue for the presence of market power in the illicit drug sector by looking at actual data on a Chicago gang. They note that the use of violence plays a major role in sustaining market power.

Does increased market power mean increased social harm? There are actually arguments to be made both for and against such a hypothesis. One might feel that society should be trying to minimize the amount of consumption in these markets. Since market power is often associated with a *reduction* in sales, it may actually be preferable to have a few criminal organizations with market power in charge of production, importation or distribution rather than facing a competitive market.[27] An organization with market power would restrict sales in order to charge higher prices and attain more profit. Imposing additional penalties for criminal organizations might seem to be counterproductive in this case. By penalizing criminal organizations more than independent criminals, the law would be encouraging competition in the market, thereby leading to greater consumption. However, this argument only holds when sellers are not able to price discriminate. When they do, sellers are able to sell more and still increase profits. As we will discuss in more detail later on, one common feature of drug markets is their high degree of price dispersion, an indication that price discrimination may be the norm.

(Footnote 23 continued)
members of criminal organizations based on an increased probability of offending in the future since the likelihood of recidivism can already be factored into the sentencing.

24. G. Fiorentini and S. Peltzman, 'Introduction', in *The Economics Of Organised Crime*, ed. G. Fiorentini and S. Peltzman (Cambridge, NY: Cambridge University Press, 1995): 1–26.

25. D. Gambetta and P. Reuter, 'Conspiracy Among the Many: The Mafia in Legitimate Industries', in *The Economics Of Organised Crime*, ed. G. Fiorentini and S. Peltzman (Cambridge, NY: Cambridge University Press, 1995): 116–36.

26. S.D. Levitt and S.A. Venkatesh, 'An Economic Analysis of a Drug Selling Gang's Finances', *Quarterly Journal of Economics* 115 (2000): 755–89.

27. See A. Mansour, N. Marceau and S. Mongrain, 'Gangs and Crime Deterrence', *Journal of Law, Economics & Organization* 22 (2006): 315–39 as well as Schelling, 'Economic Analysis and Organized Crime'.

Further, minimizing consumption may not be the appropriate objective. In contrast to property or violent crimes, it is not obvious that illegal trades impose any direct costs.[28] Many arguments as to why any markets should be illegal often turn on the presence of externalities; for example, in the case of prostitution, the market could lead to an increased transmission of sexually transmitted infections. In the case of drugs, addicts may resort to property crime in order to support their habit. Drugs are expensive; Caulkins and Reuter compare the price of drugs to the price of gold.[29] In 1997, marijuana was worth as much as gold, while cocaine and heroin were respectively 10 and 100 times more expensive than gold. Some argue that it is the high price that leads addicts to commit crimes in order to support their habits.[30] Indeed, some estimates of expenditures run as high as $12,000 a year for hardcore cocaine and heroin users.[31] Would prices be as high if drugs were legal? When drugs are illegal, prices tend to be high due to the direct and indirect costs imposed by law enforcement. Market power only pushes those prices up further, whether it occurs in production or in distribution. Moreover, if price discrimination is possible, as suggested by data on price dispersion,[32] then this is the worst of all worlds. Quantities sold are high, and so is the average price. Laws aimed at criminal organizations could thus be effective at reducing property crimes by controlling prices through the promotion of more competitive markets. In general, however, while the presence of market power almost certainly has an impact on the price and quantity of illegal goods and services, there does not appear to be a strong argument that social harm is increased through these avenues.

Another feature of market power, however, is increased profits. As alluded to above, with increased profits comes increased incentive to use violence in order to protect them. Such violence may be directed at members of other organizations, within an organization or against customers that try to default on payments.[33] Innocent bystanders may also be victims. The costs associated with the use of violence in drug markets are considerable. Caulkins estimates that compensation for physical risk accounts for more than 30% of the price of cocaine.[34] Bookkeeping information about a gang in Chicago collected by Levitt and Venkatesh[35] indicates that members of this particular gang faced up to a 30% chance of death over a three year period.

---

28. This observation is probably less objectionable to economists, who generally hold that trade makes all parties involved better off and that the law does not need to protect people from themselves.

29. J.P. Caulkins and P. Reuter, 'What Price Data Tell Us About Drug Markets', *Journal of Drug Issues* 28 (1998): 593–613.

30. See R.A. Posner, *Economic Analysis of Law*, 7th edn (Austin, TX: Aspen Publishers, 2007), at p. 242.

31. These estimates are for 1995 in the United States by W. Rhodes, P. Scheiman, T. Pittayathikhun, L. Collins and V. Tsarfaty, 'What America's Users Spend on Illegal Drugs, 1988–1995' (Washington, DC: Office of National Drug Control Policy, 1997).

32. See M. Galenianos, R. Pacula and N. Persico, 'A Search-Theoretic Model of the Retail Market for Illicit Drugs', mimeo (2008).

33. See, for example S.H. Decker, C.M. Katz and V.J. Webb, 'Understanding the Black Box of Gang Organization: Implications for Involvement in Violent Crime, Drug Sales, and Violent Victimization', *Crime & Delinquency* 54 (2008): 153–71; and C. Morselli, D. Tanguay and A.-M. Labalette, 'Criminal Conflicts and Collective Violence: Biker-Related Account Settlements in Quebec, 1994–2001', in *Organized Crime: Culture, Markets and Policies*, ed. D. Siegel and H. Nelen (New York: Springer Science + Business Media, LLC, 2008).

34. Caulkins and Reuter, 'What Price Data Tell Us About Drug Markets'.

35. Levitt and Venkatesh, 'An Economic Analysis of a Drug Selling Gang's Finances'.

The threat of violence is also integral to extortion as well as other crimes against the population. Recall, however, that the economic theory of punishments states that, if criminal organizations should be subjected to higher penalties because they cause greater social harm, it must be on a per act basis, not because they use violence or commit other crimes to a greater degree.[36] Why should there be greater social harm associated with the violent acts of criminal organizations as compared with the same crimes committed by an individual? The answer may be that there is more harm per act because gangs are better organized in their attempts to commit those crimes. The key to this insight lies in a proper definition of the harm caused by a criminal act. Note that the social harm must be greater than the loss to the victim, for many reasons: goods may be destroyed in the act of theft, or physical injury may accompany property crimes. Perhaps more importantly, the threat of crime causes individuals to take precautions to avoid being victimized as well as causing stress and fear among the population. Precautions could involve monetary expenditures, such as the purchase of an alarm system, or they could involve changes to one's lifestyle, such as avoiding certain parts of town.

Consider the following adaptation of the simple model outlined above.[37] As before, gains to criminals are given by g, so that a criminal would like to commit an illegal act if $g \geq \pi s$. Potential victims, however, can take precautions to prevent the act from occurring. Suppose that expenditures, e, by the potential victim reduce the probability of a successful crime by $\alpha(e)$, where $\alpha'(e) > 0$ and $\alpha''(e) < 0$. Potential victims thus choose e to minimize their expected losses (comprising losses to criminals and expenditures e). As the threat of crime increases, potential victims spend more in order to avoid encounters with criminals. If criminal organizations represent a greater threat to potential victims, then victims will spend more, thereby increasing the social harm per act. In this case, it would be socially optimal to have higher penalties for crimes committed by members of criminal organizations.

Probability of detection

Another reason to penalize criminal organizations more than independent criminals is because they face lower probabilities of arrest and conviction. We now consider how this might be the case. In particular, we consider how market power can have important implications for the probability of detecting a criminal act. Recall the hypothetical case of a perfectly competitive market for an illegal good, such as drugs. It would be characterized by free entry with a large number of small suppliers making zero economic profits. For a given quality, the price of the drug would be set equal to the marginal cost of production and distribution, which includes all expected costs related to enforcement. The presence of market power brings two important features: lower quantity supplied and higher profits or surplus. Each of these two features influences the probability of detection.

Fewer offences

In a market dominated by a small number of suppliers, output tends to be smaller. In the case of a legal and homogeneous good, fewer transactions imply that the marginal

36. It is possible that they engage in these activities to a greater degree than independent criminals because they have a lower chance of being caught. This is discussed in the next section.
37. Taken from P.A. Curry, 'Malice Aforethought', mimeo (2008).

transaction is done at a higher price and with individuals who have a higher valuation for the product. In other words, with fewer transactions, each transaction is more profitable solely due to higher prices. Illegal markets, and those for addictive goods in particular, operate very differently.[38] With illegal markets the goods traded, and even the actual transactions themselves, are rarely homogenous. Caulkins gives a clean example to support this affirmation: 'The amount of heroin in a "dime bag" might change over time and location, but by definition a dime bag always costs $10 ("dime" being street argot for $10)'.[39] In the same article, Caulkins also gives many examples where purity varies from one transaction to another instead of quantity. Negotiation on prices is time consuming, and so it increases the risk. Dealers sell at a fixed price, but ultimately it is the quantity and the quality that determine their per unit profits. For the point of view of the consumers, however, the benefit of every transaction is difficult to evaluate *a priori* because of asymmetric information problems. Drug markets also often exhibit quantity discounting, where per unit prices on larger transactions are significantly lower. While such price discrimination is also common in legal markets, the magnitude of the discount seems to be more drastic for illegal markets, in the order of 40% for cocaine.[40] These facts suggest that a higher price is not the only way by which suppliers earn greater surplus. Drug traders may increase the surplus they extract from a transaction by cheating on quantity, by diluting their product, or by even by concentrating on transactions that are less risky. It is on this last point that we wish to focus.

Consider first the example of quantity discounting. Imagine an individual with 100 grams of an illegal substance to distribute. Suppose for simplicity that the probability of detection π does not depend on the size of a transaction, but the penalty might. We also assume that, once caught, a dealer loses the rest of his supply. If p is the price per gram of the illegal substance, then the expected profit from a single (1 gram) transaction is $p - \pi s$, where s is the sanction for selling 1 gram. The expected profit from trying to sell 100 grams in a hundred transactions is:[41]

$$\sum_t (1 - \pi)^t [p - \pi s]$$

Alternatively, the dealer could sell the entire 100 grams in a single transaction at a total price P, and make an expected profit of $P - \pi S$, where S is the sanction for selling a full 100 grams of the substance. Thus the dealer would be willing to offer a single transaction price of

$$P = \left[\sum_t (1 - \pi)^t\right] p + \pi\left[S - \sum_t (1 - \pi)^t S\right]$$

38. See J.P. Caulkins and P. Reuter 'Illicit Drug Markets and Economic Irregularities', *Socio-Economic Planning Sciences* 40 (2006): 1–14.
39. From J.P. Caulkins, 'Price and Purity Analysis for Illicit Drugs: Data and Conceptual Issues', *Drug and Alcohol Dependence* 90 (2007): 61–8.
40. Estimations for cocaine can be found in J.P. Caulkins, 'What is the Average Price of an Illicit Drug?', *Addiction* 89 (1994): 815–19. Significant quantity discounts are also found for the case of marijuana by K.W. Clements, 'Pricing and Packaging: the Case of Marijuana', *Journal of Business* 79 (2006): 2019–44.
41. Note that we do not consider the price of the illegal substance itself. This is because we assume that it has already been purchased, and therefore a sunk cost. There would therefore be no marginal cost to selling an additional 1 gram.

Consider the following parameterization: let the probability of arrest be 7%, as approximated by Bouchard and Tremblay.[42] While it is common to normalize the price to 1, it is more difficult to determine the appropriate values for s and S, since the penalties are generally in terms of prison time. In Canada, the maximum penalty for possession of cocaine or heroin (first conviction) is 6 months in prison and a $1000 fine. The maximum penalty for possession for the purpose of trafficking is life imprisonment.[43] Suppose that when dealing a single gram, the dealer receives the former penalty but life imprisonment when dealing all 100 grams. Given that 1 gram of cocaine retails for just under $100, s would be approximately 10. The appropriate value for S is difficult to ascertain, but suppose that life imprisonment is 1000 times worse than 6 months in prison and a $1000 fine. In that case, S would be 10,000. Using these parameter values, we find that $P = 704$, or approximately a 30% discount.

The reason dealers are willing to discount so heavily is because they like to reduce risk, and quantity discounting is one way in which they can select less risky transactions. The presence of market power can have similar effects. A simple supply and demand model can demonstrate how a reduction in the number of transactions can lead to lower probabilities of arrest. Figure 1 displays the demand for an illegal good (or service). Curve D is the standard downward-sloping demand curve, while curve MC represents the marginal cost of supplying an additional unit of the illegal good. This marginal cost is made up of two components: the actual cost of production and distribution, which is assumed to be equal to a constant c, and the additional expected cost due to law enforcement. This additional expected cost may be increasing even when the actual sanction remains constant.

Consider an environment in which times and locations for transactions vary in their discreetness (visibility to the police, perhaps). If a dealer makes a low number of deals in a month, he would choose to transact in the more discreet locations/times. As the number of deals increases, they will have to occur in more visible places, thus increasing the probability of detection. This yields the upward sloping MC curve depicted in Figure 1.

Imagine that a given transaction carries a probability π of being detected, where π is between 0 and 1. Dealers who are detected receive a sanction s. If those probabilities of detection are observable, suppliers will select less risky transactions first. The marginal cost is then given by $MC = c + \pi(Q)s$, where $\pi(Q)$ is the probability of detection attached to transaction Q. Hence, π is an increasing function of Q.

Now consider the two extreme forms of market structure: perfect competition and monopoly. Perfect competition is characterized by free entry, so the number of transactions is determined through a zero profit condition. In a competitive market, dealers enter (transacting in riskier and riskier locations) until the price is equal to marginal cost. This yields a number of transactions q^{c} and a market price p^{c}. A monopolist, however, maximizes profits by setting marginal revenue equal to marginal costs. In Figure 1, curve MR represents marginal revenue, while p^{m} and q^{m} represent the monopoly price and quantity. Obviously, in a monopolized market the price is higher and the quantity distributed is lower. More importantly, the total marginal cost of the last transaction is lower, meaning that the probability of detection is lower.

While this simple supply and demand model may capture some features of the market for illegal goods and services, there are other characteristics particularly relevant to the

42. M. Bouchard and P. Tremblay 'Risks of Arrest Across Drug Markets: A Capture–Recapture Analysis of 'Hidden' Dealer and User Populations', *Journal of Drug Issues* 35 (2005): 733–54.
43. Taken from http://www.defencelaw.com/printversion-chart-contents.html.

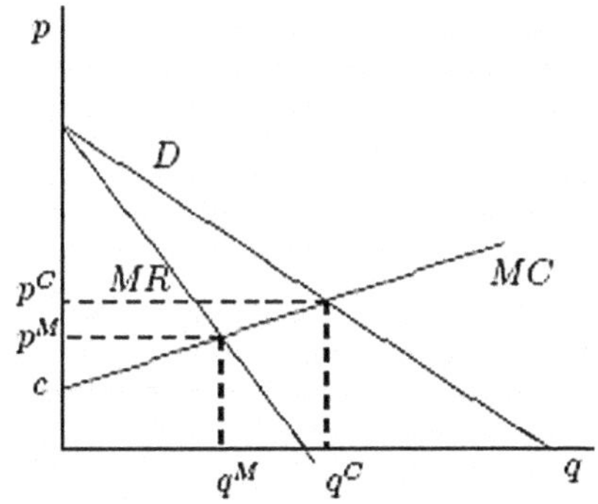

Figure 1. Marlet power reduces output, leading to less risky transactions on average.

market for illegal drugs that are worth examining. Drugs can be described as experience goods, in the sense that quality is difficult to observe prior to consumption. As mentioned above, a 'dime bag' always costs $10, but it is not always the same 'dime bag'. With unobservable quality, a uniform price can prevail, even though quality varies as suppliers dilute their product. This environment can perhaps be best described using a search model in which consumers and drug dealers are matched at random, and trade only if both side agree.[44] In such an environment, agents make separate decisions on price, quality and other characteristics such as the riskiness associated with the transaction. Reputation and the prospect of future transactions provide the supplier with the incentive to maintain some level of quality. However, there could be heterogeneity in quality and even in price in equilibrium. More importantly for this paper, more market power allows suppliers to be more selective when accepting or declining a transaction. Since the riskiness of each transaction contributes to the overall expected surplus, one can expect that, with an increase in market power, suppliers will move away from more risky transactions. Building a complete search model describing a drug market is beyond the scope of this paper, but some important implications can be stated without a formal model.

Greater surplus

Criminals, or criminal organizations, have incentive to expend resources (financial or otherwise) in order to reduce the probability of detection and conviction (or even potentially reduce the sanction). Malik discusses expenditures that directly reduce the probability of apprehension,[45] while Lott argues that wealthier individuals (or organizations) are harder to convict because they can hire more costly and potentially better lawyers.[46] Finally, Beck and Maher examine the case of bribery to suggest that competition can reduce the incentive to take bribes (thereby increasing enforcement).[47]

44. For example see Galenianos et al., 'A Search-Theoretic Model of the Retail Market for Illicit Drugs'.

45. A.S. Malik, 'Avoidance, Screening, and Optimum Enforcement', *RAND Journal of Economics* 21 (1990): 341–53.

46. Lott, J. Jr, 'Should the Wealthy Be Able to "Buy Justice"?', *Journal of Political Economy* 95 (1987): 1307–16.

47. P.J. Beck and M. W. Maher, 'Competition, Regulation and Bribery', *Managerial and Decision Economics* 10 (1989): 1–12.

When a criminal organization is able to create barriers to entry, and therefore able to enjoy a degree of market power, additional profits are generated. With greater profit comes higher costs of seeing inventory being confiscated by the authorities. For example, on 7 October 2007, in what was the third biggest seizure of ecstasy in the United States, the DEA confiscated 1.4 million tablets worth an estimated US$42 million. In 2005, a record year for cocaine seizures, the DEA confiscated more than 118,000 kg.[48] Some studies clearly show that costs associated with seizure are surely non-negligible. For example, costs associated with seizure account for about 10% of the final price of cocaine in the United States.[49] In some cases, the loss of revenue is almost the only cost incurred by the supplier. Easton[50] highlighted the following facts: in a sample of Vancouver marijuana-growing operations 'busted' by the police, most (55%) of those who were convicted received no jail time. Five per cent were sentenced to a single day or less and another 8% received sentences of between one day and 31 days. Of those who received longer sentences, 8% received 60 days and 11% were sentenced to 90 days. Of those who were repeat offenders, half were re-apprehended within the year. Of the 55% who were fined, the average fine amounted to less than $1200: a small amount considering the size of most marijuana operations. Thus the major component of the penalty associated with conviction is the loss of product: police destroy nearly 3000 marijuana-growing operations a year.

In summary, since organizations with market power are able to command a higher price than competitive agents, they forego more profit from seizure. As such, one should expect that they expend more resources to avoid detection and conviction. Whether criminal organizations should receive greater penalties thus seems closely tied to the question of whether they have market power. The analysis thus far suggests that there is little reason to have additional punishments for criminal organizations without market power, such as a typical street gang. Since violence is still associated with such gangs, we now consider the use of violence in a more in-depth manner.

The use of violence

While all means by which an organization tries to reduce the probability of detection are socially wasteful activities, some can impose serious costs on others. The use of violence is the best example. Criminal organizations can use the threat of violence on their victims (and other witnesses) in order to reduce the probability of being caught. If an independent criminal threatens to kill a person if they testify against him, that person still may do so, knowing that they will be safe at least for the duration that the criminal is in jail. If a gang member makes such a threat, however, then it is much more immediate, as it may be carried by another gang member while the offender is in prison. Consider the 1996 indictment of Clarence (Preacher) Heatley, a gang leader from Harlem.[51] Mary Jo White, the United States Attorney in Manhattan, gave the following explanation for why it had taken a long time to get to Heatley: 'They were careful. They were smart and they intimidated all those around them, drug dealers and citizens alike'. Further, in 1989,

48. See the DEA web site at http://www.usdoj.gov/dea/pubs/states/newsrel/2002/nyc100902.html and http://www.usdoj.gov/dea/statistics.html#seizures for more information.
49. See Caulkins and Reuter 'What Price Data Tell Us About Drug Markets' for estimates using 1990 data.
50. S. Easton, 'Marijuana Growth in British Columbia', in *Public Policy Sources*, vol. 74 (Vancouver: The Fraser Institute, 2004).
51. '18 Indicted on Murder and Drug Charges,' *New York Times*, November 15, 1996.

another member of Heatley's gang had been acquitted of a killing in Baltimore after witnesses changed their testimony. Thus it would appear that gang members are better able to commit violence in order to reduce their probability of conviction.

Criminal organizations can also use violence to keep their members in line. Such organizations may suffer from an agency problem in that the incentives of its members individually may not be perfectly aligned with the incentives of the gang as a whole.[52] As such, violence is an instrument that may be used in order to overcome the moral hazard problem. While such violence is a quintessential feature of many movies and books, there are many real examples as well: in 1985, the internal purge done by the Quebec chapter of the Hells Angels resulted in the murder of five of their own members.[53] Note that one aspect of the agency problem that gangs try to overcome is the incentive for members to provide evidence against each other in exchange for reduced sentences for themselves. Thus violence, or its threat, may be a key instrument in controlling the flow of information and preventing, for example, testimonies in order to reduce the probability of conviction.

In general, violence may be used to try to either obtain or maintain market power, or it may be used simply to reduce the probability of conviction. The use of violence (or the threat of violence) would thus seem linked to many of the reasons why criminal organizations should receive greater penalties. We therefore propose that the demonstration of violence beyond levels commensurate with those of independent criminals be a key part of obtaining enhanced sentencing.

So how should the law define a criminal organization?

We have thus far considered reasons for the law to penalize crimes committed by members of an organization more severely than those committed by independent criminals. It is worth noting that all arguments entail that the organization perpetrate multiple crimes. Thus it would seem sensible to somehow include the permanence of the group in the definition of a gang, as per the Canadian Criminal Code.

Also of note is that many of these arguments centre on the presence of market power in an illegal market (either in the market for crimes within a defined area, or in a market for a specific illegal good or service, or both). None of the arguments require a particular structure on behalf of the organization. Laws that require demonstration of a particular structure to the organization would thus seem to exclude some organizations that should receive additional punishment and perhaps even include some that do not. Figure 2 presents the type of information required in Canada to have a group classified as a 'criminal organization'.[54]

Note that all of the reasons discussed above fall into the category of 'Indicators of Benefit'. Requiring prosecutors to provide evidence for 'Indicators of Membership' and 'Indicators of Organization' would thus seem to merely increase the costs of prosecution while reducing the effectiveness of the legislation. As such, we propose that the definition of a criminal organization be linked to the demonstration of market power and/or the use of violence. Prosecutors should *not* have to demonstrate a particular structure or internal organization. In addition, it should be possible to prove the presence of market power

52. This point was also made in Levitt and Venkatesh, 'An Economic Analysis of a Drug Selling Gang's Finances'.
53. 'Parole a Step Closer for Hells Angel', *Montreal Gazette*, October 16, 2007.
54. Courtesy of the Combined Forces Special Enforcement Unit of the Lower Mainland in British Columbia.

PROVING THE CRIMINAL ORGANIZATION

Section 467.1 - Canada Criminal Code

"Criminal Organization": Composed of three or more persons, involved in the **facilitation or commission of serious offences,** and results in the **receipt of a material benefit,** by the **group** or **persons who constitute the group.**

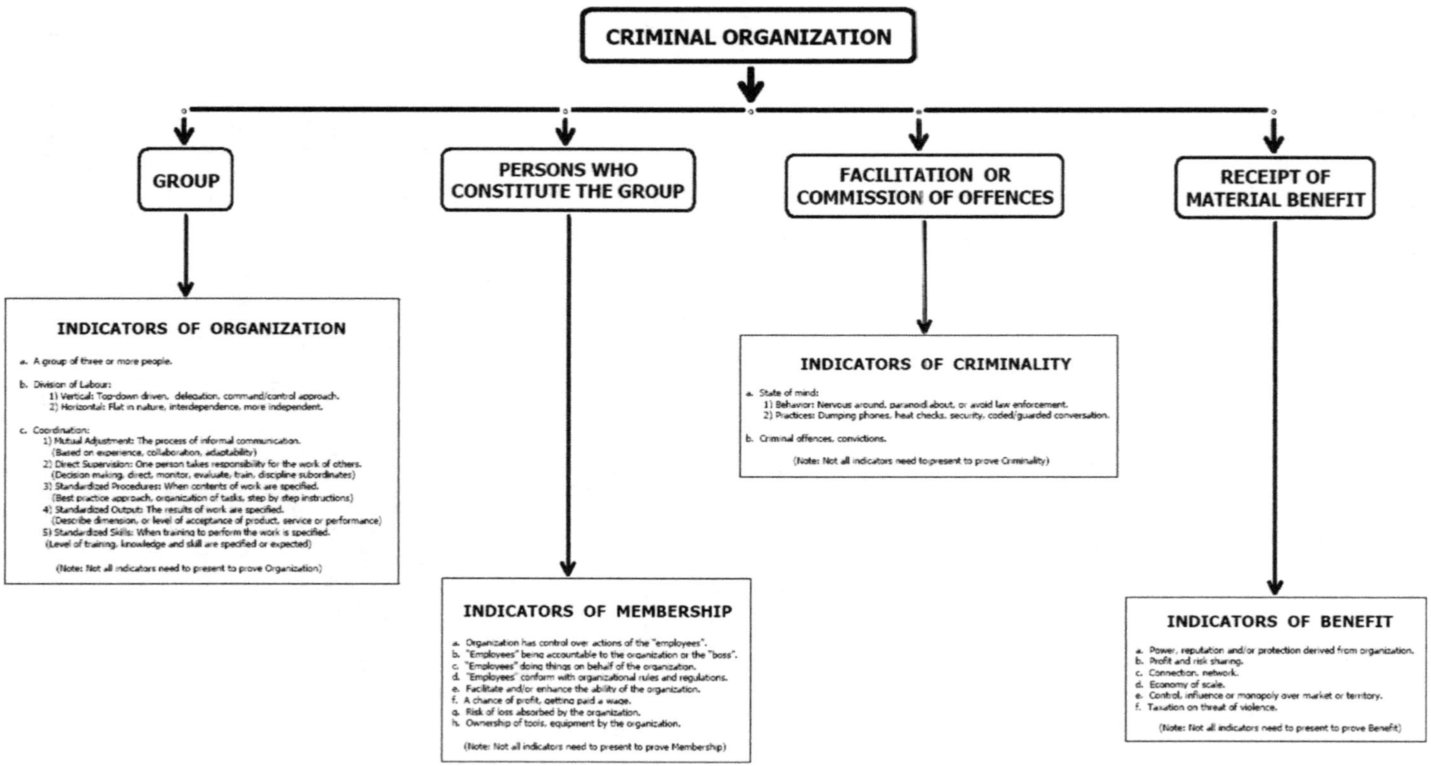

Prepared by: Policy & Strategic Directions
Combined Forces Special Enforcement Unit, B.C.
12 August, 2008

without having to establish the extent of the organization. That is, if a subset of a greater organization can be proved to have committed crimes while enjoying the benefits of market power, or to have used violence beyond what one would expect from independent criminals, then they should receive greater punishment.

There are both advantages and disadvantages to this proposal. One advantage is that fewer costs need be incurred demonstrating membership and organization. A disadvantage is that, if some members of an organization are convicted, other members are no longer necessarily liable. Thus additional costs may be necessary to convict the entire organization. It is not clear that this disadvantage is severe, however. The idea that other members of an organization would be guilty by association if some members are convicted has presented problems in obtaining convictions in Canada with the Hells Angels.[55] Indeed, it is not obvious that one would want to implicate other members of an organization when some have been found to have committed a series of crimes. For example, if a subset of a social group were to commit crimes (and exercise market power in doing so), they should receive enhanced sentencing without implicating the rest of the social group as members. Automatic implication the rest of the group may lead to inefficiently few people joining social groups.

We recognize that the demonstration of market power is not an easy exercise, particularly for illegal markets. Market power may differ widely depending on where you stand in the production and distribution chain. It would be wrong to imagine the drug market as being populated by vertically integrated organizations that produce, import and distribute their products. Even if being sheltered from antitrust regulations could push for integration, the risks associated with enforcement strongly promote independence. Just by the nature of the activity, one expects to see more market power at the import stage compared with street retailing, for example. Market power may also vary from product to product, and from one location to another; this may partly explain the extreme dispersion in prices that we observe.[56] While prosecutors are currently attempting to demonstrate market power as well as violence and intimidation, as indicated by Figure 2, there are undoubtedly cases where this proves to be excessively difficult. As such, it may be helpful for the law to employ a two-pronged approach in which it is sufficient to demonstrate *either* market power (or the use of intimidation) *or* that the group exhibits a certain organizational structure. Note that our proposal has the effect of reducing the number of things required to be shown while actually targeting those organizations that *should* receive greater penalties more accurately.

Acknowledgements

We would like to thank Steve Easton as well as Martin Bouchard and two anonymous referees for very helpful comments. We would also like to thank Mike Gavin for excellent research assistance.

55. See 'Hells Angel Says he Feels Shunned', http://www.cbc.ca/canada/british-columbia/story/2006/10/17/bc-hells-angels.html.
56. See Caulkins and Reuter, 'Illicit Drug Markets and Economic Irregularities'.

Appendix A

Table 1. Anti-gang legislation by state.

	DB	ES	FP	PAR	RTI	CBS	FS	GRA	RM	PN	CJ	DBS	LD	PRO
Alaska		Y	Y		Y							Y		
Arizona	Y	Y		Y	Y		Y	Y	Y			Y		Y
Arkansas		Y			Y					Y		Y	Y	
California		Y		Y	Y	Y	Y	Y		Y	Y	Y	Y	Y
Colorado	Y						Y	Y		Y		Y	Y	
Connecticut							Y							Y
Delaware		Y		Y			Y	Y			Y			
D.C.				Y	Y			Y			Y			
Florida	Y	Y	Y		Y				Y	Y	Y		Y	
Georgia		Y		Y	Y		Y	Y		Y	Y	Y	Y	Y
Hawaii								Y						
Idaho		Y			Y			Y						
Illinois	Y		Y	Y	Y		Y	Y					Y	Y
Indiana		Y		Y	Y		Y	Y	Y		Y			Y
Iowa				Y	Y	Y	Y		Y	Y				
Kansas		Y			Y				Y	Y				
Kentucky					Y				Y					
Louisiana		Y	Y	Y	Y			Y	Y	Y	Y	Y	Y	Y
Maryland				Y	Y		Y	Y			Y			
Massachusetts					Y						Y			
Michigan							Y				Y			
Minnesota	Y	Y		Y				Y		Y		Y		
Mississippi		Y	Y				Y			Y	Y	Y	Y	Y
Missouri		Y		Y		Y	Y		Y	Y		Y		
Montana		Y			Y									
Nevada		Y	Y			Y	Y	Y				Y		
New Hampshire					Y			Y						
New Jersey		Y			Y	Y	Y	Y			Y			
New Mexico			Y					Y	Y	Y	Y	Y		
New York								Y						
Noith Carolina		Y												
North Dakota	Y	Y			Y									

Table 1 – *continued*

	DB	ES	FP	PAR	RTI	CBS	FS	GRA	RM	PN	CJ	DBS	LD	PRO
Ohio		Y		Y						Y		Y		
Oklahoma					Y		Y	Y				Y	Y	Y
Oregon								Y				Y		
Pennsylvania								Y						
Rhode Island							Y	Y				Y		Y
South Carolina	Y		Y		Y			Y			Y		Y	
South Dakota		Y												
Tennessee		Y				Y		Y	Y		Y			
Texas	Y	Y		Y	Y	Y	Y	Y		Y				Y
Utah		Y				Y	Y	Y				Y		
Vermont					Y									
Virginia	Y	Y	Y	Y		Y	Y	Y	Y	Y	Y	Y		
Washington					Y	Y	Y		Y	Y		Y	Y	
Wisconsin			Y					Y		Y				

Notes: Database (DB), the state administers and maintains a computerized criminal gang investigative data system. Enhanced sentencing (ES), gang members receive additional penalties. Forfeiture of property (FP), property used in the commission of an offence is confiscated. Participation (PAR), membership in a street gang is punishable in and of itself. Recrutiment, threats, intimidation (RTI), recruiting and coercing others to join is an offence. Clothing ban at school (CBS). Regarding schools (RS), gang members that commit an offence on school grounds may be suspended or expelled. Graffiti (GRA). Regarding minors (RM), recruitment of minors is an offence. Public nuisance (PN), property used for the criminal purposes of a gang member constitutes a public nuisance. Carjacking (CJ). Drive-by shooting (DBS). Legislative declarations (LD), the Legislature has made a public declaration concerning gangs. Programmes (PRO), there exist state committees or programmes devoted to the deterrence of gangs.

The size and influence of a criminal organization: a criminal achievement perspective

Pierre Tremblay[a], Martin Bouchard[b] and Sévrine Petit[a]

[a]*École de criminologie, Université de Montréal;* [b]*School of Criminology, Simon Fraser University*

Introduction

Criminal organizations are likely to be large in settings where states are weak and corruption opportunities abundant and small in settings where states are strong and corruption opportunities scarce and costly.[1] When criminal organizations are large, they can provide public goods such as security or even law,[2] or contribute to the economic welfare of a significant segment of the labour force. Whether this welfare is optimal or ensures sustained economic growth in the long run is another matter. In countries where illegal markets cannot rely as much on corruption opportunities, organizations face, as Reuter[3] has argued, more risks and uncertainties. For illegal entrepreneurs, the consequences of product illegality include unreliable audit procedures, restricted access to credit and insurance markets and inability to take advantage of advertisement and customer loyalty; because criminal careers are relatively short and offenders generally

---

1. P. Tremblay, M. Cusson and C. Corselli, 'Market Offenses and Limits to Growth', *Crime, Law and Social Change* 29 (1998): 4–29.
2. D. Gambetta, *The Sicilian Mafia: The Business of Private Protection* (Cambridge, MA: Harvard University Press, 1993); P.B.E. Hill, *The Japanese Mafia: Yakuza, Law and the State* (Oxford: Oxford University Press, 2003); F. Varese, *The Russian Mafia: Private Protection in a New Market Economy* (Oxford: Oxford University Press, 2001).
3. P. Reuter, *Disorganized Crime: the Economics of the Visible Hand* (Cambridge, MIT Press, 1983).

lack conventional human capital, illegal entrepreneurs are unlikely to invest in employee–employer relationships. Moreover organizational growth and success comes with a severe price tag as it increases the number of law enforcement agencies ready to devote time and energy to 'removing' the more entrepreneurial members. In such a context, illegal entrepreneurs are likely to adapt and keep their organizations relatively small. This in turn could explain why illegal drug markets are surprisingly resilient.[4]

One reason why Reuter's argument is persuasive is that the size of co-offending networks is typically small. This is true both for juvenile delinquents[5] and committed adult offenders.[6] Crime-specific work groups are also relatively small: four to 10 co-offenders for groups involved in the resale of stolen vehicles;[7] about 12 co-offenders for those involved in organized credit check frauds;[8] and three to six persons for outdoor, indoor and hydroponic cannabis cultivation sites.[9] Given the subject matter of the current paper, it is also relevant to mention that among the 63 outlaw biker gangs that were 'well known' to Québec's law-enforcement agencies during the 1974–1988 period, only six groups heavily involved in criminal activities were considered by outlaw bikers interviewed to have achieved continuity (having lasted as a club for 12 years or more) and size (a membership of 40 persons or more).[10]

Strictly focusing on the small size of the majority of illegal organizations (in number of co-offenders or employees) can make one lose sight of two important things. First, the economic influence[11] of criminal organizations is not necessarily captured by the size of its membership. Productivity levels, for instance, are likely to vary within and between organizations of similar size. Second, even if we accept that small criminal organizations are more efficient than large ones, it does not imply that large criminal organizations do not exist. It only implies that, if they do exist, they are likely to be inefficient. Levitt and Venkatesh[12] managed to study in

4. M. Bouchard, 'On the Resilience of Illegal Drug Markets', *Global Crime* 8 (2007): 325–44.

5. D. Sarneki, *Delinquent Network* (Stockholm: National Council for Crime Prevention, 1986); M. Warr, 'Organisation and Instigation in Delinquent Groups', *Criminology* 34 (1996): 11–37.

6. C. Morselli and P. Tremblay, 'Criminal Achievement And The Benefits Of Low Self-Control', *Criminology* 42 (2004): 773–804.

7. P. Tremblay, B. Talon and D. Hurley, 'Body Switching and Related Adaptations in the Resale of Stolen Vehicles: Script Elaborations and Aggregate Crime Learning Curves', *British Journal of Criminology*, 41 (2001): 561–79; C. Morselli and J. Roy, 'Brokerage Qualifications in Ringing Operations', *Criminology* 46 (2008): 71–98.

8. J. Lacoste and P. Tremblay, 'Crime and Innovation: a Procedural Analysis of Patterns in Check Forgery', in *Theory for Practice in Situational Crime Prevention. Crime Prevention Studies*, ed. M.J. Smith and D.B. Cornish (Monsey, NY: Criminal Justice Press, 2003), 169–96.

9. M. Bouchard, 'A Capture–Recapture Model to Estimate the Size of Criminal Populations and the Risks of Detection in a Cannabis Cultivation Industry', *Journal of Quantitative Criminology* 23 (2007): 221–41.

10. P. Tremblay, S. Laisne, G. Cordeau, B. MacLean and A. Shewshuck, 'Carrières criminelles collectives: évolution d'une population délinquante (les groupes motards)', *Criminologie* 22 (1989): 65–94.

11. In this paper, 'economic influence' and 'sphere of influence' are used interchangeably, and broadly refer to the same thing: the extent to which an organization has some control over other participants in a given market. Influence is measured specifically here as the number of offenders directly and indirectly depending on the organization to sell or obtain drug supplies. In other contexts, 'economic influence' refers to the ability of an organization to influence market price, which is not the case here, although one can expect a strong association between different 'types' of market influence.

12. S. Levitt and S.A. Venkatesh, 'An Economic Analysis of a Drug-selling Gang's Finances', *Quarterly Journal of Economics* 115 (2000): 775–89. Membership of the particular gang investigated in this study reaches 1000 individuals. But this particular belongs to a federation of 10 gangs of about the same size.

detail the behaviour of a large criminal organization that incorporated about 10,000 employees. What the authors observed is that entrepreneurs paid their employees unsatisfactory wages, offered limited opportunities for advancement and relied on violence as a means to increase their share of the market. Reuter's racketeering study,[13] which examined the role of the mafia in New York's garbage and waste disposal industry, illustrated how reputation is not a good proxy for economic influence: far from controlling the waste disposal market, the mafia was only allowed to collect a 5% commission for their services; and these services were mainly designed to maintain an obsolete and inefficient distribution of clients among the 150 firms that comprised this local market.

If it is true that size of criminal organization does not provide conclusive evidence of significant economic influence, it should also be the case that relatively tight organizations may in fact exercise a much larger influence than suggested by the number of individuals who actually 'belong' to these enterprises. Organization A may boost its membership by providing affiliation to all offenders willing to 'work' on its behalf: affiliation provides some street status yet status may not translate into tangible rewards. Organization B may opt for more stringent membership criteria and accept affiliation only to offenders having demonstrated considerable wits, prudence and entrepreneurial drive. Yet the economic influence of organization B is likely to be much 'larger' than that of organization A. In this paper, we argue that size of economic influence, which captures a network of interdependencies embedded in various criminal markets, may be conceptually[14] more important to analyse than actual 'membership size' of criminal organizations operating in these markets.

The influence of type A organizations can be assessed by offenders who defiantly advertise their affiliations. For example Cook et al.[15] described the structure and dynamics of gun markets in an urban environment where currently affiliated gang members represent 10–20% of male arrestees (as in Chicago or Los Angeles). Widespread affiliation characterizes some cities but not others. Assessing the economic influence of type B organizations requires a more roundabout procedure. In ideal conditions, one would first need to estimate a population of relevant offenders involved in various markets, extract a representative sample of offenders from this population, develop some intimacy with offenders interviewed and ask them if they have worked 'for' a particular organization; or better still, wait for the interviewees to bring up the subject matter. The final step would be to use the attributable fractions or proportions of offenders mentioning they worked for a given organization to assess its economic influence in such markets. Of course ideal conditions rarely exist. We nonetheless attempt, in this paper, to approximate these conditions.

If the economic influence of a criminal organization is to be captured 'outside' its boundaries, analysing how this influence structures the behaviour of all offenders servicing these markets becomes a central concern. A related topic is how criminal organizations may successfully widen their influence. Organized crime scholars typically consider size as a fixed or substantive attribute of criminal organizations and/or their global political and economic environment. Because their main interest is to describe how organizational status affects the rise and downfall of specific upper level entrepreneurs,

13. P. Reuter, *The Cartage Industry in New York*, in *Beyond the Law: Crime in Complex Organisations*, ed. Michael Tonry and Albert J. Reiss (Chicago, IL: University of Chicago Press, 1993), 149–202.

14. Membership estimates are important concerns however for law enforcement and prosecutorial purposes.

15. P.J. Cook, L. Jens, S. Venkatesh and A.A. Braga, 'Underground Gun Markets', *The Economic Journal* 117 (2007): F1–F29.

what these organizations actually achieve or how criminal markets affect their behaviour becomes somewhat irrelevant. From Chicago to Naples, from Naples to Moscow to Cali, Tokyo, Amsterdam and back again to Chicago, most in-house (and law-enforcement) intrigues share similar endings, and it does not matter much whether these intrigues occurred in the 1930s, the 1950s, the 1980s or the 2000s. However, just like conventional markets, criminal markets do change: prices of illegal commodities and services increase and decrease, sometimes dramatically,[16] barriers of entry change over time and across settings,[17] new products hit the market and new technologies change communication and distribution arrangements.[18] These market changes affect the behaviour of both affiliated and unaffiliated offenders servicing the markets, as well as the economic influence achieved by individual criminal organizations. Economic influence, then, is not assumed to be an attribute of criminal organizations, but a relational outcome of how they actually react and adapt to their environments and their contingencies.

In this paper, self-report survey and size of population methodologies are combined to assess the regional economic influence of a criminal organization (Hells Angels) in three illegal drug markets (the cocaine trade, the cannabis trade and the cannabis cultivation industry) in the province of Québec. The next section presents the data necessary for such estimates, and describes our analytical strategy. The findings are then divided in three sections. The first section argues that the economic influence of a relatively small organization can be large and provides some data to estimate its scope. The second section explains why this influence expanded over a relatively short period of time. The last section explores some of the consequences that rapid growth in organizational influence may have had on the levels of dispute within Québec's criminal milieu.

Data and analytical strategy

A drawback of mainstream criminological research has been, as Hagan[19] pointed out, that 'schools have replaced streets as sites for data collection', 'delinquency replaced crime as the behaviour to be explained' and 'common self-reported indiscretions' replaced 'the crimes of more general concern to citizens'. There have been, however, noteworthy efforts to improve 'street' criminology and auto-referential sampling procedures,[20] or to use

---

16. J.P. Caulkins and P. Reuter, 'What Price Data Tell us About Drug Markets', *Journal of Drug Issues* 28 (1998): 593–612.
17. V. Ruggiero, 'Drug Economics: A Fordist Model of Criminal Capital', *Capital and Class* 55 (1995): 131–50.
18. Ric Curtis and T. Wendel, 'Toward the Development of a Typology of Illegal Drug Markets', in *Illegal Drug Markets: From Research to Prevention Policy*, ed. Mangai Natarajan and Mike Hough (Monsey, NY: Criminal Justice Press, 2000); J. Riley, *Crack, Powder Cocaine, and Heroin: Drug Purchase and Use Patterns in Six U.S. Cities* (National Institute of Justice and Office of National Drug Control Policy, 1997).
19. J. Hagan, 'The Poverty of a Classless Criminology, The American Society of Criminology 1991 Presidential Address', *Criminology* 30 (1992): 1–19 at 4.
20. P. Biernacki and D. Waldorf, 'Snowball Sampling: Problems and Techniques of Chain Referral Sampling', *Sociological Methods & Research* 10 (1981): 141–63; D.D. Heckathorn, 'Respondent-driven Sampling: a new Approach to the Study of Hidden Populations', *Social Problems* 44 (1997): 174–99; R. Wright, S.H. Decker, A.K. Redfern and D.L. Smith, 'A Snowball's Chance in Hell: Doing Fieldwork with Active Residential Burglars', *Journal of Research in Crime and Delinquency* 29 (1992): 148–61; S. Jacques and R. Wright, 'Intimacy with Outlaws: the Role of Relational Distance in Recruiting, Paying and Interviewing Underworld Research Participants', *Journal of Research in Crime and Delinquency* 45 (2008): 22–38.

self-report surveys as a means to reach out for samples of experienced offenders involved in specific kinds of criminal activities.[21]

In this study, we engaged in the partial codification of a set of interviews with 'relatively successful adult offenders' conducted by 183 undergraduate students over a 10 year period (1996–2007). Students were asked to seek but not necessarily find 'relatively successful adult offenders' (namely who had achieved meaningful criminal earnings for some period of time). Each of these students were required to 'find' such an offender, preferably in their entourage (friends, relatives, acquaintances, friends of these friends, relatives of these relatives, acquaintances of friends or relatives). They were instructed to perform detailed interviews regarding their subjects' main offending activity and the length of time during which the offender was involved in the activity, and explore the many details of their favoured crime scripts. Because of the time allocated to the interviews (2–3 hours), students were advised to focus on a relatively short time frame (e.g. a three year window period for example), to concentrate on the criminal activity the subject knew best, to avoid going back into childhood and adolescent experiences, and to avoid discussion on 'general topics' or 'world view opinions'. They were then asked to present in class a synopsis of the criminal 'career' of the offender interviewed, respond to additional queries and details that other people in the classroom felt relevant and then write out their paper. As interviews accumulated, all new students were asked to take a sample of 15 interviews conducted by prior cohorts of fellow students enrolled in the course and explain why certain interviews were more 'interesting' than others. Essays did not require verbatim transcriptions (nearly all interviews were taped) but required extensive 'citations' and detailed accounts of crime scripts and significant turning points affecting the offender's ability to manage 'his crime life'.

We used content analysis of interview summaries (which had between 15 and 20 pages) to create the dataset used in this paper. Interviews were codified on variables and topics relevant for the purpose of this paper, most notably the type of crime involvement and the presence of organizational affiliation. Lack of instruments (questionnaire, detailed interview schedules) is partially compensated for by the common perspective driving these interviews. As shall be seen below, the majority of students were able to find a relatively successful offender. We still included the less successful offenders in this sample to preserve heterogeneity in the distribution of offenders interviewed.

Very few of these offenders were female (9 or 5% of 183), even if the majority of interviewers were female (67%). Offenders were 33 years old on average and nearly all were French Canadian (93%), a characteristic they shared with the interviewers themselves. Most offenders interviewed (80%) were embedded within the close or distant entourage of the students who interviewed them (relatives, friends or acquaintances, friends of friends or relatives or acquaintances, etc.). Students who lacked any 'eligible' offender in their circle of friends or acquaintances searched for subjects in halfway houses (rather than prisons) because they had friends working there and access was less troublesome and more informal. In a few cases they received some help from police officers they knew (three cases) or adopted other means (three cases).

21. J.D. Wright and P.H. Rossi, *Armed and Considered Dangerous: A Survey of Felons and Their Firearms* (New York: Aldine de Greyer, 1994); C. Morselli, P. Tremblay and B. McCarthy, 'Mentors and Criminal Achievement', *Criminology* 44 (2006): 17–43; P. Reuter, R. MacCoun and P. Murphy, *Money from Crime: A Study of the Economics of Drug Dealing in Washington, D.C* (Santa Monica, CA: Rand, 1990).

Some of the offenders interviewed were involved in property offences (robbery, 12 cases; break-and-enter and theft, 14 cases; credit card or check frauds, 16 cases; vehicle thefts, 14 cases;[22] cyber offences, eight cases). The majority of offenders interviewed (70% or 127 out 183), however, has been involved in market offences: fencing stolen goods or vehicles (five cases), or the cannabis trade (31 cases of retailing; three cases of wholesale; 16 cases of cultivation[23]). Others had been active in the cocaine trade (15 cases of retailing, 13 cases of upper level distributions, three cases of importing). Some offenders, but not many (seven cases), sold both cocaine and cannabis. (They were nonetheless classified as cocaine dealers.) Some were involved in other drug markets (hashish, three cases; amphetamines and ecstasy, two cases; steroids and benzodiazepine, two cases; and crack, one case only) or other kinds of criminal markets (prostitution, 10 cases; loansharking, four cases; smuggling of illegal immigrants, one case; illegal production of alcohol, one case, etc.) The proportion of offenders involved in market offences in this sample is not unusual. We found a similar proportion (67%) among offenders incarcerated in Canadian federal prisons who had stated having criminal earnings during the three years preceding their incarceration.[24]

Reaching out for offenders in the cannabis trade was expected to be easier for these students than interviewing offenders involved in selling cocaine, heroine or crack. This was partially true, as students were unable to access offenders supplying the crack market and heroine markets, but the ratio of cannabis and cocaine dealers interviewed (2 for 1) was quite similar to the ratio of cannabis and cocaine arrests for trafficking offences.[25] Detailed monthly and annual criminal earnings were provided in 103 of these interviews:[26] subjects who had some direct or indirect intimacy with the subjects were more likely to elicit explicit data on criminal earnings (61%) than those who conducted one-shot interviews in institutional settings (33%). The median annual income of offenders interviewed was $46,000 (geomean of $51,000): 25% had an income under $22,000, and 25% had an income above $75,000. Annual earnings of a random sample of Canadian federal inmates[27] who had been involved in property or marking offences during the three years prior to their current incarceration, were quite similar (an annual geomean of $42,000).

About one-half of the offenders interviewed (85 of 183) were criminally active at the time they were interviewed.[28] Among those who stated they were no longer active, 72% had been active during the five years preceding the interview. The average duration of their

22. Many of these interviews were a source of additional information for the analysis of investigation files of professional networks of motor vehicle thefts (Tremblay et al., 'Body Switching and Related Adaptations in the Resale of Stolen Vehicles').
23. These growers cultivated, on average, 100 plants per site, most of which were soil-based (in three cases they were hydroponic sites). Many interviews were a source of additional information for an analysis of the cannabis cultivation industry.
24. M. Charest, 'Classe sociale et réussite criminelle' (PhD diss., School of Criminology, University of Montréal, 2007).
25. M. Bouchard and P. Tremblay, 'Risks of Arrest Across Drug Markets: A Capture–Recapture Analysis of "Hidden" Dealer and User Populations', *The Journal of Drug Issues* 35 (2005): 733–54.
26. The proportion of offenders in market offences was similar in interviews that provided no data on criminal earnings. They were also more likely to belong to the earlier cohorts of student when confidence in the ability of students to reach out for relevant offenders had yet to be proven. Many of these interviews had chosen to focus on other features of crime life such as crime scripts.
27. Morselli and Tremblay, 'Criminal Achievement and the Benefits of Low Self-control'.
28. When interviews did not mention whether or not the subject was still active in crime (10.9% of interviews), we assumed that they were.

adult criminal career was 6 years: for 25% of subjects, offending activities spanned less than 3 years; for another 25%, duration spanned more than 8 years. Duration of involvement was higher for offenders interviewed in institutional settings (9.5 years) than for offenders recruited in the students' circle of friends and acquaintances (5.5 years). These figures are consistent with available estimates of average duration of adult criminal careers.[29] Patterns in impunity indicated that many had never been arrested (48%), and nearly two-thirds had managed to avoid incarceration (67%). Because relatively few offenders were interviewed in halfway houses or prisons, the apprehension avoidance rate of offenders embedded in the circle of friends and acquaintances of the interviewers was higher (84% had never been sentenced to prison, and 58% had never been arrested). Rates of impunity observed in this sample are not very different from those observed by Wright et al.[30] in their snowball sample of street-efficient burglars. Referral samples provide some shelter from potential self-selection biases that might contaminate inmate prison self-report surveys. Although this data set is not a chain referral sample – all interviewers reached out for only one eligible offender – the interviewers all shared some intimacy with the interviewees, conducted the interview at their place or the offender's place and were already known by interviewees as trustworthy or presented by friends or relatives of their entourage as people they could freely talk with.

Because this sample was composed of adult offenders (a) who were experienced in what they were doing, (b) had achieved meaningful returns from crime, if only for a few years, (c) had often managed to escape prison, (d) were all involved in what may viewed as 'common crimes' (very few 'white collar' offenders were recruited in this sample) and (e) were all well acquainted with the illegal drug markets, they provide a relevant sample of *'relatively' successful offenders* for the purpose of this study.

Data on the size of offender populations

The second data set used in this study is very different. The distribution of offenders arrested one or more times for cocaine or cannabis trafficking, or cannabis cultivation, during a period of three years in Québec from 1997 to 1999, was used to estimate the number of dealers and growers at risk of arrest but not arrested. The most robust estimation strategy[31] argues that arrests are rare events that occur randomly and that the distribution over time of arrests fits a homogeneous Poisson distribution.[32] If the research interest is in targeting the population of high-rate offenders likely to be arrested frequently over a relatively short period of time, or to fit existing arrest recidivism distributions, this model is inappropriate. If the research interest, however, is in providing a realistic estimate of the overall size of the population of offenders active in a given line of criminal activity, the Zelterman strategy of removing heterogeneity (excluding from the calculation of average arrest rate the subset of offenders arrested three or more times during the period of observation) has been shown to be robust and appropriate. Offenders who have been

29. A. Blumstein, J. Cohen, J.A. Roth and C.A. Visher, (eds), 'Criminal Careers and "Career Criminals"' (Washington, DC: National Academy of Science, 1986).
30. Biernacki and Waldorf, 'Snowball Sampling: Problems and Techniques of Chain Referral Sampling'; Heckathorn, 'Respondent-driven Sampling'; Wright et al., 'A Snowball's Chance in Hell'; Jacques and Wright, 'Intimacy with Outlaws'.
31. D. Zelterman, 'Robust Estimation in Truncated Discrete Distributions with Applications to Capture–Recapture Experiments', *Journal of Statistical Planning and Inference* 18 (1988): 225–37.
32. See Bouchard, 'A Capture–Recapture Model to Estimate the Size of Criminal Populations' for a detailed technical exposition.

arrested only once during an observation period are more likely to 'resemble' those who have not been arrested than offenders arrested many times, and the odds of being arrested only once more during this time interval are likely to approximate the odds of being arrested just once.

The model's second assumption requires that offenders who participate at various lambda rates in a given line of activity do so throughout the period of observation, or that those who choose to get involved and those who choose to 'leave' be roughly equal. The period of observation can be shortened when the arrest base rate is high, but needs to be extended when the arrest base rate is low. Since the average duration of criminal careers is about five years for many early adult offenders[33,34] and odds of arrest for drug dealing are typically low, we settled for a period of observation of three years. Violations of ecological boundaries are not a major concern in this study since the jurisdiction of the arrest data set is relatively wide (the province of Québec at large). The model's third assumption requires that offenders be sufficiently active to be at risk of arrest throughout the period of observation. This assumption is not appropriate when the target population involves individuals who commit 'three thefts of less than $100 during their lifetime', but these 'paper and pencil offenders' have little criminological interest and are not, in any meaningful way, 'at risk' of arrest.

Table 1 combines findings already published elsewhere.[35] The main focus of interest, at the time, was to assess cumulative odds of arrest over a one year period across various drug markets for both users and sellers. Cumulative odds of arrest for offenders servicing various illicit drug markets are estimated to be relatively low since they range from 2.6 to 7.1%. In this paper, however, we draw attention to the size of the labour force involved in these markets. Table 1 estimates that there were, in the late 1990s, about 46,000 cannabis dealers, 19,000 cocaine dealers and 30,000 offenders who produced domestic cannabis. These estimates are market-specific. It may well be that some offenders spread out their activities in more than one market. If so, the number of individuals servicing all three markets should be somewhat lower than the sum of persons working in each of one of them. In our interviews, crossovers were not extensive. In addition, in this paper, we are seeking orders of magnitude not precise estimates.

Linking these figures to consumer surveys is interesting. In the late 1990s these markets serviced about 800,000 cannabis and 200,000 cocaine users. This implies that about 70,000 producing and selling cannabis supplied 800,000 users and that about 19,000 persons serviced 200,000 cocaine users. In both cases we find one seller for 10 consumers. Similar ratios were found by MacCoun and Reuter in the United States.[36] Because these markets require little influx of capital or conventional human capital and can take advantage of inflated prices (a direct consequence of illegality), they are clearly labour-intensive. Given offenders' paramount concerns for apprehension avoidance, they also show very low productivity when compared with legitimate markets. This state of things, of course, is perfectly consistent with Reuter's[37] model of 'disorganized crime'.

33. See note 28.
34. Kazemian Lila and David P. Farrington, 'Exploring Residual Career Length and Residual Number of Offences for Two Generations of Repeat Offenders', *Journal of Research in Crime and Delinquency* 43 (2006): 89–113.
35. Lacoste and Tremblay, 'Crime and Innovation'. See note 23.
36. MacCoun, R., & Reuter, P. (2001). *Drug war heresies: Learning from other vices, times, and places*. New York: Cambridge University Press.
37. Reuter, 'Disorganized Crime: the Economics of the Visible Hand'.

Table 1. Estimating the total population of arrested and non-arrested dealers across illegal drug markets, Québec, Canada, *ca* 1998.

	Cannabis dealers	Cocaine dealers	Cannabis growers (soil-based)	Cannabis growers (hydroponic)
Number of dealers with k arrests[a]				
0	43,849	17,353	21,153	7904
1	2127	224	880	205
2	55	47	18	3
3+	14	4	1	0
Parametric Z estimates[b]	46,046	18,626	22,053	8112
Number of arrests	2281	1326	899	208
Z-derived arrest risks	5.0%	7.1%	4.1%	2.6%

[a] Data for the years 1997 to 1999 were used to generate a moving average of re-arrests distributions *ca* 1998.
[b] The parametric estimate for one year is obtained by adding the number of people with zero, one and more arrests.

These raw figures are important for the purpose of this study since our main goal is to roughly measure the number of offenders working for criminal organizations embedded in these markets.

The economic influence of a criminal organization

We now go back to the interviews to evaluate the prevalence of offenders who mentioned working for criminal organizations. Note that interviewers were not asked to seek out offenders who were associated with a criminal organization, or to target certain criminal organizations more than others. Their only instruction was to search for a person who, in their close or distant entourage, had been able to pursue for some time a relatively successful criminal career. They were asked to enquire if the offenders they interviewed acted 'solo' or not, and if not, to examine how assistance and cooperation from other co-offenders had an impact on their individual performance. Co-offenders included all offenders who helped them accomplish their activities before, during and after the transactions of events in they were directly involved.[38]

For the purpose of this study, we distinguished explicit affiliation associations (working for an identifiable criminal organization) from other co-offending work group associations (unaffiliated or independent groups of offenders). Thus, respondents who reported buying their drug supplies from a specific organization and re-selling them were defined as being 'associated' with that organization.[39]

Of the 183 offenders interviewed, 74 mentioned working for a criminal organization (about 40%). In 37 interviews, offenders explicitly declared their association to the Hells Angels, that is, to members of the five chapters established in Québec or to their affiliated clubs.[40] In three interviews, however, subjects mentioned having been threatened or

38. P. Tremblay, 'Searching for Suitable Co-offenders', in R.V. Clarke and M. Felson (eds) *Routine Activities and Rational Choice. Advances in Criminological Theory*, vol. 5 (New Brunswick, NJ: Transaction Press, 1993), 17–36.
39. A limitation of this data is the possibility that respondents have exaggerated their 'associations' to criminal organizations. While we cannot rule out that possibility, we also cannot rule out the opposite possibility that some respondents failed (purposely or not) to mention an existing association. And others may not have been aware of the affiliations of their business partners.
40. The Hells Angels have 34 chapters in Canada, of which five are in the province of Québec.

ordered to cease their unaffiliated competition with offenders affiliated to the Hells Angels, and rather than accept affiliation, they had abandoned their activities (selling cocaine or cultivating cannabis). This left 34 interviews in which offenders mentioned working for the Hells Angels. In three interviews, subjects said they worked for a rival biker gang (the 'Rock Machines'[41]) and in eight interviews, subjects said they worked for 'bikers' without specifying whether the affiliation referred to the Hells Angels or to other biker clubs.[42]

When we eliminated the 35 interviews with offenders who were not recruited within students' entourage, the number of references to associations with criminal organizations decreased from 74 to 63, and explicit references of a working association with the Hells Angels decreased from 34 to 28. The relative number of references to criminal organizations was the same (44%) as the dominant position of references to the Hells Angels. We conclude that the influence of this particular organization cannot be explained away as a selection bias of offenders incarcerated in halfway houses or prisons or contacted through law enforcement officers. Interviews did not provide detailed information on characteristics of those they believed to be affiliated with the Hells Angels or their status (members in good standing or 'prospects' of a Hells Angels chapter or an affiliated club). We know, however, that nearly all these local chapters and affiliated clubs are located outside the Montréal region (and its suburbs). As it happens 56% of offenders who said they worked for people affiliated with the Hells Angels conducted their criminal activities outside of Montréal, whereas this was true of only 27% of subjects who said they were associated with other criminal organizations (or who did not specify their affiliations).

Table 2 combines two data sources. First, it cross-tabulates affiliation associations[43] and self-reported criminal activities derived from the interviews. These activities were broken down into four categories: the cannabis trade, the cultivation industry, the cocaine trade and other illicit activities. Second, it incorporates (from Table 1) aggregate workforce estimates for the three markets. The size of offender populations involved in 'other criminal activities' is unknown. Table 2 indicates that offenders affiliated with criminal organizations are predominantly involved in the cocaine trade (72%), and to a lesser degree in the cannabis trade (53%), or in cannabis cultivation (37%). This is not very surprising: cocaine is an imported good and because the market is smaller, and it is easier for upper level entrepreneurs to control its distribution, and because the cannabis cultivation sites are spread out across a large territory, it also makes sense that its 'industrial relations' be somewhat more 'disorganized' than its retailing.

The results presented in Table 2 show that the economic influence of a criminal organization can be large: 8940 of the 18,626 cocaine dealing jobs (nearly 50%) can

41. Dominant group of a short-lived coalition of dissidents (the 'Alliance') who were briefly associated with the Bandidos during the 'war' that opposed them to the Hells Angels from 1994 to 2001: C. Morselli, D. Tanguay and A.-M. Labalette, 'Criminal Conflicts and Collective Violence: Biker-Related Account Settlements in Québec, 1994–2001', in D. Siegel and H. Nelen (eds) *Organized Crime: Culture, Markets, and Policies* (New York: Springer, 2008), 145–164. A number of these dissidents eventually joined the ranks of Hells Angels after the feud; this was also the case for some of the Outlaws who had defied the Hells Angels during the 1970s.
42. Many of the outlaw motorcycle gangs of the 1970s and 1980s have either disappeared or have been absorbed by the Hells Angels (Tremblay et al., 'Carrières criminelles collectives'). See note 10.
43. Affiliation is indirect because nearly all subjects interviewed mentioned working for another offender who belonged or acted on behalf of a member of a Hells Angels chapter or to one of their affiliated clubs. For the purpose of this article, the expression 'affiliation association' is defined as 'indirect affiliation'.

Table 2. Estimates of the economic influence of criminal organizations in three illegal markets, Québec *ca* 1998.

	Non-affiliated population		Population associated with Hells Angels		Population associatied with other organizations		Total population	
	n%	*N*	*n*%	*N*	*n*%	*N*	Total%	*N*[a]
Cannabis trade	14 66%	30,390	6 29%	13,353	5 24%	11,051	21 100%	46,046
Cannabis cultivation	10 63%	19,004	4 25%	7541	2 12%	3620	16 100%	30,165
Cocaine trade	8 28%	5215	14 48%	8940	7 24%	4470	29 100%	18,626
Other activities	76 67%	–	11 10%	–	26 23%	–	113 100%	–
Total (respondents)	108		34		43		183	

[a] From Table 1.

be related to the Hells Angels, as can be 13,353 of the 46,046 cannabis dealing jobs, and 7451 of the 30,165 cannabis cultivation jobs. Their influence on the sale of cannabis is about equal to the sum of influences all other criminal organizations combined. Even though the cultivation industry is largely 'freelance' or 'disorganized', the Hells Angels have a direct influence on 25% of the workforce, whereas all other criminal organizations influence only 12% of jobs available. Given the uncertainties regarding the precision of each one of the parameters used to generate such proportions, these numbers should be considered for what they are: rough estimates. The important point is that, even if these calculations overestimate the influence of the Hells Angels by 25 or 50%, the overall result remains the same: the organization has an influence on the livelihood of thousands of cannabis growers and drug dealers at all levels.

Reuter[44] argues that criminal firms are typically small in size, local in geographical scope and short-lived. What we have here is an organization that is regional in scope and has a direct impact on half of the jobs in the cocaine trade and about a quarter of the jobs involved in the sale and domestic cultivation of cannabis. Reuter's argument, however, emphasizes only that the size of criminal organizations is small. It does not imply that its economic influence should necessarily be 'small'.[45] We may view the Hells Angels as a chamber of commerce that incorporates, in Québec, about 100 affiliated or 'franchised' entrepreneurs who share the same trademark, logo or banner.[46] 'Franchisees' or 'affiliates'

44. Reuter, 'Disorganized Crime: the Economics of the Visible Hand'.
45. Investigative material provides an illustration: 'Upon examination of Hells Angels accounting, we are stunned to see that they were able to dispose of their drugs with lightning speed. For example, a 350kg order of cocaine, valued at $14 million was disposed of in less than three weeks. In addition to the drug sold to other criminal organizations, the Nomads supplied their own dealers, as well as Hells Angels dealers, with more than 2000kg of cocaine annually and at least as much hashish'. Julian Sher and William Marsden, *La route des Hells: comment les motards ont bâti leur empire* (Montréal: Les Éditions de l'Homme, 2003), 186.
46. Ibid., 431: 'With the Hells, there is no godfather, no singular chief who can be eliminated in order to topple the whole empire. The Hells function a bit like McDonalds: even if you close a franchise, other franchises continue to prosper'.

are themselves relatively autonomous entrepreneurs seeking partners to conduct business. If we grant each franchisee a network of 10 partners, and if any given partner either directly supervises 40 employees or, more realistically, supervises about 10 employees, who themselves supervise four employees each, the aggregate network extends to 40,000 people. In short, under specific circumstances, there is no logical reason why criminal organizations of limited size (about 100 members) cannot achieve in criminal markets the kind of economic power granted to large firms in conventional markets.

Explaining organizational growth

It is one thing to argue that a criminal organization can achieve decisive influence in one or several illicit markets. It is quite another to explain this influence or understand its growth. For Levitt and Venkatesh,[47] violence or predatory competition emerge as the main mechanisms for organizational growth. This is surely part of the answer. However, other factors should also be considered. It may be that some organizations differ in their competing ability to take advantage of local or regional opportunities.

Official crime data suggest that, during the 1990s, business opportunities in the cocaine and heroine markets were stagnant in Québec (Figure 1), but they flourished in the cannabis market (Figure 2). The turning point occurred around 1993. Bouchard and Dion[48] argued that this turning point was not a statistical artefact because the number of legitimate hydroponics supplies businesses increased sharply during that time period, with a turning point also occurring in 1993. No analogous growth pattern was observed in similar kinds of businesses (such as flower shops). Drug user surveys[49] add validity to the upward trend observed in official data: the proportion of past year cannabis consumers in the province of Québec rose from 6.5% in 1989, to 8.6% in 1994, reaching 13.5% in 1998 and 15.8% in 2004. The impact of this increase is even more striking when the raw figures are considered: a net increase of 500,000 additional cannabis users over a 10 year period (1994–2004).

What kind of criminal organizations could take advantage of such favourable circumstances? One scenario could be that that all players and all organizations benefited equally from this market opportunity. Independent entrepreneurs, however, do not have the same resources as their affiliated counterparts, and all organizations do not necessarily have the same competitive advantages in seizing this opportunity. Three elements should be considered.

First, cannabis is a mass consumption market. Its clientele crosses all social classes and is not confined to large urban centres. Because cannabis consumption is a regional market (for the purpose of this study) and rural or semi-urban regions present lower risk opportunities for entrepreneurs, a criminal enterprise with a regional grassroots distribution network is likely to be competitive. The literature on drug trafficking has

47. Levitt and Venkatesh, 'An Economic Analysis of a Drug-selling Gang's Finances'.
48. M. Bouchard and C.B. Dion, 'Growers and Facilitators: Probing the Role of Entrepreneurs in the Development of the Cannabis Cultivation Industry', *Journal of Small Business & Entrepreneurship* 22 (2009): 25–38.
49. E.M. Adlaf, P. Begin and E. Sawka (eds), 'Canadian Addiction Survey: A National Survey of Canadians' Use of Alcohol and Other Drugs, Prevalence of Use and Related Harms: Detailed Report' (Ottawa: Canadian Centre on Substance Abuse, 2005); G. Dubé, I. Traoré, and R. Tremblay, 'Recueil statistique sur le tabac, l'alcool, ladrogue et le jeu chez les élèves du secondaire de 1998 à 2004' (Québec: Institut de la Statistique du Québec, 2006).

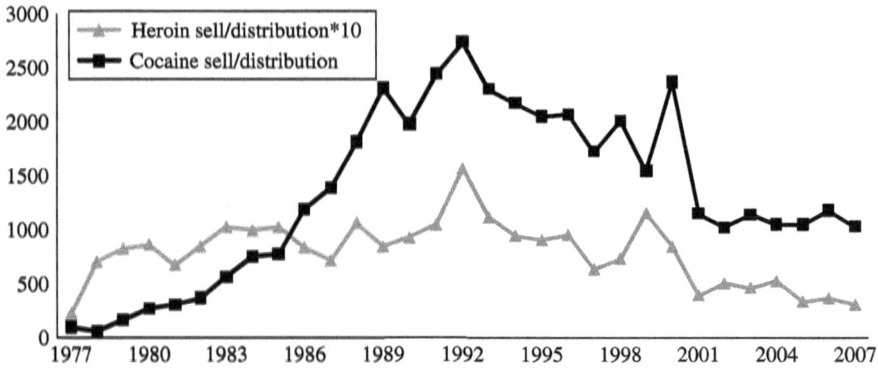

Figure 1. Number of cocaine and heroin selling/distribution offences reported by the police, Québec, 1977–2007.

largely focused on groups of offenders who have a competitive edge in supplying imported goods. Unsurprisingly the suitable groups emerged as cosmopolitan groups located in large urban centres.[50] These advantages may become handicaps when applied to the cannabis industry.[51] The Hells Angels organization, however, had spread its chapters and clubs throughout the province of Québec well before the cannabis market exploded and was well positioned to seize the opportunity when it presented itself.[52]

Second, this organization has shown a taste for innovative business practices. Whereas opportunities for 'promotion' and advancement were very limited in the organization studied by Levitt and Venkatesh,[53] a study of the 'organizational' career paths of about 20 Hells Angels 'hang arounds', 'prospects' and members during the 1996–2001 period indicated that there were numerous flexible and beneficial promotion opportunities strengthening members' dedication to the organization as well as contributing to its resilience.[54] From 1992 to 1994, precisely when domestic cannabis cultivation was developing rapidly, the Hells Angels incorporated numerous affiliated clubs (Satans Guard in the Saguenay region; the Rockers in Montréal; the Jockers in St Jean; the Rowdy Crew in Lanaudière; and the Evil Ones Drummond in Drummondville).[55] With expertise in the production of amphetamines and a solid regional cocaine distribution infrastructure in the province's bars and clubs, the Hells Angels were well positioned to take advantage of the transition from small to large cultivation sites, and the even more profitable transition from 'soil grown' cannabis to hydroponics production.[56] Commenting on the boom in cannabis cultivation in Québec, cannabis growers interviewed in a recent field study were categorical: during the 1990s,

50. For example, see D. Zaitch, *Trafficking Cocaine: Columbian Drug Entrepreneurs in the Netherlands* (The Hague: Kluwer Law International, 2002).
51. R. Weisheit, *Domestic Marijuana; A Neglected Industry* (New York: Greenwood Press, 1992).
52. G. Ouellette and N. Lester, *Mom* (Montréal, Éditions les Intouchables, 2005).
53. Levitt and Venkatesh, 'An Economic Analysis of a Drug-selling Gang's Finances'.
54. M. Leduc, *Patchwork: le rationnel du système de promotion dans l'organisation des Hells Angels* (Masters diss., School of Criminology, University of Montréal, 2005), ii, 31.
55. See note 52.
56. Bouchard, 'A Capture–Recapture Model to Estimate the Size of Criminal Populations'.

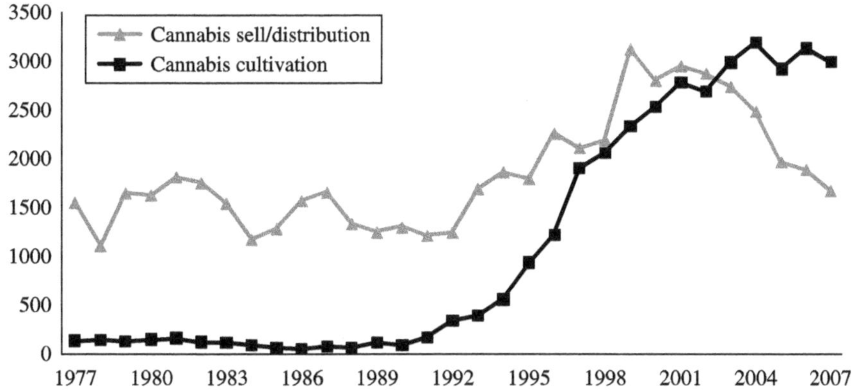

Figure 2. Number of cannabis selling/distribution and cultivation offences reported by the police 1977–2007, Québec.

the 'market price' was the 'bikers' price'; 'They bought everything'; 'Who buys 1000 pounds? That's where bikers come into the picture'.[57]

Third, outlaw motorcycle gangs, especially the Hells Angels, had acquired a reputation for warfare. Cordeau[58] noted that members affiliated with motorcycle gangs were involved in 20% of 530 account settlements (gang-related homicides) in Québec from 1970 to 1986. This proportion quadrupled in Québec during the 1990s.[59] A first major conflict between four offender groups, two of whom were motorcycle gangs (Devils Disciples and Pacific Rebels), and which lasted for three years from 1974 to 1976, ended in about 40 deaths.[60,61] The second major conflict, which opposed the Hells Angels and the Outlaws, lasted for seven years (from 1978 to 1985) and caused about 30 deaths.[62] In the third conflict, the Hells Angels were in conflict with a coalition of motorcycle gangs (the Rock Machines) and dissident rivals. The conflict lasted from 1994 to 2001, and ended with a much higher death toll (126 deaths). Note that only nine Hells Angels chapter members in good standing, and four members in good standing among their numerous affiliated clubs (about 10), were killed in these conflicts.[63] The degree of organization and resources exhibited by the Hells Angels during this conflict was striking, with theft of dynamite from construction sites, storage in various caches, remote controlled bombings and information gathering on both the police and rival gangs.[64]

57. For details on the field study involving nine marijuana growers who were active in the province of Québec between 1993 and 2005, see note 9.
58. G. Cordeau, *Les règlements de compte dans le milieu criminel québécois de 1970 à 1986* (Ph.D. diss., School of Criminology, University of Montréal, 1990), 50.
59. See note 39.
60. Leduc, *Patchwork.*
61. C. Deveault and R. Desmarais, *Donald Lavoie, tueur à gages* (Montréal: Édition du Club Québec-Loisirs, 1984); R. Desmarais, *Le clan des Dubois* (Montréal: Stanké, 1976).
62. Y. Lavigne, *Hell's Angels: Taking Care of Business* (Toronto: Deneau and Wayne, 1988).
63. D. Tanguay, *Récits motards: examen d'un conflit en milieu criminel* (Masters diss., School of Criminology, University of Montréal, 2003), 43.
64. See note 45.

Conclusion

In *Disorganized Crime*, Reuter[65] emphasized the importance of looking into employee–employer transactions and their impact on the behaviour of criminal entrepreneurs and the optimal size of criminal organizations. Levitt and Venkatesh[66] also adopted this bottom-up approach by analysing the behaviour of 'employees' in a large criminal organization that internalized their economic influence into its boundaries. Such an arrangement appears to be inefficient since members were provided with few promotion opportunities, asked to give up their tangible self-interests in exchange for intangible street 'status', to comply with artificial territorial or street corner barriers of trade, and to engage in lethal warfare that provided meagre returns on investment. In this paper, we also adopt a bottom-up perspective approach but we do so by linking macro and micro levels of analyses. We start by estimating the size of the population of job holders in illegal markets where criminal organizations are likely to have a hold. We then engage in referential self-report survey research designed to reach a relevant and diversified pool of knowledgeable participants in such markets. The views of such respondents, who are not themselves organizational insiders, are important because they provide an estimate of the economic influence of criminal organizations on the overall market in which they are embedded. Findings indicate that relatively small organizations (100 affiliates) may build a 'large', coordinated network of economic influence involving thousands of individuals working in these markets. While past studies on criminal achievement have carefully examined the factors explaining individual success in crime,[67] the current study shows that a criminal achievement perspective can also be applied to criminal organizations.

The influence of a criminal organization can increase, decrease or remain stable. What we find in this study is that enrichment opportunities during the 1990s were provided by the expanding cannabis market. Because this was a regional mass-market fuelled by domestic cultivation, a grass-roots French Canadian organization had a competing advantage over cosmopolitan organizations (located mainly in Montréal), who were confined to their network of pipeline connections required for the transnational smuggling of illegal commodities. Other factors also explains why the Hells Angels achieved dominant economic influence: entrepreneurial flair, technological innovations (e.g. hydroponics production), organizational flexibility (creation of affiliated clubs) and a well-deserved reputation of violence.

Violence may explain why a criminal organization maintains itself, but violence is just a means to an end – an adaptation to a 'situation'. It does not explain the stakes of the situation or make us understand the particular goals criminal entrepreneurs seek to achieve. Violence, in short, does not explain itself, even though it may be tempting to think so. Scholars as well as investigative reporters seem to be fascinated by eruption of lethal conflicts in the criminal milieu. There are a number of interesting monographs on the 'biker war' which, from 1994 to 2001, opposed the Hells Angels to a coalition of other outlaw motorcycle gangs. These studies describe in minute details the duration and tempo of this conflict and the impact of police interventions on monthly fatalities, but these studies do not explain the patterns they observe. For example they observe that the 1994–2001 war polarized the entire criminal milieu in the province of Québec

65. Reuter, 'Disorganized Crime'.
66. Levitt and Venkatesh, 'An Economic Analysis of a Drug-selling Gang's Finances'.
67. Morselli et al., 'Mentors and Criminal Achievement'; Morselli and Tremblay, 'Criminal Achievement and the Benefits of Low Self-control'.

(group conflicts of the 1970s and 1980s did not have such an effect). Why should that be so? Findings in this paper shed some light on the possible underlying reasons for this polarization. If, as we suspect, Hells Angels had an influence, through intermediate subcontractors, on 50% of the active cocaine dealers in the province of Québec, 25% of its cannabis growers and nearly 30% of cannabis dealers, and if this particular organization had an economic network of influence equal to all organizations in these markets, then one can understand why the polarization effect occurred, and how, in turn, this polarization explains the unusual duration and heavy toll of this particular conflict, in comparison to prior conflicts.

These same studies observe that the conflict began in 1994, but they do not attempt to explain why it occurred in the first place, or why it occurred in 1994 rather than at some other time. It is tempting to assume that the criminal milieu is 'naturally' violent, that criminal entrepreneurs lack self-control and do not need strong reasons to engage in 'warfare', or that violence is the only way in which an organization can increase its influence. Yet this only begs further questions. Our findings suggest that the creation of affiliated clubs by the Hells Angels coincided with the expansion of domestic cannabis cultivation. In fact many of these clubs were created before the conflict and designed to provide additional structure and coordination to the economic influence of the organization. Over the years (1980s and early 1990s), the Hells Angels had broadened their regional influence on the cannabis and cocaine markets, yet their influence was limited in the crowded criminal markets of the province's metropolitan area.[68] A key finding of the current study is that the economic influence achieved by the Hells Angels in the 1990s in these markets was about the same as that of all other criminal organizations combined. It may well be that the expanding cannabis market tipped over the balance of economic influence between organizations embedded in these markets. This tipping over seems to have had a fateful domino effect. It may have convinced the Hells Angels that they could move into the metropolitan market (Montréal) and that if a 'war' occurred they would win it (as indeed they did[69]). However, the balance of power also convinced the remaining organizations that they could rally a coalition and successfully preserve the status quo. Had the pattern of economic influences of criminal organizations been somewhat unbalanced, the conflict may not have occurred, or would not have occurred at that particular time, or would have not lasted so long, or would not have been so deadly.

Acknowledgements

The authors would like to thank the reviewers for their useful comments, and all the 1996–2007 undergraduate students of the course 'Formes particulières de crimes' who devoted time and ingenuity in achieving 'intimacy with outlaws'.

68. Montréal was the main location of most of the fatalities of the 1994–2001 biker conflict.
69. Despite a major law-enforcement crackdown in 2001, a majority of members were not arrested and quite a number were spared altogether: S. Petit, *Hells Angels malgré tout* (Working Paper, School of Criminology, University of Montréal, 2006), 35–7.

Understanding optimal criminal networks

Stephen T. Easton and Alexander K. Karaivanov

Department of Economics, Simon Fraser University

Introduction

For 70 years social scientists have discussed crime in the context of social networks. Hard on the heels of one of the early mathematical and empirical studies of what we now call a 'social network' by Moreno in 1934, Sutherland used the idea of a network to describe the relationships that existed and guided loose 'organizations' of thieves in their criminal endeavours.[1]

By a social network we mean a group of individuals together with the set of links that connect them. These links can represent a wide variety of social or other connections: communication channels, friendships, family relationships, criminal or business relationships, etc. The connections can be bidirectional or unidirectional and can reflect a measure of the intensity of the relationship or simply its presence.

Our purpose in this paper is to discuss and apply an economics approach to the theory of networking in the study of crime. For this purpose networks may be thought of as coming in two important varieties: (i) those that describe a set of fixed, pre-existing relationships like kinship ties; and (ii) those that arise from some behavioural process whereby the agents choose both the number of individuals participating in the network and the configuration of links. The vast bulk of analysis in social science is confined to the first variety. Consequently, the configuration of the networks, be it friendship groups or criminal organizations, is taken to be outside the scope of analysis. Most scholars are instead interested in characterizing the *observed* network for various purposes. Measures related to the number and configuration

1. J. Moreno, *Who Shall Survive?: A New Approach to the Problem of Human Interrelations* (Nervous and Mental Disease Publishing Co.: Washington, DC, 1934); E. Sutherland, *The Professional Thief: by a Professional Thief. Annotated and Interpreted by Edwin H. Sutherland* (Chicago, IL: University of Chicago Press, 1937).

of extant nodes and links such as 'centrality', 'betweenness', 'density' and other formalizations[2] are computed to help understand any number of relevant issues. In the context of crime, policy is frequently linked to identifying or removing an actor who is important in some dimension or in destabilizing a particular network.

Our approach generalizes the case in which the network structure is taken as fixed exogenously to an analysis in which the configuration of the network itself is an object of choice. We are thus interested in networks that have a *raison d'être*, as a consequence of purposeful behavioural choices made by the network members. This would seem to be particularly appropriate in the context of criminal networks. First, while there are examples of criminal activity based on kinship or regional relationships, even in these cases not every member of a family nor every person in a community is involved in the criminal activity. Writ broadly, the idea of a network as a pre-existing set of relationships in many cases begs the fundamental question as to why a particular network structure has been formed instead of any of a large number of alternative networks.

Second, once we recognize that the criminal network structure itself is an object of choice by the participants, it forces a very different perspective on the appropriateness and usage of standard measures such as connectivity and centrality. If as a prescription for crime reduction, for example, a policy based on a fixed network calls for removing the 'central' or 'key player' in the network, we want to be sure that it is the right 'key player' who is targeted if the network structure in fact is flexible. While irrelevant if the network is fixed, should criminals be aware of a particular law enforcement policy threat, they may choose to alter (ex-ante or ex-post) their network to one less vulnerable to that policy. Facing different specific threats, it would be surprising to see the same network always be formed if criminals have the ability to modify the network, even if this ability is subject to constraints.[3] Consequently, we argue that the crime combating policy strategists must recognize that criminals have the ability to alter the structure of the network itself. As a result, as we demonstrate in this paper, in general the best policies are not the same as those designed for fixed networks.

To be able to analyse the criminals' purposeful choice of network structures as well as their optimal response to various law enforcement policies and strategies, we develop a formal model of criminal networks. This model, after calibration with data on actual networks and the costs and benefits of particular criminal or terrorism activities, can be used as forecasting tool in designing crime combating policy.

The social networks approach to the study of criminal organizations

Networks in Criminology

Criminologists have used networks to frame any number of important issues such as delinquency, violence, the consequences of drug abuse among women, police socialization,

2. For an excellent review see S. Wasserman and K. Faust, *Social Network Analysis: Methods and Applications* (Cambridge: Cambridge University Press, 1994).

3. Economists typically distinguish short-run from long-run responses on the basis of various constraints on possible choices characterizing the short-run. Analogously, we might imagine an observed network as a short-run outcome of a process in which the players are unable for some time to change the size or the number of links in the network. Further, this is not to say that networks are not influenced by exogenous relationships like family or social ties. What is important is that the actual choice of the size and structure of the network, possibly subject to those constraints (which are not absolute) has not been modelled.

co-offending, criminal intelligence gathering and criminal displacement to name but a few.[4] Quintessentially, social network theory has been used as a way to understand organized crime ranging from mafia families to street-level drug dealing. For instance, Bruinsma and Bernasco[5] suggest that 'the traditional view of criminal groups as centrally controlled organizations has been replaced by the notion of criminal networks' while Kenney provides extensive list of references and a guide to the use of social networks for analysing crime.[6]

Economic sociologist Ronald Burt, one of the 'fathers' of network theory, introduced the idea that gaps between two different groups connected through a single key agent ('broker') can be thought of as 'structural holes' in social networks. Burt studied supply chain managers and hypothesized that people who span such structural holes are those who 'live at the intersection of social worlds', and are 'at higher risk of having good ideas' as they are exposed to more diversity, while people who are part of more cohesive social networks (e.g. colleagues in the same office) tend to think and act the same. Burt's theory implies that among networks with a given number of non-redundant links, those who span more diverse sets of players (sub-networks) provide more information. Burt's theory has been widely used in sociology and criminology and brings important insights as to the benefits and costs of different network structures that we use in our analysis.[7]

There are several important aspects of organized crime that have been successfully analysed using network theory, although some authors have reservations. The works of McIllwain and McGloin[8] aptly illustrate these differences of opinion. McIllwain explicitly treats organized crime from a social networking perspective, in contrast to what he argues has been its major characterizations from institutional or organizational perspectives: as a set of patron–client relationships, or as part of the 'business of organized crime'. His take on the mafia is reminiscent of Burt's[9] as he finds that, 'they serve as brokers of information and services between various subgroups' and consequently, the network they inhabit is fundamental and serves as an underpinning to all of the earlier approaches. McGloin, on the other hand, while arguing that network analysis is useful for the study of gangs in the broad sense, maintains that it is not necessarily useful for characterizing all gangs.

4. J. Sarnecki, *Delinquent Networks: Youth Co-offending in Stockholm* (Cambridge: Cambridge University Press, 2001); C. Schreck, B. Fisher, J. Miller and J. Mitchell, 'The Social Context of Violent Victimization: A Study of the Delinquent Peer Effect', *Justice Quarterly* 21 (2004): 23–47; S. James, J. Johnson and C. Raghavan, 'I Couldn't go Anywhere: Contextualizing Violence and Drug Abuse: A Social Network Study', *Violence Against Women* 10 (2004): 991–1014; M. Sato, 'Police Recruits' Training and the Socialization Process: From the Network Perspective', *Police Journal* 76 (2003): 289–303; L. Hoffer, *Junkie Business: The Evolution and Operation of a Heroin Dealing Network* (Ann Arbor, MI: UMI Press, 2002); M. Sparrow, 'The Application of Network Analysis to Criminal Intelligence: an Assessment of the Prospects', *Social Networks* 13 (1991): 251–74; S. Deutsch, J. Jarvis and G. Parker, 'A Network Flow Model for Forecasting and Evaluating Criminal Displacement', *Evaluation Quarterly* 3 (1979): 219–35.

5. G. Bruinsma and W. Bernasco, 'Criminal Groups and Transnational Illegal Markets: A More Detailed Examination on the Basis of Social Network Theory', *Crime, Law and Social Change: An Interdisciplinary Journal* 41 (2004): 79–94.

6. M. Kenney, 'The Architecture of Drug Trafficking: Network Forms of Organisation in the Colombian Cocaine Trade', *Global Crime* 8 (2007): 233–59.

7. R. Burt, *Structural Holes: The Social Structure of Competition* (Cambridge, MA: Harvard University Press, 1992).

8. J. McIllwain, 'Organized Crime: A Social Network Approach', *Crime, Law and Social Change* 32 (1999): 301–23; J. McGloin, 'Policy and Intervention Considerations of a Network Analysis of Street Gangs', *Criminology and Public Policy* 4 (2005): 607–36.

9. R. Burt, *Structural Holes*, 311.

In particular, she has reservations about the relevance of the 'key player' approach for analysis and intervention. If the gangs in question can easily re-form or are sufficiently loosely associated, then they are far less structured than a simple relationship mapping suggests.

Morselli and Tremblay[10] use a network approach to examine the gains from criminal earnings. By emphasizing the theory of 'non-redundant' networking derived from Burt's theory of structural holes, they find that 'brokerage-like' networking raises offenders' market earnings. However, networking does not affect non-market incomes or 'predatory' offenders' incomes. When engaged in illegal market-oriented offences, criminals who stand between different networks that have no additional contacts with each other are the participants who generate income higher than that of the other members of the network. We find similar results in our theoretical model.

In yet another application, Albanese argues for a generic network approach by function, rather than looking at particular individuals, in his application of the network approach to human trafficking.[11] He suggests that tasks of recruiting, transporting and exploiting, while variable among individuals, reflect fundamental characteristics of a network of required activities to permit the 'white slave' trade to persist. He contrasts networks with 'traditional crime groups', arguing that the associations made up of networks are less persistent and less well-organized.

The role of networks is distinct and stands in contrast to approaches that emphasize simple association. For example, Haynie[12] argues that network 'density' (the frequency of links among players) plays an important part in delinquency behaviour – peer association with higher network density is associated with greater delinquency. Consequently, the structure of the network, as well as simple peer effects (which are usually thought of as averages of associates' attitudes), is germane to observed criminal behaviour. Location in the network, which can be quantified through measures of density, centrality and popularity, provides a better predictor of delinquent involvement than simply knowing the attitudes of peers. Haynie also finds that an adaptation of Sutherland's theory of differential association and Akers' emphasis on peer behaviour is consistent with evidence found by knowing the intensity of association as a function of the location in the network.[13]

Natarajan emphasizes the network structures associated with different phases of criminal activities.[14] She uses telephone intercepts to explore network density, cut-points and centrality in the context of heroin dealing. She finds that while the 'star' topology reflects best the dealer and his distributors, and that dealers alone are connected to suppliers, the suppliers themselves are also connected to each other. Most of the players

10. C. Morselli and P. Tremblay, 'Criminal Achievement, Offender Networks and the Benefits of Low Self-Control', *Criminology* 42 (2004): 773–804.
11. J. Albanese, 'Criminal Network Approach to Understanding & Measuring Trafficking in Human Beings', in *Measuring Human Trafficking* (New York: Springer 2004).
12. D. Haynie, 'Delinquent Peers Revisited: Does Network Structure Matter?', *American Journal of Sociology* 106 (2001): 1013–57; D. Haynie, 'Neighborhood Characteristics, Peer Networks, and Adolescent Violence' *Journal of Quantitative Criminology* 22 (2006): 147–69.
13. E. Sutherland, *Principles of Criminology*, 4th edn (Philadelphia, PA: J. B. Lippincott, 1947); R. Akers, *Deviant Behavior: A Social Learning Approach*, 3rd edn (Belmont, CA: Wadsworth, 1985).
14. M. Natarajan, 'Understanding the Structure of a Large Heroin Distribution Network: A Quantitative Analysis of Qualitative Data', *Journal of Quantitative Criminology* 22 (2006): 171–92.

in the network have a single contact (208 out of 294 participants), and only about 38 of 294 players were active in the sense of having multiple phone calls to each other. The nature of the organization itself is not well defined by traditional forms of top-down hierarchical structure, and Natarajan speculates on the possibility that there may be little organization other than that imposed by prosecutors. Without an 'organization' it is particularly difficult for law enforcement to make a case.

While it may be difficult to prosecute organizations that are characterized by a network rather than by a more formal structure, more instrumentally, Dombroski et al.[15] propose using network theory to identify such covert organizations. By using theories about triad closure and adjacency, they are able to show that, under some circumstances, it is possible to identify elements in the network that are unobserved.

In a paper close to what we are analysing here, Carley et al.[16] ask the question: what is important for destabilizing networks? They input various measures of network flows, centrality, cut-points and the like, into a computer program (ThreatFinder) that assesses the risk to the intrinsic structure of an organization. Although their interest is primarily in large-scale networks, there are many policy experiments that they explore to examine the features that lead to group stability. They find that centrality measures point to those actors who should be removed to destabilize the network in the most efficient way.

Tsvetovat and Carley[17] carry the analysis somewhat further by examining what leads covert networks that have been attacked to re-juvenate. They consider the effect of policies that have focused on centrality, betweenness and the like to harm the network by partitioning the cells. Although directed toward networks in which the participants display some degree of isolation, simulations suggest that the existence of latent resources in the network is key to their recovery. Those networks in which it is possible to bypass the 'gatekeeper' and contact a member of a disrupted cell recover relatively quickly while those that have no additional contact points other than the gatekeeper (who has been removed in the experiment) remain disrupted.

The economics approach to social networks

Much of the early work analysing the trade-offs between the costs and benefits of creating and maintaining links within a network originated in economic sociology. In a seminal contribution, the economic sociologist Mark Granovetter introduced the distinction of 'strong' vs 'weak' ties in a job search context, observing that people who obtained jobs through social contacts often did so through 'strong' ties, i.e. through people they knew well and with whom they had considerable interaction, but, even more often, they obtained jobs through contacts with whom they had 'weak' ties: people with whom they had looser interactions.[18]

15. M. Dombroski, P. Fischbeck and K. Carley, 'Estimating the Shape of Covert Networks', *Proceedings of the International Command and Control Research and Technology Symposium*, Washington, DC (2003).
16. K. Carley, J.-S. Lee and D. Krackhardt, 'Destabilizing Networks', *Connections* 24 (2002): 79–92.
17. M. Tsvetovat and K. Carley, 'Bouncing Back: Recovery Mechanisms of Covert Networks', *NAACSOS Conference*, 2003, Day 3, http://www.casos.cs.cmu.edu/events/conferences/2003/proceedings.html.
18. M. Granovetter, 'The Strength of Weak Ties', *American Journal of Sociology* 78 (1973): 1360–80.

For the last 15 years research using networks in economics proper has gradually been building. Jackson summarizes many of the theoretical developments.[19] The economist's paradigm is somewhat different from the criminologist's described in the previous section. Economists typically start with the assumption that the observed network is a result of forces that lead to an 'optimal' outcome. The economic approach therefore models networks as the result of strategic and intentional interaction among agents. The main postulate is that members of the network receive payoffs that are dependent on the network structure.

Sharing this common assumption, one strand of research takes the network structure as given and analyses or compares outcomes achieved in a strategic equilibrium for different network structures.[20] Another, more recent, approach that we build upon attempts to model network formation itself as the result of a (strategic) optimization process. Links are formed at the discretion of the individuals involved and game theory is used to predict what types of 'stable' networks emerge.[21]

The literature associated with network stability is primarily interested in whether 'socially optimal' networks are stable, and if not, what mechanisms may ensure stability. In one stylized example that shares common elements with our model, Jackson and Wolinsky model a communication network in which being connected to another player carries benefits that deteriorate with distance. Like in our findings below, they show that, for different configurations of cost and benefit parameters, different stable networks emerge – the 'full' network, the 'star' network or the 'empty' network.[22] Further contributions extend these ideas in various directions, e.g. in Brueckner, who endogenizes the probability and cost of links, Calvo-Armengol, who studies probabilistic job information networks, and Calvo-Armengol and Zenou, who examine job matching.[23]

In applied work, most authors take the networks as extant and report implications for agents' behaviours. For example, Munshi finds that social networks play a significant role

19. M. Jackson, 'The Economics of Social Networks', chapter 1 in *Advances in Economics and Econometrics, Theory and Applications*, ed. R. Blundell, W. Newey and T. Persson (Cambridge: Cambridge University Press, 2006); M. Jackson, 'The Study of Social Networks in Economics', in *The Missing Links: Formation and Decay of Economic Networks*, ed. J. Rauch (New York: Russell Sage Foundation, 2007); M. Jackson, 'Network Formation', in *The New Palgrave Dictionary of Economics and the Law* (Macmillan Press, 2008).

20. Examples of this approach are: C. Ballester, A. Calvo-Armengol and Y. Zenou, 'Who's Who in Networks: Wanted the Key Player', *Econometrica*, 74 (2006): 1403–17; Y. Bramoulle and R. Kranton, 'A Network Model of Public Goods: Experimentation and Social Learning', mimeo (University of Toulouse, 2005); and A. Calvo-Armengol and M. Jackson, 'The Effects of Social Networks on Employment and Inequality', *American Economic Review*, 94 (2004): 426–54.

21. M. Jackson, 'The Stability and Efficiency of Economic and Social Networks', in *Advances in Economic Design*, ed. S. Koray and M. Sertel (Springer: Heidelberg 2003); M. Jackson, 'A Survey of Models of Network Formation: Stability and Efficiency', in *Group Formation in Economics: Networks, Clubs and Coalitions*, ed. G. Demange and M. Wooders (Cambridge: Cambridge University Press, 2004) are two excellent reviews.

22. M. Jackson and A. Wolinsky, 'A Strategic Model of Social and Economic Networks', *Journal of Economic Theory*, 71(1996): 44–74; V. Bala and S. Goyal, 'A Non-cooperative Model of Network Formation', *Econometrica* 68 (2002): 1181–230 extend this analysis to directed networks with similar conclusions.

23. J. Brueckner, 'Friendship Networks', mimeo (University of Illinois, 2003); A. Calvo-Armengol, 'Job Contact Networks', *Journal of Economic Theory*, 115 (2004), 191–206; A. Calvo-Armengol and Y. Zenou, 'Job Matching, Social Network and Word-of-Mouth Communication', CEPR Discussion Paper 2797 (2001).

in job information transmission among Mexican immigrants to the United States. Further, smaller and 'younger' networks reduce the chance of finding a job.[24] Calvo-Armengol and Jackson model the process of job information transmission, allowing for varying intensity in social contacts (à la Granovetter) and directed links. These findings emphasize the recognition that policy interventions such as unemployment insurance need to reflect the structure of the network in which people find themselves.[25]

Criminal networks and our approach

One significant contribution economics has made to network theory is the focus on 'why' we observe the networks with specific features that have been reported by criminologists, sociologists and others. A fundamental requirement for understanding why certain types of networks form and others do not is to have a model of how the network structure affects individual behaviour. Our approach to characterizing crime networks lies in between the approaches of 'characterizing behaviour in a given network' and 'identifying which networks would arise optimally' discussed above. We first model the costs and benefits of being in a criminal network and derive the equilibrium crime level that arises in any particular network structure. We then find which network structures arise as consequence of maximizing a meaningful criterion, which in our case is 'total profits' (benefits minus costs) received by the criminal organization.

We define the concept of an *optimal network* as the profit maximizing network structure that will be attained as a result of competition among criminal groups. The idea is that free entry (or the threat) of new, competitor networks ensures that only profit maximizing structures survive. Equivalently, the same outcome can arise from the operation of a criminal 'boss' who optimizes over possible network structures and selects the organizational structure that generates highest profits.[26]

In a pioneering example of the economics approach of characterizing criminal networks, Ballester, Calvo-Armengol and Zenou (hereafter BCZ) model the incentives of individuals to engage in crime as explicitly dependent on the structure of links among them.[27] Each criminal chooses a level of 'effort' (criminal activity) for the given network structure[28] and given the effort levels of all other members in the network. The chosen effort level determines the criminal's net payoff, defined as the benefits from doing crime

24. K. Munshi, 'The Identification of Network Effects: Mexican Migrants in the U.S. LaborMarket' (Working Paper, University of Pennsylvania, 2002).
25. A. Calvo-Armengol and M. Jackson, 'Networks in Labor Markets: Wage and Employment Dynamics and Inequality', *Journal of Economic Theory* 132 (2007): 27–46; A. Calvo-Armengol and M. Jackson 'The Effects of Social Networks on Employment and Inequality', *American Economic Review* 94 (2004): 426–54; See also Y. Ioannides and L. Loury, 'Job Information Networks, Neighborhood Effects, and Inequality', *Journal of Economic Literature* 42 (2004): 1056–93 for an extensive review on networks in labour economics, with applications to job information dissemination, neighbourhood effects and inequality.
26. Profits here should not be interpreted literally as monetary rewards and can include other goals (e.g. maximal damage, recognition, etc., which are perhaps more relevant for terrorist groups).
27. C. Ballester, A. Calvo-Armengol and Y. Zenou 'Who's Who in Crime Networks. Wanted: the Key Player' (Working Paper, 2004). See also A. Calvo-Armengol and Y. Zenou, 'Social Networks and Crime Decisions: The Role of Social Structure in Facilitating Delinquent Behavior', *International Economic Review* 45 (2004): 939–58 who use a similar model to analyse entry into crime.
28. Unlike in our model, in BCZ the configuration of links and nodes is fixed and not allowed to change.

less the costs – which are not explicitly modelled but might include being captured and penalized if caught, the psychic costs of being a criminal, out-of-pocket costs, etc. The configuration of the individual criminal efforts and the aggregate crime level are determined in Nash equilibrium[29] and, importantly, depend on the assumed network structure. BCZ find that individuals with higher 'Bonacich centrality',[30] i.e. those who have the highest number of direct and (appropriately weighted) indirect links with all others, exert the most crime. They also define 'key players' in the network as those who are the most influential in terms of the overall crime level. This means that removing such a key player from the network will cause the maximum drop in crime, compared with removing any other player. An obvious policy implication is that crime fighting policy that directly targets such individuals, holding the network fixed, will be more successful than a policy targeting random individuals or targeting those who do the most crime.

While our theoretical model borrows liberally from the analysis of BCZ and retains some of their notation and the basic spirit of their theoretical model, we modify and extend BCZ's contribution in several significant ways. First, we adopt a different cost–benefit configuration for the players that we think better reflects the operation of actual criminal organizations. Namely, we assume that the benefits for an individual doing crime in the network depend positively on the connections the criminal has with others and on their crime efforts, while the costs of doing crime depend on aggregate criminal activity. The interpretation is that better connected criminals and/or criminals whose 'partners' are more active should have higher productivity and obtain higher payoffs. On the other hand, higher aggregate crime is likely to draw more attention by law enforcement and increase everyone's costs.

Second, while we characterize the Nash equilibrium in crime levels within a given network, we do not stop there. Instead, our primary objective is to look for the 'optimal network' not only for a given number of agents, but also over various network sizes – a variable number of agents. We define the 'optimal network' as the network that maximizes aggregate profits from doing crime for the criminals involved. This does not have to coincide (and in fact does not coincide, as we describe below) with the network maximizing aggregate criminal activity. That is, on top of the within-network optimization with everyone choosing their crime level, we add a second important layer of optimization: searching for the optimal network structure that will arise. The network structure includes both the pattern of links among agents and the number of agents themselves.

Third, not unlike BCZ's original motivation, we are also interested in the effect of crime fighting policies for observed crime levels. However, with the addition of the extra layer of optimization that now includes the network structure, this question is not as straightforward as finding BCZ's 'key player'. Specifically, when analysing crime fighting policy, we recognize that the criminals' knowledge of the policy will affect the structure of the network being formed. While, by definition, it is true that taking out the 'key player' will cause the greatest reduction of criminal activity for any given network, should criminals be aware of such a policy, our optimization suggests that they will adapt their network structure in such a way as to reduce (or minimize) the impact of the policy. As a result, we show examples, in which a 'myopic' crime combating policy targeting the network's key player performs worse

29. Nash equilibrium is a solution concept of a game involving two or more players, in which each player is assumed to know the strategies of the other players. In Nash equilibrium no one has anything to gain by changing one's strategy unilaterally given the strategies of all others.
30. P. Bonacich, 'Power and Centrality: A Family of Measures', *American Journal of Sociology* 92 (1987): 1170–82.

than targeting another player! We elaborate further on this 'Lucas critique'[31] argument below. To understand the framework necessary to develop these points we move first to a formal characterization of our approach and then turn to the way in which policy would be different. Rather than look exclusively at a general framework, we develop the theory in the context of a manageable and limited example.

A theoretical model of criminal networks

Basic setting

At the most abstract level, suppose that there are N agents whose interaction we model as a social network. A network is defined as a list of nodes and the links between them. We assume only bi-directional links so that if agent i is connected to agent j then the reverse is also true.

For a particular network structure, the agents decide on a level of criminal activity to undertake, which we term their criminal 'effort', and which can be either zero or positive. The efforts chosen maximize the agent's 'utility' or net income: their benefits less their costs. While choosing their effort, each agent takes the structure of the network and the efforts of the other agents as given and maximizes his/her net payoff, solving the following maximization problem:

$$\max_{e_i} U_i(G,e) = y_i(G,e) - c_i(G,e) \tag{1}$$

where criminal i's income is y_i, his costs are c_i, and **e** is the vector of all agents' efforts, $e = (e_1, e_3, \ldots, e_N)$. G is the criminal network's 'adjacency matrix': a square, N-by-N matrix made up of zeros on the diagonal and zeros and ones symmetrically on the off-diagonals. The positions of the ones in G correspond to pairs of agents that are linked. That is a '1' element g_{ij} of G means agents i and j, $i, j = 1, \ldots, N$ with $i \neq j$ are linked, while $g_{ij} = 0$ would mean that agents i and j are not linked.

The next step is to flesh out the determinants of the costs and benefits of crime. To explore the consequences of networking on crime levels and payoffs, we assume: (a) that the benefits increase in the number of links a player has; (b) that through these links a player's effort interacts with other players' efforts and this interaction raises the level of income above that obtained simply by one player on his or her own; and (c) that the total amount of crime created by others in the network generates a congestion effect, increasing each agent's costs, arising (say) from a greater likelihood of being detected.

Specifically, individual i's income, y_i is given by:

$$y_i(G,e) = e_i\left(1 + \gamma\sum_{j=1}^{N} g_{ij}e_j\right) \tag{2}$$

31. The 'Lucas critique' is named after Nobel Prize winning economist Robert E. Lucas Jr, who argued that, if we want to study the effect of a certain policy, we should model the structural parameters (relating to preferences, technology and resource constraints) that govern individual behaviour. We can then predict what individuals will do when they take the policy into account, and then aggregate these individual decisions to calculate the macroeconomic effects of the policy change. Designing policy based on current or historical data alone, without accounting for the expected change in people's behaviour resulting from the proposed policy, is inherently flawed and can have unintended consequences.

while individual costs, c_i, are defined as:

$$c_i(G, e) = \pi e_i \left(1 + \lambda \sum_{j=1}^{N} e_j + \delta \sum_{j=1}^{N} g_{ij} \right) \tag{3}$$

The benefit from participation in the crime activity has two components. The first is the direct effect of the individual's own activity. The second results from the interaction of the individual's own criminal effort and the sum of the efforts of other agents with whom he/she is connected. The strength of the positive effect of connectedness on the individual i's income is captured by the parameter $\gamma > 0$. The benefits of participation in crime are a function of the efforts of other criminals in the network and the structure of the network itself. The effect of an increase in individual effort is to raise an individual's income in proportion to the connections he has with the rest of the network.

The costs from the criminal activity depend on the effort that an individual makes and its interaction with the aggregate activity level (the sum of the *e*s). The logic is that a higher level of activity is more likely to attract unwanted 'attention' to the criminal network, either from law enforcement authorities or rival organizations, which makes it costlier to do business. This 'congestion cost' of higher levels of crime is captured by $\lambda > 0$. As more people participate at higher levels of activity, the costs to all individuals rise proportionately.

In addition, we allow for direct costs accruing from the number of links agent i has to maintain – the parameter $\delta \geq 0$. This captures the idea that a connection is not 'manna from heaven', but may be a choice or depend upon a costly process of ongoing assessment. Finally, there is the scaling parameter π that determines the stand-alone cost of effort for an unconnected single player. We assume $\pi\lambda > \gamma$ to make sure that the maximum in equation (1) exists – otherwise, if the benefits of linking with others are too high, payoffs may grow out of bound since individual efforts are complements to each other.

Note that increases in individual effort increase costs quadratically. Increases in the number of connections raise cost in proportion to the number of connections and the effort level of the individual who is maintaining those connections.[32] Also, an increase in the activity level of others implies an increase in costs to the individual that is proportional to the individual's own level of activity.

Nash equilibrium

The particular configuration of efforts that simultaneously solves all the individual maximization problems in equation (1) is determined in Nash equilibrium. The basic notion of a Nash equilibrium is the idea that, given all other players' actions, player i does not want to deviate from her/his optimal action, e_i^* to any other criminal effort level. Moreover, in Nash equilibrium this must be true for all players. That is, given what everybody else is currently choosing, nobody finds it optimal to choose a different level of effort. This is why we refer to such a situation as 'equilibrium'. The assumption here is that individual players choose their efforts simultaneously and independently in a non-cooperative manner. This is more natural in a non-hierarchical criminal organization; however, below we also consider the potential role of a 'boss' (or competition among criminal organizations) in optimizing the network structure. An alternative would be to allow individual criminal levels to be optimized in a centralized way, e.g. as in a close-knit

32. Since both parties maintain a connection, we assume that both incur a cost per unit of effort.

mafia or terrorist structure. We discuss ways to extend our approach to permit multiple hierarchy levels below.

The dependence of each agent's benefits and costs on the network structure implies that in the Nash equilibrium the criminals' effort levels will be interdependent and co-determined by the specific configuration of the network. The equilibrium crime levels depend on the structure of the network and so individual payoffs also depend on the network configuration.

With the costs and benefits given in equations (2) and (3) above, each individual chooses her/his optimal crime level. For a particular network and the choice of effort by each of the others, person *i* makes an optimal choice of effort by maximizing the difference between benefit and cost in equation (1). The optimization implies that, for each participant, the additional benefit of supplying one extra unit of effort, the marginal benefit (depending on the number of agents with whom agent *i* is connected and their effort levels), must be equalized to the marginal cost of supplying an extra unit of effort. The marginal cost depends on the congestion cost and the cost of maintaining links. We are then able to calculate the equilibrium levels of effort for all the participants.[33]

In contrast to specific results tied to particular networks, there are some general results that characterize the solutions to the optimal network problem. These theoretical results characterize the Nash equilibrium in criminal activities and payoffs and their dependence on the cost and benefit parameters. To keep things non-technical and accessible we only provide heuristic, intuitive 'proofs' here.[34] The first result tells us about the way in which effort and reward are linked in the model.

Result 1: *The maximized individual payoffs from crime are quadratic in the individual's own optimal crime effort.*

This is an interesting result in that it tells us that the payoff from crime is not linear in effort.[35] A greater effort increases the reward more than proportionally. We discuss the significance of this further in conjunction with Result 3 (see below) as it is extremely important for the interplay between aggregate profits and aggregate crime level.

Our second result characterizes the dependence of the equilibrium crime levels on the cost and benefit parameters.

Result 2: *The optimal individual and total crime levels are decreasing in the stand-alone cost, π and the cost of links, δ for any network. In addition, if the network is symmetric (regular), the optimal individual and the total crime levels are decreasing in the congestion cost, λ, and increasing in the benefit of links, γ.*

The intuition for the first part of Result 2 should be clear: higher values of π scale up the costs without affecting the benefits for all players. Thus, individual crime levels and,

33. Writing out the equilibrium conditions for all agents we obtain a linear system of N equations in N unknowns that can be solved for the optimal effort levels, e_i^*. We solve analytically an example for $N = 3$ in the Appendix. In general, however, the solution is complicated and we approach the problem numerically although even this approach faces limitations arising from the complexity of optimizing over network structures networks (see more on this below).

34. The full details can be found in Easton and Karaivanov, 'The Economic Structure of Crime Networks' (Working Paper, Simon Fraser University, 2008), hereafter EK.

35. This follows from the linear-quadratic structure of the costs and benefits of crime. Intuitively, all dependence on other criminals' efforts and the network structure is embedded in one's optimal effort, e_i*, which yields that the individual's payoff is quadratic in their own effort.

by extension, total crime, decrease when π increases. Further, higher costs of maintaining links, δ have a similar effect since, for any given configuration of links embodied in G they impose a higher burden on the criminal if he tries to extend his contacts. Interestingly, the effects of the marginal benefit parameter γ and the congestion cost λ cannot be assigned in a simple unambiguous way for any possible network. The reason is that there is a complicated interaction between individual efforts and their dependence on the configuration of links (described by the matrix G). For example, higher λ increases the direct costs per unit of other players' efforts but if, in equilibrium, the sum total of other players' efforts decreases at the same time, this may actually make it more beneficial for an individual agent to supply more effort. Similarly, if G is not regular (where regular means that all members have the same number of links), an increase in the congestion cost variable λ has asymmetric effects on different agents, through the interaction with efforts of others in generating income, y_i.

The latter complications do not arise in the case of a regular (symmetric) network in which the Nash equilibrium conditions imply that all criminals will supply the same level of effort. This fact can be used to solve for the optimal crime level using the first-order optimality conditions.[36]

Optimizing over the network structure and size

What separates our approach from that of criminologists, sociologists and most other social scientists who have used networks in the study of crime and other applications hinges on the assumption that, in choosing to maximize net income, the players implicitly start with the 'correct' network. Those who have analysed networks have explicitly chosen a particular network and then asked the question, what is the level of activity that maximizes net income? This is a reasonable assumption in situations in which the links among actors are fixed or at least in part exogenously determined. One can see family ties, social relationships or even class or caste relationships as being environments amenable to such a modelling strategy. In addition, criminal networks and offenders' positions within them can be structured by neighbourhood factors, kinship or other ties outside the criminal connections; individual factors such as gender, age, etc., and outside influences such as incarceration. We might term these 'predetermined' links.[37]

However, in a broader context actors can equally choose with whom they interact. This means that the nature of the choice facing a network participant is not simply to choose a level of effort confronted by a particular pattern of links, but rather that each participant must also choose the links that will maximize net income.

We therefore add a second layer of optimization to that of the choice of effort and study the network structure that maximizes some meaningful performance measure. That is, we search over all possible networks (of fixed or variable size) to find the 'optimal' network structure.[38] Naturally, in realistic settings the optimization can be constrained – some links

36. We show analytically (see EK) that the crime levels satisfy the properties listed in Result 2. The Appendix derives a sample case.
37. These predetermined links are relevant in some cases, but they will differ by context. We are more interested in those links chosen by the participants as described below.
38. In this paper, we study connected networks only. These are networks in which each actor is linked with at least one other actor. No criminals stand alone. In principle, our theoretical model and computation methods allow us to analyse more general structures, with both connected and unconnected criminals, but given our emphasis on networks, we rule those out in this paper.

can be fixed or the number of criminals can be fixed, at least in the short term. Our method allows us to take such constraints into account and, in fact, this makes the problem easier, since it reduces the number of network structures we need to search over.

The optimization over network structures can be thought of as the result of the process of free entry of new, competitors' networks which would ensure that only the best, profit-maximizing structure survives – in the same way as perfect competition results in zero economic profits for firms. Alternatively, the optimal network can be thought of as arising from the operation of an overarching criminal 'boss' who optimizes over all possible network structures and chooses the network generating highest aggregate profits. Which of the two interpretations is more suitable depends on the particular application.

In general, finding the optimal network is a hard mathematical problem, especially for large numbers of participants. This is discussed in more detail in the next section. However, for some particular cases we are able to derive more specific results. For instance, consider the situation in which there are no direct costs of maintaining or using links. We obtain:

Result 3: *For any given network size N, if the cost of links δ is zero, the network structure that maximizes overall equilibrium crime is the full network where all criminals are connected.*

We have proved this result formally.[39] Intuitively, if links are not costly, the gain of being connected with everyone offsets the additional marginal cost of congestion. We know from equations (2) and (3) that the agents' efforts are strategic substitutes. That is, holding other things constant, an increase in someone else's effort e_j reduces criminal i's crime effort. Moreover, this substitutability is stronger if two agents are not connected ($g_{ij} = 0$ in equation (2)). Connections between participants tend to counter substitutability in efforts. Thus, when the number of direct connections is maximized, which happens in the full network, the total crime effort level is highest.

However, finding the network that maximizes total crime is not our primary goal. Instead, the economics of the problem suggests that we are likely to observe networks that maximize total payoffs. This is a result of competition among criminal organizations. The more profitable drive out the less profitable. Consequently, the payoff of doing crime and not crime *per se* is what is relevant.

Combining Results 1 and 3 identifies a trade-off that is intrinsic to the solution of the optimal profit-maximizing network. From Result 1 we know that, for a given level of total crime in equilibrium, total profits are proportional to the sum of the squares of individual crime levels. This implies that, the more 'asymmetric' the effort structure is, the higher total profit tends to be.[40] On the other hand, we know that (if link costs are zero), it is the symmetric full network structure that maximizes total crime and asymmetric structures lead to less crime, which can reduce profits. The interplay of these two effects – the former favouring asymmetric structures, like the 'star' network, and the latter favouring the full network, will depend on the particular cost and benefit structure. We show representative examples of optimal networks in the next section.

39. EK as per footnote 34.

40. The quadratic structure means that, if a criminal supplies a disproportionate fraction of total effort, this is likely to generate higher profits. In the extreme, one criminal has to do everything, but this is inconsistent with equilibrium. To see this tendency, imagine total effort of 12 with three participants. If each has an effort of 4, total profit is 3 times 4-squared or 48. If one participant supplied the same total effort instead, 12 times 12 is 144.

We can further extend the analysis to what we term 'full optimization' by permitting the number of agents in the network also to be a choice variable. To analyse this, we compare the maximized aggregate profits networks of different sizes. Depending on the costs and benefit parameters the optimal network may be large or small. This highlights the role that choice plays since not only the configuration of the links but number of players is now a matter of choice.

Let us summarize. Our research strategy looks at networks as outcomes of a behavioural process. Traditionally, the network has been taken as exogenous to the players in the network, and analysis has answered questions in the context of that network. We believe that a more fruitful approach treats the network itself as the outcome of an optimization process. Further, the size of the network is also a potential object of choice. However, there are pitfalls in our approach. The fundamental complexity of networks is a stumbling block to extensive application.

Computation and complexity

Because networks and individuals, as opposed to just individuals are our units of analysis, there is a fundamental complexity. Keeping track of the network structure in addition to the 'usual' prices and quantities creates substantial analytical difficulties while solving for static optima and equilibria even in standard economic problems. In addition, even if all agents in the network have exactly the same preferences and technology, their position in the network or how many and which other players to whom they are connected effectively makes them heterogeneous, adding another layer of complication. Further, the externalities among the agents embedded in a network interaction can be the cause for multiple equilibria – yet another additional known source of complexity. Computational power sufficient for the analysis of these more complex problems has become generally available only recently.

In our particular setting, it is optimizing over the network itself that makes the problem complex. One of the main contributions of this paper is that we study 'optimal networks' – networks that maximize aggregate profits among all possible networks of a given size, and then across different sizes. In principle, there are $2^{N(N-1)/2}$ networks of size N. This means that, even with a small number of players, the potential number of networks becomes very large. For example, with only seven nodes there are already 2^{21} (2,097,152) networks. Thus, if we were to compute the equilibrium for every network, the computational time required would grow faster than exponentially with network size. On the other hand, it is clear that many of the possible networks are effectively the same, requiring only the re-labelling of nodes. For example, for $N = 7$ there are only 1044 unique networks. Thus, to avoid costly duplication of time and effort we only need to compute the equilibria for the different, or as they are known in graph theory, non-isomorphic networks.[41] In EK we explain the details of the numerical algorithm we use to search for the optimal profit-maximizing network in the general case.

Examples

We use numerical methods to find the optimal network. We set our four benefit and cost parameters – connectedness (γ), congestion (λ), the cost of links (δ) and stand-alone costs

41. However, even simply generating all non-isomorphic networks of given size is a difficult problem in graph theory and computer science that has not been solved for any N. See B. McKay, 'Practical Graph Isomorphism' *Congressus Numerantium* 30 (1981): 45–87.

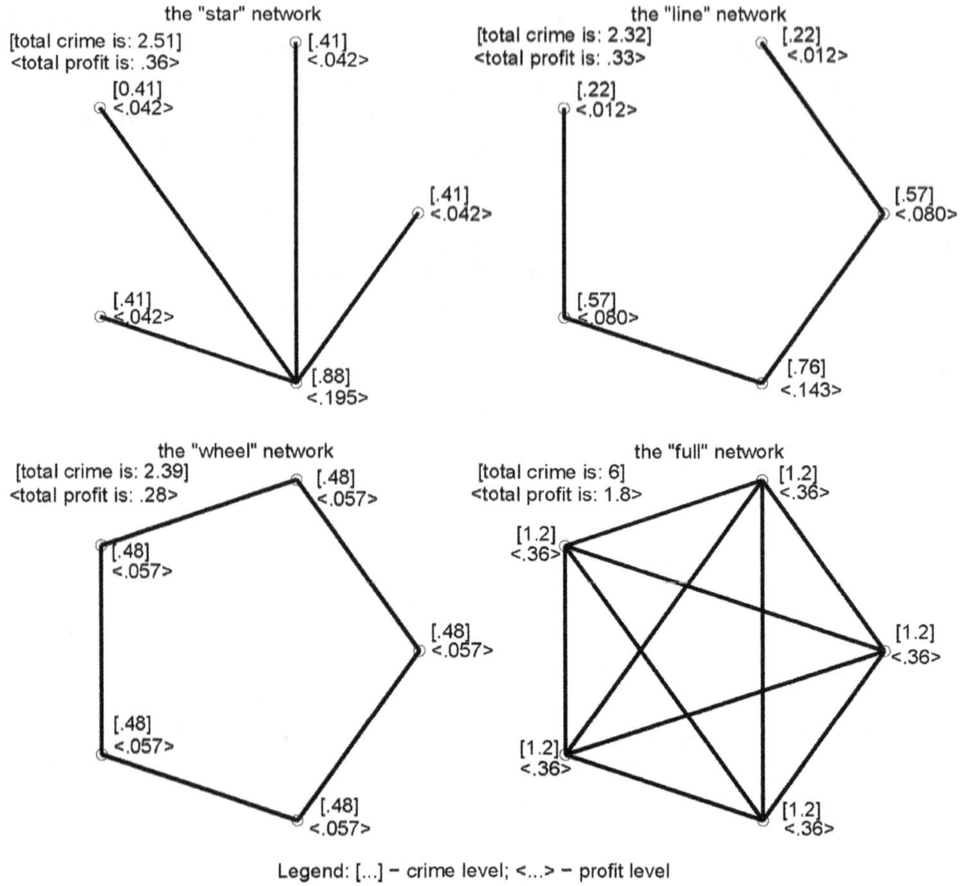

Figure 1. Nash equilibrium individual crime and profit levels (constant parameters).

of crime (π) – and calculate the levels of effort and profit for every network. The result of the optimization yields a set of profit maximizing effort (crime) levels selected over all possible networks.[42] Below we provide several representative examples[43] of optimal networks and the effects of parameters on the network structure. These examples demonstrate and further clarify the general analytical results from above.

To fix ideas, Figure 1 displays a number of different five-player networks reporting the total crime (the sum of individual efforts) and the total profit (the sum of individual profits) obtained in Nash equilibrium associated with a particular set of parameters ($\delta = 0.07$, $\gamma = 0.3$, $\lambda = 0.5$ and $\pi = 0.5$), as well as the effort and profit levels associated with each player. The configurations displayed in Figure 1 include some well-known networks: the 'star', 'line', 'wheel' and 'full' networks.

Figure 1 demonstrates that different network structures affect crime levels and profits in a significant way, both at the individual and the aggregate level. For example, for the

42. For the more technically oriented, the Appendix solves a specific example for a three-player network.

43. The chosen parameters are arbitrary but the changes in them across the examples are deliberately picked to illustrate the general trends and outcomes discussed above.

chosen parameters the 'full' network, in which each criminal is connected to everyone else, achieves a total crime level of 6. This is more than twice the amount of crime generated by the 'wheel', 'star' or 'line' configurations. Further, the figure also illustrates that there is no simple one-to-one mapping between aggregate profits and the aggregate crime level. For instance, the 'wheel' network produces more crime than the 'line' but lower overall profits. This is important because we argue that it is likely that criminals would choose (or competition will ensure the survival of) organizational forms that maximize overall net income ('profits') and not necessarily those that maximize the crime level. This should be kept in mind when we discuss policy implications in the next section.

Finally, Figure 1 also illustrates how an individual player's position in the network implies a different crime (and profit) level for that individual. For example, observe the agent in the 'star' network connected to everyone else. His key position gives him a large share of total profits (he generates more than half of the aggregate profit), while he is only responsible for about a third of the total crime. Similarly, in the 'line' network the end players (those connected to a single other person only) put in the lowest effort and contribute the least to total profits, while naturally the criminal who is farthest from the end players contributes the most. The 'wheel' and 'full' structures are symmetric in terms of the connections that network members have with each other. Naturally, in equilibrium, everyone optimally creates the same amount of crime and generates the same share of income and profit.

We next illustrate the forces determining the equilibrium crime efforts (which in turn determine the choice of the optimal network structure) by exploring the inner workings of the model through varying the parameters of the environment as in Result 2 above. Holding the number of criminals in the network constant, Figure 2 displays the way that changes in the cost and benefit parameters affect the structure and total crime and profits in the optimal, profit-maximizing five-person network.

For the same parameter values as in Figure 1 ($\delta = 0.07$, $\gamma = 0.3$, $\lambda = 0.5$ and $\pi = 0.5$), the top-left panel of Figure 2 plots the optimal five-person network. The optimal structure is the 'full' network which achieves total profits of 1.8 and an aggregate crime level of 6. In contrast, the top-right panel depicts the optimal network structure when we keep δ, γ and π at the same level, but increase the congestion cost parameter λ to 1.5. This not only dramatically reduces realized total crime (it is now 0.55) and total profits (down to 0.05), but more importantly the 'full' network is no longer optimal. Instead, the optimal structure is the 'line'. What this shows is that a different environment with higher costs of doing crime (captured by the congestion cost of being directly and indirectly associated with others) no longer leads to a network structure in which all agents are connected to each other. The reason is that now the 'full' network (not depicted in the new environment) generates lower total profits (by about 12%) than the 'line' structure.

Moving to the bottom-left panel of Figure 2, now we keep values for δ and γ as before, but let congestion costs increase to $\lambda = 0.78$ (from 0.5), and the stand-alone costs rise to $\pi = 0.64$ (from 0.5). The result is an optimal network structure resembling a 'cell' structure, that is a 'full' network (a 'cell') of four agents plus a fifth one connected to only one of the four. This structure is, in some sense between the line and full networks we had above. It has fewer links than the full network (because of the higher costs), but not as few as in the 'line' structure that arose for very high λ. Total profits and crime achieved are also in between the levels in the top-row panels of Figure 2.

Finally, the bottom-right panel of the figure depicts the optimal network structure (the 'star' network) that arises for $\delta = 0.07$, $\gamma = 0.3$, $\lambda = 2.3$ and $\pi = 0.5$; i.e., for even higher congestion costs, relative to the previous examples. Naturally, the result of the cost

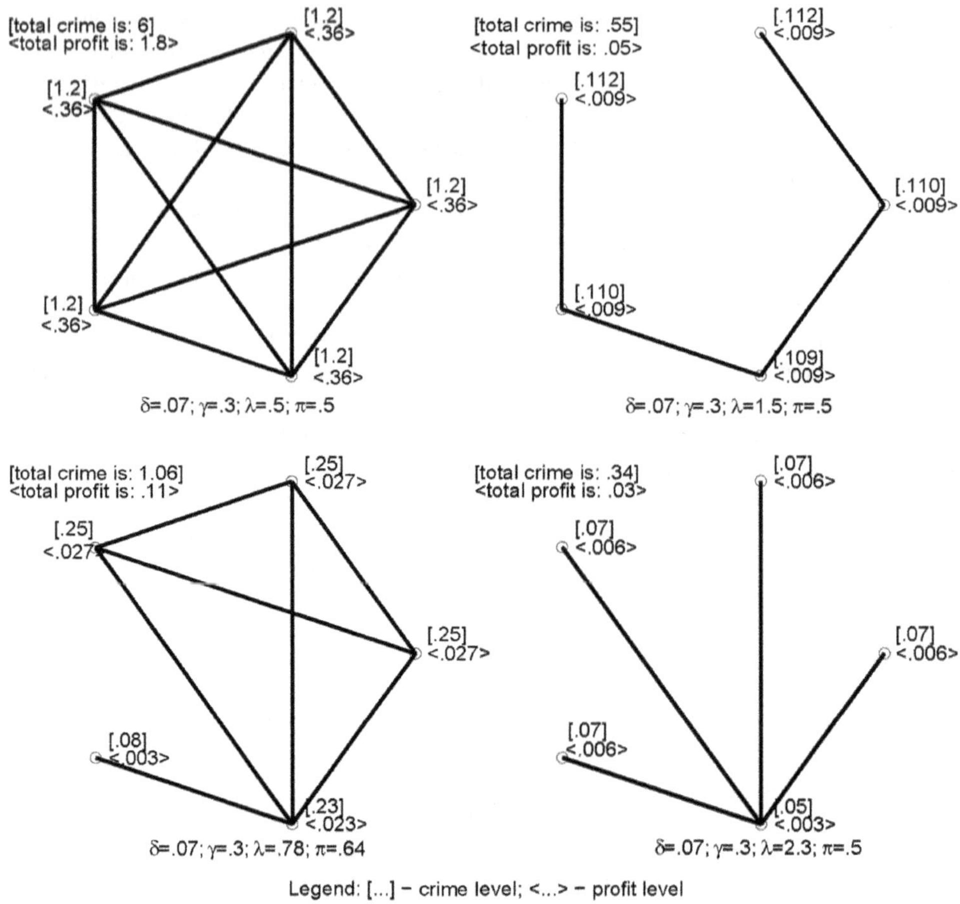

Figure 2. Optimal networks for different cost–benefit parameters.

increase is even lower total crime and profits, while more importantly, the optimal network structure shifts shape again.

The cost and benefit parameters significantly affect not only the equilibrium crime effort levels chosen but also the resulting optimal network. Higher costs are, on average, likely to lead to network structures with fewer links (recall the network size is held constant), while lower costs or (not shown in the figure) higher gains from being in the network, tend to lead to networks with more links among members.[44]

Yet what if the network size is also endogenous and can be chosen and consequently optimized to generate maximum profits? To illustrate the consequences of this requirement for full optimality, we again hold the cost and benefit parameters fixed at some representative values[45] and investigate how the optimal network structure, the total crime level, and total profits change as we vary the network size N. Figure 3 displays the optimal networks for $N = 2$ through $N = 7$.

44. EK as per footnote 34 explore those relationships in much more detail for a set of 10,000 parameter combinations.

45. For this example we use $\delta = 0.039$, $\gamma = 0.2$, $\lambda = 0.78$ and $\delta = 0.64$.

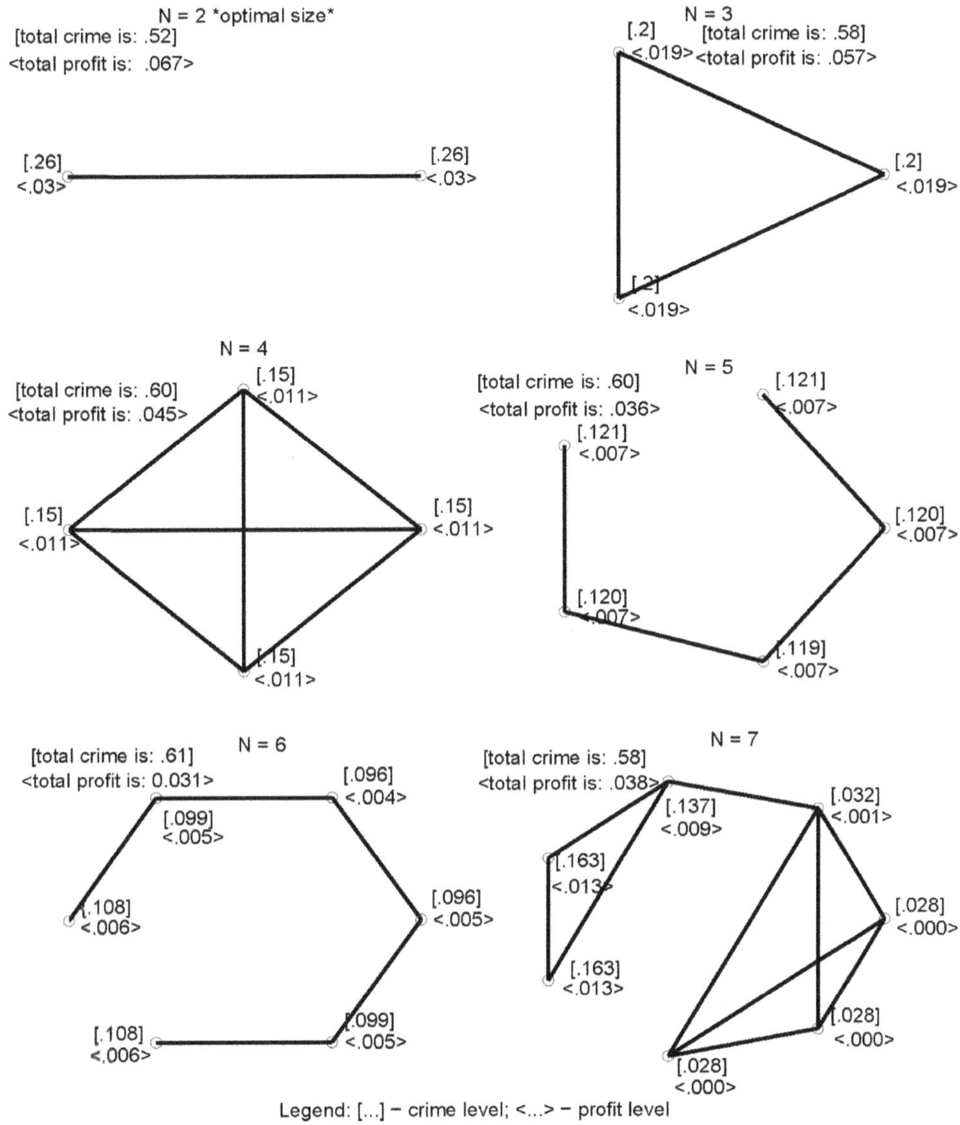

Figure 3. Optimal networks for different numbers of agents (constant parameters).

For a small number of agents (two to four), the optimal network structure is the 'full' network in which any two criminals are connected to each other. While the optimal structure remains the same, the group size does affect the total crime generated – it increases from 0.52 for $N = 2$ to 0.60 for $N = 4$, while the total net income for the network members in this example decreases from 0.067 to 0.045 as the size of the network rises from two to four. If the network expands further, to five or six agents, we notice a change in the optimal structure which transforms into the 'line' network. The total crime level still rises a little, to as much as 0.61 for $N = 6$, but total profits go down to 0.031 at the same time as the number of links necessary to maintain a connected network adds to the costs. Finally, for $N = 7$, the optimal seven-criminal structure is the 'cell'-type network depicted on the bottom-right panel which consists of one full network of four members (on the right) and one full network of three members (on the left) connected via a single bridging link.

Over all network sizes we see that (in this parameterization) the two-agent network generates the maximum net income for the criminals (benefits minus congestion costs and costs of links), followed by the four-player and seven-player structures. That is, if one could choose over both the network structure for given network size, and also over the network size, or if competition among criminals would result in the most profitable structure, there would be two criminals operating.

Another point worth noting is that the network size that maximizes total profits does not have to coincide with the network size that would generate the highest aggregate crime level. As seen in Figure 3, total crime is maximized at $N = 6$ while such large networks are not likely to be observed if maximizing aggregate profits is the criminal organization's objective. This point has important policy implications – understanding that the criminals' objective is not maximizing total crime or harm but instead their net income should be part of designing optimal crime combating policies. We return to this issue in much more detail in the next section.

Understandably, these examples are just illustrative and in practice we would need data on actual networks and the relative size of costs and benefits involved to calibrate the exact parameter values. The point we are making here is that in our model the optimal network structure adjusts in a natural, predictable way to changes in the costs and benefits of crimes. Thus, after a proper calibration, our model has predictive power about expected changes in criminal structures arising from changes in the environment in which they operate.

Implications for crime combating policy

Within our analytical model we can study the relative effectiveness of various policies to reduce the overall crime level. That is, we can study the effects on network choice and aggregate crime from removing individual network members, increasing the probability or penalty associated to the apprehension of criminals, intercepting information flows by severing communication links or even infiltrating the criminal networks. These various crime-combating policies can be analysed quantitatively by varying the model parameters. This policy analysis can be done for any exogenously given network structure, consistent with much of the literature reviewed above, but an important next step we take here is to describe what optimal network structures would arise endogenously as a result of law enforcement using or intending to use a particular deterrence policy.

Further, our model provides testable predictions about changes in the optimal network structure arising from changes in the environment in which criminals operate. As the theoretical analysis indicates, changes in the various costs and benefits of doing crime affect both the equilibrium crime level and the types of structures chosen.

The fundamental insight is simple. When deciding on a crime-combating strategy, law enforcement or anti-terrorism authorities must take into account the criminals' likely reaction to the policy, which potentially depends upon the time frame in question. If criminals would have chosen a particular network structure without the crime fighting policy in place, there is no guarantee that the same structure would be chosen or maintained if that particular crime fighting policy is pursued. This implies that simply analyzing and classifying currently observed network structures that exist in the field, and using such historical data as a basis for deciding the policies that will make the greatest impact on the crime network, may both be flawed and have unintended consequences.

To be clear, historical data are generated by an underlying process that includes the policies of the past. Once these policies change, then one cannot expect new data to reflect old policies. Instead, we should expect them to reflect the new policies.

To deal with this profound difficulty we have developed our structural model of criminal networks exposing some of the 'deep' cost and benefit parameters of criminals' behaviour. It is capable of modelling and, subject to proper calibration, predicting the criminals' reaction to various policies used by law enforcement authorities that can be represented in a formal way within the model setting. The main point is that the predicted reaction of criminals can be explicitly accommodated in a forward-looking fashion to design the optimal crime fighting policy.

Naturally, the criminals can be constrained in various ways when reacting to possible crime combating policies. Our model allows us to study both short-term or 'constrained' responses by criminals,[46] when the network remains fixed, as well as long-term responses when the network adapts optimally (or learns) about impending or current policies. Depending on the particular network in mind, its level of sophistication, its power/hierarchical structure or degree of specialization of its members, the ability of the criminal structure to quickly adjust to policies may vary. We believe policy design should be forward looking and anticipate changes in criminal behaviour.

We clarify this general conceptual point with a specific example. Consider two possible crime-combating policies. Suppose one possible policy is to remove the 'key player' in the criminal network, as in BCZ. For the purpose of this example assume that the network players do not (or are unable to) re-optimize after the policy has been enforced (e.g. think of this as the short-term response in the terminology above).[47]

For any given network, the 'key player' policy fingers for elimination the single agent whose removal reduces total crime by the greatest amount. This is not necessarily the agent who does the most crime in the network, although it may be. The second possible policy we consider is that of removing a criminal with a probability proportional to his level of crime. This could be interpreted as removing a criminal based on his 'exposure' to the risk of being caught.

Now let us compare the effectiveness of the above two policies. For any given network structure, by definition, removing the 'key player' (as opposed to any other player) is optimal in generating the greatest reduction in crime. However, this view assumes that criminals are myopic.[48] That is, while the criminals understand that their key player is targeted, they stick with the same original network for which this key player was identified. Although information about police objectives and strategies may be secret, frequently they are highly public and part of the political process. We believe it is a reasonable conjecture to consider that (at least the most resilient and successful) criminal organizations would take the crime fighting policy (or their best prediction thereof) into account and as a result may choose a different, policy-specific, 'robust' network structure, with a different key player whose removal may not be as effective in reducing crime.

Next we provide a concrete example of the idea described above in the context of our criminal network model. This example is purposely extreme in the sense that we assume that the criminals know perfectly the direction of the policy change. Nevertheless, as long

46. For example, initially a secret change of policy direction or targeting a particular network may 'surprise' the criminal organization.
47. The case allowing for re-optimization is developed more fully in EK as per footnote 34.
48. Alternatively, it may be that the costs of information are too high.

as the criminal groups are not completely surprised, and the network structure adapts to policy to some degree, then the thrust of our example goes through.

Specifically, suppose the cost–benefit parameters are $\delta = 0.054$, $\gamma = 1$, $\lambda = 3$ and $\pi = 0.547$ and there are $N = 6$ agents in the original network. For these parameters, assuming that initially there is no crime-combating policy in place, the optimal network which maximizes aggregate profits for the criminal organization is depicted on the top panel (labelled 'no policy') of Figure 4. It is a 'cell' network consisting of four inter-connected criminals connected with two others through a bridging agent. The total

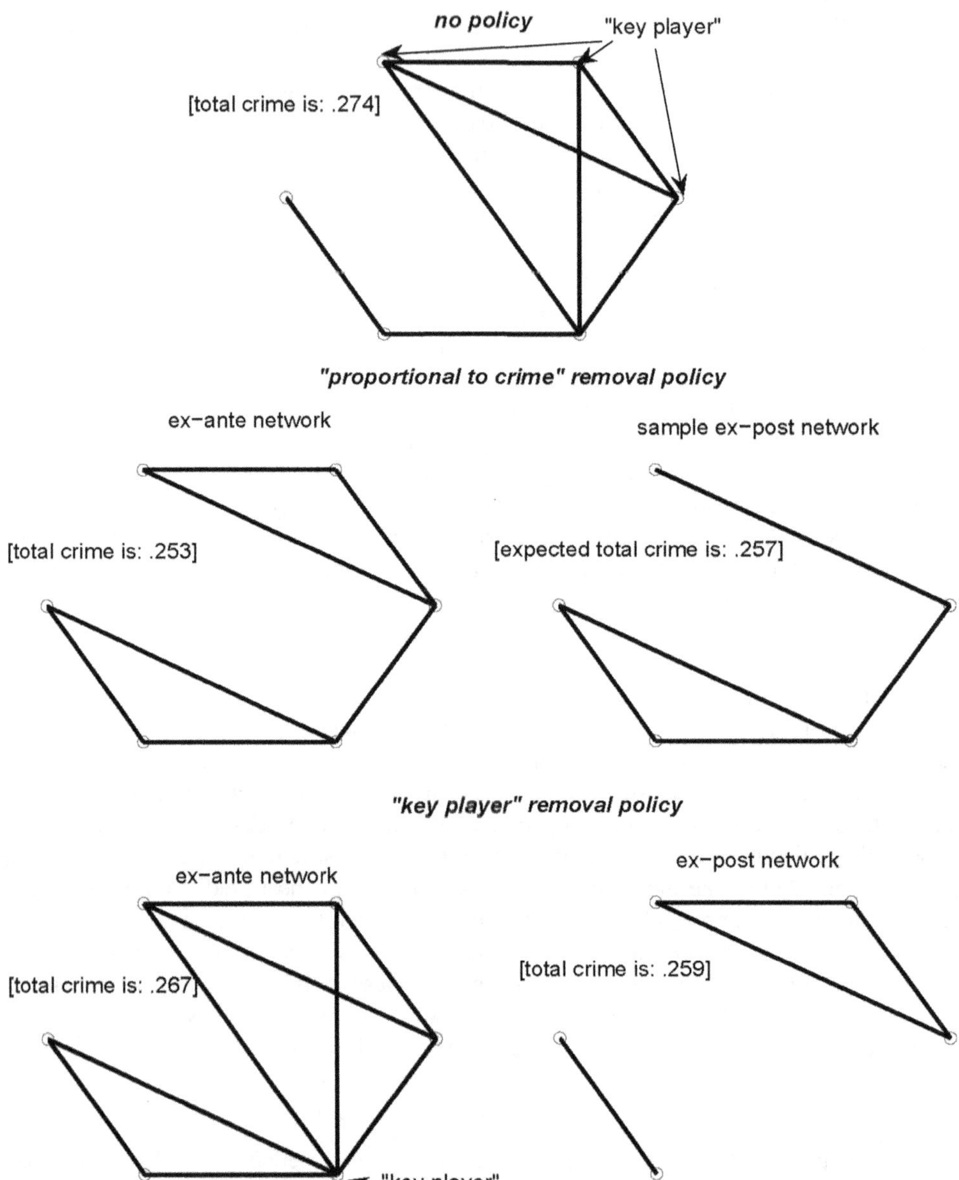

Figure 4. The effect of different crime combating policies on optimal network choice.

crime in this benchmark network is 0.274. Now consider the effect of the two possible crime reduction policies discussed above.

Suppose first that the police decide to pursue the policy of catching and removing players with a probability proportional to their crime level. Assume also, for simplicity, that this policy is effective with probability 1. That is, one criminal will always be removed and it is the 'right' criminal who is caught. If the criminals are aware (or, at some point become aware) of this policy, the optimal structure they will choose is no longer the network displayed in the top panel of Figure 4. Instead, the network structure in the middle-left panel (which we call the 'ex-ante network') will be chosen, consisting of two full three-agent networks connected with a single connection between them. Once a player is removed, the middle-right network (the 'ex-post network') is left, and expected total crime will be 0.257, a 0.017 or 6.2% reduction in crime relative to the 'no policy' benchmark.[49]

Now, compare this 'proportional to crime level' removal policy to what would happen if the 'key player' removal policy were to be enforced instead. This is the policy that targets the removal of the criminal whose departure will reduce crime the most. Again, assume for simplicity that the key player will be caught with probability 1. The criminals will then choose a different network structure which is depicted in the bottom-left ('ex-ante') panel of Figure 4. After removing the key player of that structure, we are left with the split network in the bottom-right panel which results in total crime of 0.259. Notice that this number, the resulting total level of crime, is *higher* than that which would result from the 'proportional to effort' policy. The reduction in crime relative to the 'no policy' baseline is therefore smaller.

While it is true that for a fixed network the key player removal policy is by construction the most effective policy in reducing crime, when the forward-looking optimizing behaviour of the criminal organization is taken into account, the resulting network structure may be different. We argue that the policy choice should reflect this. The particular example is simply representative and naturally extremely simplistic. What is important is that the criminals' reaction to the policy (as long as it exists and no matter how constrained) should necessarily be taken into account when choosing the crime-combating strategy. A structural model of criminal behaviour like ours, incorporating the benefits and costs of criminal activity, is therefore indispensable in assessing the effectiveness of various policies and strategies to fight crime or terrorism.

Conclusions and future research

We study the network structures that arise endogenously as a result of the interaction between a deterrence policy and the networked agents' responses in adapting the crime network itself. The 'Lucas critique' that we formalize here in the context of criminal networks argues that using history to forecast the future can be misleading. Outcomes and data from the past are predicated on policies that were present in the past. Therefore, developing current crime fighting policy requires that we understand the behavioural responses to policy at a deeper level than simply observing past outcomes. If there is a

49. The relevant comparison for the expected crime rate is between the no-policy crime level and the post-policy crime level in the ex-post network. The ex-ante network will not be observed as the probability of removal is a certainty. In Easton and Karaivanov, 'The Economic Structure of Crime Networks', we allow for any probability of the policy being effective, ranging between 0 (completely ineffective) to 1 (fully effective).

change in policy, criminals' responses will change too. Our model provides one possible framework that can be used to forecast outcomes when the participants have varying degrees of policy awareness. While this approach has made an important contribution to understanding people's and organizations' behaviour in a variety of macroeconomic policy environments, and we are confident that this perspective is useful theoretically, it remains to be proven as a basis for understanding criminal behaviour.

An important policy-related problem for analysing criminal networks is the lack of or sparseness of available data with respect to their operations or structure. Within the framework of our model, we can study the equilibrium restrictions arising from theory and generate predictions as to how much can be learned about the entire structure from observing only pieces of the network. In particular, we are interested in what is the minimum amount of information (about nodes or links in the network) that would be sufficient to combat criminal activity efficiently.[50] We also plan to investigate the potential usefulness of various summary statistics developed in the literature (measures of centrality, 'betweenness', etc.) in obtaining approximations of total crime activity without knowing the complete structure of the network. Understanding the consequences of a hierarchy within the criminal enterprise is another logical extension to the flat networks discussed thus far.

The networks approach to crime we advocate here is, of course, not without its critics. For instance, Peter Klerks argues that 'sophisticated network analysis methods need to enable investigators to identify positions of power and to attribute these to specific individual traits or to structural roles that these individuals fulfill.' Yet in doing so, he also worries that 'criminologists still need to ask the deeper question about the usefulness of theory for practical applications: if we as researchers come up with "better" knowledge and explanations of empirical phenomena, does this have consequences for the practitioners? Does such criminological research have any relevance and influence on the "real" world?'[51]

Our approach is only partly ready to meet this challenge. There are two things that need to be done to bring it to a point of practical use. First, we need to identify networks and discover whether the parsimonious numbers of parameters we have chosen are useful for predicting the formation of networks and their changing configuration. Second, we need to test whether the underlying model of criminal behaviour is itself a useful one for describing the forces playing on criminals. Is our simple formulation capable of capturing undoubtedly complex behaviour sufficiently well to be useful? In the long run it is important that we confront our model with data. Yet without a model, sophisticated or not, data have no use.

Acknowledgements

We would like to thank Professor Martin Bouchard and three anonymous referees for the generous and substantial comments that have made our paper more comprehensible and useful to the broader criminological community. We, of course, are responsible for any errors and omissions.

50. See Dombroski et al., 'Estimating the Shape of Covert Networks', for another approach to identifying missing or hidden links among participants.

51. P. Klerks, 'The Network Paradigm Applied to Criminal Organisations: Theoretical Nitpicking or Irrelevant Doctrine for Investigators? Recent Developments in the Netherlands', *Connections* 24 (2001): 53–65.

Appendix

In this Appendix we describe our general analytical approach and then solve completely a three-player network example to further illustrate our methodology. EK[52] provide more details for the interested reader.

For a particular network G and choices of efforts of all others, criminal i makes his optimal choice of effort by maximizing the difference between his benefits and costs of crime given in equations (2) and (3). Optimality implies that for each participant ($i = 1, \ldots, N$), marginal benefits of doing crime are equalized to marginal costs of doing crime. These are characterized by the first order conditions (FOC):

$$1 + \gamma \sum_{j=1}^{N} g_{ij} e_j = \pi \left(1 + \gamma \sum_{j=1}^{N} e_j + \lambda e_i + \delta \sum_{j=1}^{N} g_{ij} \right) \tag{FOC}$$

For each network of a given number of participants, we solve for the optimal effort level given the parameters. We then search over all possible networks of fixed size N to find the 'optimal' network structure – the optimal G that maximizes network profit.

Formally, if $e^*(G)$ are the optimal Nash equilibrium crime levels that result from a given network structure G, we solve the problem of finding the optimal network, defined as the network G maximizing aggregate profits among all possible networks of a given number of participants.

$$\pi^*(N) = \max_G \sum_{i=1}^{N} \left[y_i(G, e^*(G)) - c_i(G, e^*(G)) \right]$$

Finally, we can extend the analysis even further with what we term 'full optimization', by permitting the number of agents in the network, N, to be also a choice variable. To achieve this, we compare the maximized aggregate profits, $\pi^*(N)$ for various network sizes, N. Depending on the costs and benefit parameters, it could be that small or large networks are optimal – see the discussion in the text.

In the remainder of this Appendix we show how to solve for the equilibrium effort levels explicitly in a simple three-player example. Assume a particular network, G:

$$G = \begin{pmatrix} 0 & 1 & 1 \\ 1 & 0 & 1 \\ 1 & 1 & 0 \end{pmatrix}$$

52. EK, 'The Economic Structure of Crime Networks'.

where G describes the ('full') network in which individuals 1 and 2 and 3 are linked. Use the optimality condition (FOC) to solve for the optimal crime levels, $e^*(G)$:

$$1 + \gamma(e_2 + e_3) = \pi + \pi\lambda(e_1 + e_2 + e_3) + \pi\lambda e_1 + 2\pi\delta$$

$$1 + \gamma(e_1 + e_3) = \pi + \pi\lambda(e_1 + e_2 + e_3) + \pi\lambda e_2 + 2\pi\delta$$

$$1 + \gamma(e_1 + e_2) = \pi + \pi\lambda(e_1 + e_2 + e_3) + \pi\lambda e_3 + 2\pi\delta$$

which is a system of three linear equations in three unknowns to be solved explicitly for $e^*(G) = (e_1^*, e_2^*, e_3^*)$. In this particular example, since G is a symmetric matrix, we obtain a symmetric Nash equilibrium in the optimal individual crime levels:

$$e_1^* = e_2^* = e_3^* = \frac{1 - \pi - 2\pi\delta}{4\pi\lambda - 2\gamma}$$

Of course, we can (and do) solve the problem for every other possible network structure G as well. In the solution for efforts (crime) above, notice that an increase in the direct cost of links (δ) reduces crime as does an increase in congestion costs (λ). Higher benefits from connectivity (γ) increase crime, while higher overall costs (π) reduce it. For the given network, the solution reveals sensible outcomes, exemplifying the general results in the text.

How illegal drugs enter an island country: insights from interviews with incarcerated smugglers

Jonathan P. Caulkins, Honora Burnett and Edward Leslie

Qatar Campus and H. John Heinz III School of Public Policy & Management, Carnegie Mellon University

Introduction

Worldwide, governments consider illegal drugs to be a serious problem, including in the UK.[1] With the important exception of diverted pharmaceuticals, in most countries the majority of drug-related social costs are associated with substances that have been smuggled in from abroad.[2] Furthermore, international borders present unusual opportunities for authorities trying to apprehend drug traffickers, and considerable funds are invested in trying to interdict the flow of drugs across borders. Hence, understanding how drugs are smuggled is of great interest.

The mechanics of importation has only rarely been a focus of past research, and this paper tries to fill that research gap by exploiting interviews with 110 people incarcerated in UK prisons who were involved in smuggling drugs. The objective is to describe how these

---

1. United Nations Office on Drugs and Crime (UNODC), *2005 World Drug Report* (Oxford: Oxford University Press, 2005); and Nicola Singleton, Rosemary Murray and Louise Tinsley, 'Measuring Different Aspects of Problem Drug Use: Methodological Developments', *Home Office Online Report* 16/06 (2006), http://www.homeoffice.gov.uk/rds/pdfs06/rdsolr1606.pdf.

2. Social costs are hard to pin down. The statement is certainly true with respect to so-called Cost of Illness (COI) estimates, but is probably true more generally. Domestic production of cannabis is common, but cannabis generates far fewer social costs per user or per kilogram than do other drugs. T.J. Moore, *The Social Costs of Illicit Drugs in Australia. Report for the Australian Federal Police* (Fitzroy: Turning Point Alcohol and Drug Centre 2006).

respondents and their organizations brought drugs into the UK and to shed some light on incentives.

The respondents are a subset of 222 inmates interviewed by Matrix Knowledge Group as part of its project *The Illicit Drug Trade in the United Kingdom*, conducted for the UK Home Office. Almost all inmates were serving sentences of 7 or more years, suggesting most respondents were involved with relatively large quantities and/or Class A drugs, although some also describe lower-level importation from earlier in their career.

The UK is an interesting case study because it is a populous country with significant use of all major classes of illegal drugs and a relatively strong data and research base concerning illegal drug use and related problems. Importantly, the UK is also an island, so the range of smuggling options is more circumscribed.

The focus here is on how – and to a lesser extent why – the drugs were imported. We develop a typology based on the 'technology' or methods used to bring drugs across the border, focusing on what skills or resources were needed to undertake the operation. To use the jargon of economics, smuggling technologies are distinguished based on the 'barriers to entry'.

Technology in this sense is not synonymous with vehicle type. For example, we distinguish between simple courier operations, organizations that corrupted airline or airport employees and an individual who flew his own cargo plane. Even though all three involved air transport, the latter two required resources (access to corruptible officials and a plane, respectively) that the first did not.

The majority of respondents were associated with the technology that posed the fewest barriers to entry – passengers carrying drugs on regularly scheduled commercial transit (66 on commercial airlines, but also 15 via ferry or tunnel). Some were self-employed couriers or managers of operations employing many couriers, but most were simple couriers hired on a fee-for-service basis. The 30 who were not involved in courier-based operations collectively accounted for substantially greater smuggling throughput capacity and fell into five groups: operations that involved corrupt lorry drivers; covertly shipping drugs intermingled with legitimate commerce; organizations that transported drugs via commercial airlines with the assistance of corrupt officials; mailing drugs into the UK; and classic smuggling via boats landing between ports of entry.

After reviewing relevant literature and describing the data and analysis methods, the two Results sections review findings pertinent to those two broad groups (courier-based operations and other). The paper concludes with a discussion of implications, including very rough estimates of how the returns to crime vary by smuggling modality.

Literature review

A fair amount is now known about lower-level drug distribution, but as Desroches observes, the literature on high-level drug trafficking remains slim.[3] In particular, there has been very little research about drug importing based on systematic interviews with incarcerated offenders. This study adds to that small but important literature. The goal is not to test a theory. Rather, the goal is simply to document the operational practices of a large number of smugglers.

3. Frederick Desroches, 'Research on Upper Level Drug Trafficking: A Review', *Journal of Drug Issues* 37 (2007): 827–44.

A progenitor of the present study is Reuter and Haaga's exploratory study of high-level drug markets in the United States, whose subjects included nine importers.[4] Our respondents' statements were mostly consistent with their primary conclusions, namely that dealing does not require scarce or specialized skills, enduring organizations or recourse to violence, and that the upper levels of the market are national, not regional. The partial exception was that it sometimes seemed important to be in the right place – socially or professionally – which we elaborate on below.

Decker and Chapman offer an excellent more recent analogue, based on interviews with 34 high-level drug smugglers incarcerated in the United States.[5] Decker and Chapman's typology differs by focusing on vehicle type, differentiating among private vessels (18, with 15 using hidden compartments), commercial vessels (10), private planes (12), commercial planes (6) and land vehicles (2). As we elaborate below, there were fascinating differences in organizational structures between what our respondents describe and what Decker and Chapman report.

Ruggiero and Kahn studied the spread of drug use and distribution in British South Asian communities.[6] Their data collection net was wide, incorporating interviews with Pakistani and British law enforcers and treatment staff, as well as 42 interviews of incarcerated drug offenders. Their study addressed all drug-related activities among a particular demographic group, whereas the present study focuses on a particular activity (importation) by all eligible respondents, regardless of ethnicity. Nevertheless, Ruggiero and Kahn offer some observations about importation by this community. Apparently the key issue is locating an international supplier, not bringing the drugs across the border, and those suppliers can be found readily in Amsterdam and Rotterdam, even if one does not already have such connections. That is, the typical pattern is local importation from just across the channel, although some move up the chain to purchase directly in Turkey, where prices are considerably lower.

Dorn et al. and Desroches review the larger literature that studies importation through methods beyond interviewing incarcerated high-level traffickers.[7] One theme of that literature is organizational structure. Desroches's study of 70 high-level, Canadian traffickers found that 33% of the interviewees had originally been in legitimate importing and exporting businesses before getting involved with the drug trade.[8] Such knowledge of how a business works, from efficiency to employee trust to terminology, was used in both the illegitimate and legitimate market. Zaitch's fieldwork on The Netherlands' cocaine industry showed how Colombian smugglers were rarely self-employed.[9] They initiated partnerships and social interactions (i.e. subcontracting), resulting in reliance on organized

---

4. Peter Reuter and John Haaga, *The Organization of High-Level Drug Markets: An Exploratory Study* (Santa Monica, CA: RAND 1989).
5. Scott Decker and Margaret Chapman, *Drug Smugglers on Drug Smuggling: Lessons from the Inside* (Philadelphia, PA: Temple University Press 2008).
6. Vincenzo Ruggiero and Kazim Kahn, 'British South Asian Communities and Drug Supply Networks in the UK: A Qualitative Study', *International Journal of Drug Policy* 17 (2006): 473–83.
7. Nicholas Dorn, Michael Levi and Leslie King, 'Literature Review on Upper Level Drug Trafficking', *The Home Office of the United Kingdom Online Report* 22/05 (2005); Desroches, 'Research on Upper Level Drug Trafficking', http://www.homeoffice.gov.uk/rds/pdfs05/rdsolr2205.pdf
8. Frederick Desroches, *The Crime that Pays: Drug Trafficking and Organized Crime in Canada* (Toronto: Canadian Scholars' Press 2005).
9. Damian Zaitch, *Trafficking Cocaine: Colombian Drug Entrepreneurs in the Netherlands* (The Hague: Kluwer Law International, 2002).

networks to transport the cocaine. Briefly, respondents in the present study paint a picture that is entirely consistent with the prevailing view reflected in these earlier studies that drug trafficking is dominated by relatively small and loosely structured organizations, and that its leaders think of what they do as a business activity and use associated terminology. Further information about the structure of the respondents' organizations is available from Matrix Knowledge Group.[10]

Beyond these close analogues to the present study, there is a larger literature on drug importation that can broadly be divided into two halves. Ethnographic studies, journalistic accounts and case studies give great detail on a small number of organizations.[11] Studies using simulation, systems analysis, modelling and policy analysis aim to provide a comprehensive description of a significant segment of the market, but usually abstract away from the mechanics of how drugs are imported.[12] The present study fills a gap between these two types of analyses. Unlike ethnographies, journalistic accounts or case studies, we describe the operations of a large number of disparate organizations. Our sample is in no way a representative or random sample of importers, but it is diverse with respect to drug, method, number of successful importations before arrest, etc. That variety and detail enriches, in a complementary way, insights provided by the more abstract analyses, which often reason based on expected values and typical organizations. To some extent this study challenges the very idea that there is a typical importing organization. Although simple couriers were sufficiently homogeneous in their operations to aggregate, most of the other respondents were not; we provide a brief paragraph on each of these respondents to illustrate the diversity of importing organizations that would otherwise be lost if we reported only averages of quantitative metrics.

---

10. Matrix Knowledge Group, 'The Illicit Drug Trade in the United Kingdom', *Home Office Online Report* 20/07 (2007), http://www.homeoffice.gov.uk/rds/pdfs07/rdsolr2007.pdf

11. Ethnographic studies: Patricia Adler, *Wheeling and Dealing: An Ethnography of an Upper-Level Drug Dealing and Smuggling Community* (New York: Columbia University Press, 1985). Journalistic accounts: James Mills, *The Underground Empire: Where Crime and Government Embrace* (New York: Doubleday 1986). Case studies: Joseph R. Fuentes, 'Life of a Cell: Managerial Practice and Strategy in Colombian Cocaine Distribution in the United States' (PhD diss., City University of New York, 1998); and Carlo Morselli, 'Structuring Mr. Nice: Entrepreneurial Opportunities and Brokerage Positioning in the Cannabis Trade', *Crime, Law and Social Change* 35 (2001): 203–44.

12. Simulation: Gordon Crawford and Peter Reuter, *Simulation of Adaptive Response: A Model of Drug Interdiction* (Santa Monica, CA: RAND, 1988); Jonathan Caulkins, Gordon Crawford and Peter Reuter, 'Simulation of Adaptive Response: A Model of Drug Interdiction', *Mathematical and Computer Modeling* 17 (1993): 37–52; and Peter Reuter, Gordon Crawford and Jonathan Cave, *Sealing the Borders: The Effects of Increased Military Participation on Drug Interdiction* (Santa Monica, CA: RAND 1988). Systems analysis: Keith Gardiner and Raymond Shreckengost, 'A System Dynamics Model for Estimating Heroin Imports into the United States', *System Dynamics Review* 3 (1987): 8–27; and Peter Rydell and Susan Everingham, *Controlling Cocaine. Supply Versus Demand Programs* (Santa Monica, CA: RAND 1994). Modeling: Jonathan Caulkins and Rema Padman, 'Interdiction's Impact on the Structure and Behavior of the Export–Import Sector for Illicit Drugs', *Zeitschrift fur Operations Research* 37 (1993): 207–24; and Jonathan Caulkins and Haijing Hao, 'Modeling Drug Market Supply Disruptions: Where Do All the Drugs *Not* Go?', *Journal of Policy Modeling* 30 (2008): 251–70. Policy analysis: Peter Reuter, 'Quantity Illusions and Paradoxes of Drug Interdiction: Federal Intervention into Vice Policy', *Law and Contemporary Problems* 51 (1988): 233–52; Peter Reuter, *Eternal Hope: America's International Narcotics Efforts* (Santa Monica, CA: RAND 1985); and Claudia Costa Storti and Paul De Grauwe, 'Modeling the Cocaine and Heroin Markets in the Era of Globalization and Drug Reduction Policies', Mimeo.

Data and methods

The matrix study and sample

Matrix Knowledge Group, a London-based public policy research and analysis firm, conducted the interviews. Its final report for the UK Home Office contains a complete description of the data collection, but the key attributes are as follows.[13] All inmates in 22 prisons who had drug-related convictions resulting in sentences of 7 years or more were invited to participate. These are fairly long sentences by UK standards, so the sample is skewed toward higher-level offenders. Link workers appointed by prison governors identified other individuals who could provide relevant information even though they were serving sentences less than 7 years. In total, Matrix invited 1390 prisoners to participate, but only 263 inmates signed consent forms. From among these 263 volunteers, Matrix conducted 222 interviews. Reasons for not completing an interview ranged from scheduling difficulties to interviewers aborting interviews when they did not feel physically safe.

The Matrix sample is not random, because some effort was made to recruit people who were prepared to discuss their activities and/or who were considered to be particularly important. Furthermore, only 19% (263 of 1390) returned signed consent forms indicating a willingness to participate, so there is ample room for sample selection bias. Nevertheless, in terms of broad descriptors (ethnicity, charge, sentence length and age) it matches well the population of all drug offenders serving sentences of 7 or more years.

The interviewees were predominantly male (95%). The majority were white and British (47%), but otherwise were diverse, with the next largest groups being Black Caribbean (14%), Black African (11%) and other White European (5%). They were not particularly young (mean age = median age = 40, with 90% between 25 and 59 years old).

The interview protocol contained both structured and semi-structured questions, and interviewers were trained on concepts related to the fields of business, economics, and social networks. Interviews were conducted in a private room and typically lasted 1.5 hours. Matrix validated the interviews by consulting stakeholders and knowledge-holders familiar with the inmates, including discussions with law enforcement, customs and asset recovery staff, and by reviewing case materials. Matrix generated 1–10 page summaries of most interviews, but not for some of the couriers. We received the summary when one existed, and otherwise received the raw transcripts.

Matrix reported four principal limitations of the data. First, individuals were self-selecting, potentially biasing the sample. Second, respondents dealt in a range of drugs and market levels over a range of years, so sample sizes for any given drug, market level and time period are small. Third, inmates spoke about different themes to different extents, so not all themes were covered in all interviews. Thus, the absence of a response cannot be inferred to be a negative response. Lastly, while Matrix undertook extensive efforts to validate interview information, the possibility of false reporting remains.

The subset of the Matrix sample examined here

Matrix converted the 222 interviews into 230 records and labelled them by 'role' played. Some interviewees played multiple roles over their career; hence, the 230 records from 222 interviews.

Many of the 222 were only involved in domestic distribution and so were not of interest to our study. To identify the records containing information about importation,

13. Matrix Knowledge Group, 'The Illicit Drug Trade in the United Kingdom'.

Table 1. Number of respondents by smuggling technology.

Technology	Number	%
Courier operations		
Commercial air couriers and their manager/organizers	66	60.0%
Couriers using other means of transport	15	13.6%
Other operations		
Operations that involved corrupt vehicle operators	15	13.6%
Hiding drugs among unaccompanied legitimate commerce	6	5.5%
Corruption-facilitated transport on commercial air flights	3	2.7%
Mailing drugs into the UK	3	2.7%
Classic smuggling by boat between ports of entry	3	2.7%

we read the 140 whose role label mentioned 'international' or was ambiguous. For example, we read records of roles Matrix described as 'bosses' but not the 'retailers'. Some of the 140 were not informative, e.g. because the boss was boss of a purely domestic operation. Conversely, some convicted of a charge other than importation nevertheless described in detail importation activities of others in their organization and/or their own import activities from a different stage in their career. In the end, 110 respondents were relevant. Eighty-one described courier-based operations, and 30 described other technologies. (One interview record covered both.)

As mentioned, we classified importers by reference to what special skill, talent or access was needed to employ the smuggling technology. This makes sense from an industrial organization's perspective. It also recognizes the fact that drug distribution is a consensual crime, so incarcerated offenders can be replaced – but some more easily than others.[14]

We distinguish first between operations using couriers who accompanied the drugs as passengers on commercial passenger services versus other methods. The majority of respondents were involved in courier operations, but the other importers are interesting because of their diversity and their success in terms of quantity imported per person and apparently lower arrests rates per kilogram delivered. Among the 30 not involved with courier operations, we distinguish five modalities and offer brief vignettes for most of those individuals, whereas we present only general patterns and aggregate statistics for the couriers. Table 1 shows the number of respondent cases in each category.

Courier operations

Introduction

Of the 81 interviews describing courier operations, 66 pertained to commercial airline flights and 15 to drivers or pedestrians on ferries or the Eurotunnel. Most of the 81 were couriers, meaning people who carried drugs on them or in their luggage while travelling among the general public. Table 2 reports concealment strategy by region of origin for the 66 couriers involved in airline operations. These 66 included five self-employed couriers who owned the drugs they were carrying and five people who managed or organized couriers' activities. These manager/organizers might or might not accompany the couriers in transit, but did not normally carry drugs themselves The other 56 were simple couriers.

14. Mark A.R. Kleiman, 'The Problem of Replacement and the Logic of Drug Law Enforcement', *Drug Policy Analysis Bulletin*, 3 (1997), 8–10.

Table 2. Origin of plane couriers' flights, by way drugs were carried.

Origin	In suitcase	In stomach	Other	Total
Africa	9	6	1	16
Asia	3	0	0	3
Europe	3	0	0	3
South America	9	3	0	12
Caribbean and Mexico	24	1	4	29
Blank/NA/mixed	2	0	1	3
Total	50	10	6	66

The majority (36 of 56) voluntarily carried the drugs on a fee-for-service basis. The remainder claimed to have been coerced or unwitting participants or had a status that was unclear from the interview.

The key characteristic of courier-based operation is low barriers to entry. While a subset go to some trouble to camouflage the drugs, strictly speaking all couriers need to do besides locating a supplier and customer is to buy a ticket.[15] Locating suppliers abroad seems to be easy, even for self-employed couriers. Fee-for-service couriers do not even need to find customers; they simply turn the drugs over to the same organization that gave them the drugs to carry.

Information about couriers on planes

Most plane courier operations (62 of 66) were carrying cocaine. This is consistent with Green et al.'s finding that couriers carrying Class A drugs, cocaine in particular, receive the longest sentences.[16] Five carried heroin, including one who carried both cocaine and heroin and all three who originated in Asia (Bangladesh and Pakistan). Half of cocaine couriers originated in the Caribbean islands, most frequently from St Lucia (8) and Jamaica (6). Most originating in Africa came from Nigeria (9) or Ghana (3). Couriers from Africa were much more likely (6 of 16) than others (4 of 50) to carry the drugs in their stomach.

Forty-two of the 49 couriers who carried drugs for someone else claimed to have been caught the first time they acted as a courier (Table 3). One might be tempted to dismiss this as deceit, and sometimes the interviewer noted that the protestations of innocence seemed dubious. (In the extreme, one respondent claimed to have believed that what he swallowed was horse food, not cocaine.) However, even leaving aside the seven who claim to have been duped and six who say they were coerced, almost as great a proportion (30 of 36) of the people who admitted to voluntarily carrying drugs for pay reported getting caught on their first trip. Furthermore, many of them were completely forthcoming about drug dealing and other criminal activity conducted earlier in their career. Also, the manager/organizers of couriers frequently complained that recruiting couriers was an onerous chore, presumably in part because of their high attrition rate, estimated

15. Respondents who camouflaged drugs described, among other schemes, using a secret compartment or lining of a suitcase, mixing drugs into hair gel or sewing them into robes. It is not clear how often these measures fool Customs. One respondent carried liquid cocaine in bottles of hot sauce only to discover on arrival that this trick was well known to Customs.

16. Penny Green, Chris Mills and Tim Read. 'The Characteristics and Sentencing of Illegal Drug Importers', *British Journal of Criminology*, 34, no. 4 (1994): 479–86; 38% of the 342 couriers carrying Class A drugs in Green et al.'s study received sentences of 7 years or longer and, hence, would have been eligible for inclusion in the sample considered here.

Table 3. Number of trips plane couriers report taking before being arrested (for the 57 of 60 plane couriers reporting this information).

	Couriers for others				
Reported involvement as:	Total	Voluntary employee	Organizers	Self-employed couriers	Total
1st Trip	42	30		3	45
2nd Trip	1	1			1
3rd Trip			1	1	2
4th Trip	1	1			1
5th Trip[a]			1		1
First time using route/mechanism that led to arrest	2	2		1	3
Involved for months or longer	3	2	1		4
Grand total	49	36	3	5	57

[a] Respondent travelled successfully as an organizer four times, but was arrested the first time he served as a courier, filling in for a courier who did not show up.

Table 4. Average pay for couriers who volunteered to carry drugs on a fee-for-service basis.

	Average pay per trip	Number of observations	Average pay per kg	Number of observations
Heroin				
Asia	£5333	2	£817	2
Cocaine				
Africa	£3089	9	£1447	8
Europe	£1833	3	£2235	3
Caribbean	£9242	12	£4805	10
South America	£10,778	6	£6182	6

Note: average pay per kilogram not available for three respondents for whom quantity carried was unclear.

by one manager to be a one in four risk of getting caught per trip (even in his large and successful operation). There is no way to adjust for the selection biases inherent in interviewing incarcerated (i.e. failed) couriers. Overall, though, the impression one gets is that the arrest risk per trip is considerable, at least for novices.

Table 4 summarizes the average pay rate among the 36 who admitted to voluntarily serving as a courier-employee. Couriers transporting cocaine from the Western Hemisphere were paid the most. Indeed, their employers paid more per kilogram for courier services than for the cocaine. (Note: couriers were usually paid upon delivery, so they did not get paid for the trip which led to their arrest.) Since the majority reported that the trip which led to arrest was their *only* trip, this means that the actual pay received per attempted trip is lower than the figures in Table 4. Failed trips are not costless to the smuggling organization. The organization still lost the value of the drugs and plane ticket. On the other hand, some couriers – particularly European residents smuggling from the Caribbean – were given a free vacation as part of the inducement and cover story, including hotel (often 7 nights) and sometimes £500–1000 in spending money. The couriers did receive those benefits even on the trips which led to their arrest.

In our sample the five self-employed couriers on planes do not appear to have been more successful at evading arrest than the courier employees. All five were UK residents trying to import cocaine from Latin America. Four claimed to have been caught on the first try; the fifth said he was caught on his third trip. The profit per kilogram is potentially much higher than the rates described in Table 4 for these self-employed couriers because they own the drugs they carry (profit of approximately £10,000 or more per kg of cocaine). However, two carried substantially less than the average courier-employee, perhaps because liquidity constraints precluded larger purchases.

Insights into courier management

The interviews with managers of courier operations offered additional insights. For example, it is commonly observed that drugs are distributed within final market countries via networks with multiple layers of domestic wholesalers separating importers from street sellers. This puts layers of anonymity between the street sellers who are vulnerable to arrest and the higher-level dealers. Couriers are also highly vulnerable to arrest, and one respondent described a similar scheme in which he served as a buffer, protecting the organization from being brought down by couriers' arrests. In particular, he recruited the couriers and collected the drugs from them at the airport, getting paid £5000 per successful trip, nearly as much as the couriers themselves. (They earned £7000 per successful trip, plus a two-week holiday in Grenada as cover.) The respondent had only been in the business for a few months when one of his couriers was arrested. That led to the arrest of the respondent and another recruiter, but not the bosses who ran the organization.

Another respondent played a similar role on the Caribbean side of an organization, smuggling cocaine from Barbados to London, Toronto and Amsterdam. After proving himself by serving as a courier on one trip (to Toronto), he was promoted to recruiter/organizer. He managed one trip every 5–6 months four times before being caught (because a courier did not show up and he had to take the courier's place). His boss had been in the business for 16 years and was unaffected by his arrest.

Another insight is that success seemed to come from organizational strategies as much as from efforts to camouflage the drug. The respondent in the previous paragraph reported that five to 10 couriers were put on a single flight, including one as 'bait' who carried just 1 kg instead of the usual 3–5 kg. The bait courier was sacrificed by phoning ahead to tell Customs who to arrest. The respondent and at least some of the other couriers would be processed by a corrupt Customs official who was on their payroll, even though the cocaine was apparently well hidden inside souvenir ornamental plates.[17]

17. The respondent claimed the organization had revenues of £250,000 from delivering 10–15 kg to a customer in London, and that this netted the boss about £100,000. The respondent accounted for most of the £150,000 in costs implied by that level of profit. Successful couriers earned £2500 per trip for carrying 3–5 kg, suggesting courier costs of £7500–10,000. The respondent (organizer) earned £15,000–25,000 per trip and thought the corrupt Customs official might have been paid £10,000–15,000 per trip or perhaps more. Assuming the 20–30 kg of cocaine shipped in order for 10–15 kg to get through had been obtained for £3000 per kg, this suggests materials costs of £60,000–90,000. Additional costs include plane tickets, paying the artist to conceal the cocaine in plates, and other operating costs. Another respondent (a boss) described a similar operation with similar finances but slightly higher net revenues. He reported a frequency of two flights per month, suggesting a throughput capacity of several hundred kg per year and net revenues of ~£7 million per year.

Couriers not on planes

Twelve respondents admitted carrying illicit drugs into the UK by ferry or Eurotunnel without using a professional activity as a cover. These 12 do not include lorry drivers who secreted drugs in amongst their legitimate cargo. One borderline case, a lorry driver who carried the drugs in the cab with his personal belongings, is included here because the drugs were not intermingled with the cargo.

These 'non-plane couriers' are similar to the plane couriers except for their mode of transportation. Barriers to entry are low. Ten of the 12 had access to a capital asset in the form of a vehicle (typically their personal auto), but otherwise these individuals were crossing the international border along with the public, not by exploiting any special skill, role or profession.

One striking result is the utter bi-modality with respect to arrest risk among these 12. Eight reported getting arrested on their first smuggling attempt; the other four operations were never discovered by the authorities. None of the 12 reported being caught on any trip other than the first. The four successful non-plane couriers were only arrested and made it into our sample because of subsequent, different smuggling activities. In particular, three of the four were ultimately arrested the *first* time they tried importing cocaine from Latin America on a plane.

Table 5 summarizes the eight who reported being arrested on their first trip. All were employees who received payment per kilogram that was comparable to that of plane couriers, although four reported carrying 10+ kg, which is more than plane couriers carried.

We describe the four successful non-plane couriers in more detail. Two of the four seemed to operate in much the same manner as these eight failed couriers, yet were never caught for this activity. The first moved very large quantities of cocaine (100 kg per trip, two trips per year) in duffle bags in his car for 3 years without making any special effort to hide the drugs. The other imported 25 kg of hash two or three times per year over three, non-consecutive years. He simply drove a van to Morocco, bought hash for £200 per kg, and sold it for £2000 per kg in the UK. Expenses per trip were £5000 for a friend to come along, keep him company and share the driving plus £1000 for gas and miscellaneous costs. Thus he could have profited close to £40,000 per trip if he sold all of the hashish, but apparently he used and/or gave away about half of it.

The third travelled to Holland by ferry on a fishing holiday every 2–3 months for a few years. Initially he would buy 2000 ecstasy tablets for £300 and sell them for £5 each. Later he would buy two ounces of cocaine for £350 and sell it on for £1000. He stopped for 5–6 years, but then returned and expanded, ferrying to Holland every 4–6 months to buy 4–10 kg of cocaine at £13,000 per kg. He was only caught when he decided to fly to St Lucia to pick up 5 kg of cocaine there.

The fourth described a successful operation from an earlier era. From 1974 to 1984 the respondent found families who wanted to go on extended holiday. He would give them a camper and £10,000 cash. They would drive through Italy, take a ferry to Tunisia, drive through Algeria and Morocco, take a ferry to Spain, and drive back to the UK. While they were in North Africa, the respondent would buy 100 kg of cannabis at £40 per kg, press it into blocks, and hide it in the camper. He retrieved the cannabis once the family was back in the UK and let them keep the camper. The operation went undiscovered; the individual was eventually arrested for other activities.

One other individual bears mention even though he was smuggling drugs out of, not into, the UK. He would buy cars at auctions, register them either in the original owner's name or under a false name, and modify them to conceal 10 kg of cocaine. He would take

Table 5. Attributes of non-plane couriers arrested on first smuggling attempt.

Drug/quantity imported	20 kg heroin and 10 kg cocaine	0.8 kg of cocaine	9500 ecstasy tablets	4 kg of cocaine	16 kg of heroin	3 kg of cocaine	10 kg of cocaine	30 kg of cocaine
Country of residence	UK	UK	Lithuania	Austria	Ireland/UK (ambiguous)	UK	Illegally in UK from France	UK
Source	France	Spain	Belgium	Amsterdam	Netherlands	Belgium	France	Spain
Method of importation	Car by tunnel	Ferry (foot passenger)	Truck on ferry	Car by tunnel	Car on ferry	Train	Car	Car
How concealed	Hidden in cans of canned goods	In a hold-all bag	Stowed in cab	Behind radio, in bumper and under dash	Not stated	Not stated	Hidden in seats	In boot of car
Previous experience drug selling?	Yes	Convicted for drug possession and supplying guns	None reported	No	Convicted robber; one prior drug run to Scotland	Yes	Yes	Lorry driver who had imported cocaine from Spain
Pay	£1500 for expenses +£2000 per kilo	£400	€500	€10,000	£20,000–40,000	Not specified	£20,000	Not specified
Year	1999	1998	2005	2004	2002	2002	2004	Not clear

the car on a ferry to Ireland. The people to whom he was delivering the drugs would drive the car off the ferry, and he would return on the ferry as a pedestrian. He was successful in doing one of these trips per month for 2 years.

The last two individuals in this category were arrested for providing assistance within the UK to a non-plane courier operation (cars on ferries), but they provided little, if any, pertinent information.

Results concerning other smuggling technologies

This section describes the five main smuggling technologies represented in the data besides courier-based operations.

Operations that involved corrupt vehicle operators ('bent lorry drivers')

A common smuggling method was hiding the drugs among other cargo carried on trucks entering the UK by ferry or tunnel with the knowledge and cooperation of the truck driver. In the respondents' words, these were 'bent lorry driver' operations.

This importation technology combines relatively low barriers to entry and high potential for success in the sense of importing large quantities for 3–5 years without getting caught. Six individuals described organizational revenues net of purchasing costs in the range of £1–10 million per year (see Table 6).

Although the most successful individual was the wealthy owner of a trucking firm, for others the barriers to entry were modest. They merely had to locate a corrupt lorry driver. Often the drivers were friends, but long-term associations were apparently not always necessary. One respondent, himself a driver, was convinced by another driver he met at a truck stop to transport 10 kg of cocaine to England from Spain for £10,000.

Nevertheless, some of these organizations clearly did more than just toss drugs in the back of a truck and head for the border. One respondent reported doing an entire year of dry runs before attempting to smuggle any drugs. He also hauled legitimate perishable cargo and tried to hit the border at particular times (1:30–3:30 a.m.) when Customs officials were tired. He was never caught on his regular run, but was convicted as a result of doing a one-time, much larger run for a different organization.

There are minor players. One respondent described a friend's brother (hence, not in our sample) who smuggled just 1.5 kg of cannabis into the UK in his lorry for £500 per load, once or twice a month from 1998 to 2000. Our sample also included unsuccessful examples, two in particular reported being arrested on their first runs.

However, Table 6 gives a sense of the scale/importance of the more successful of these operations. In particular, when comparing their estimated annual throughput capacity with Singleton et al.'s estimates of total UK consumption, five of the six could each plausibly have been accounting for between 1–2 and 10% of the UK market for their drug.[18] Four others not included in Table 6 described activities consistent with throughput capacities of this magnitude, although missing data (e.g. on the frequency of operations) precludes stronger statements.

We include in Table 6 one individual who flew a plane rather than driving a lorry because the operations were similar (operator of a cargo vehicle knowingly participating

18. Singleton et al. 'Measuring Different Aspects Of Problem Drug Use'.

Table 6. Summary of scale of larger operations involving corrupt vehicle drivers.

Vehicle	Lorry	Lorry	Lorry	Lorry	Lorry	Plane
Years of operation	1992–1996	Pre-2002–2005	1999/2000–2005	1991–1996	1992–2000	1996–1998
Typical load	100 kg heroin (and one 500 kg load of cannabis)	20–50 kg of cocaine or heroin	30–40 kg cocaine	40–60 kg cannabis (sometimes also 50,000 ecstasy pills)	100 kg of cannabis (or 63,000 sleeves of cigarettes)	700–2500 kg cannabis
Number of loads per year	3	20–25	12	9	100 (twice a week)	12
Throughput capacity	300 kg/year	400–1250 kg/year	360–480 kg/year	~450 kg/year	10 metric tons/year	8.4–30 metric toms/year
Capacity as percentage of UK consumption in 2003/2004[a]	1.9–2.8%	2.5–11.7% for heroin or 1.1–4.9% for cocaine/crack	0.9–1.9% for cocaine or crack	0.1%	2.4%	2.0–7.3%
Source	Belgium	Holland	Holland	Belgium	Spain	Germany
Value/kg at source	£10,000[b]	Not given	£15,000	£400–550	Varied	Not given
Value/kg in UK	£17,500	Not given	£32,000	£2000–2500	£3200/kg in 1992; £600/kg in 2000	Not given
Revenue per year net of product purchase	£2.25 million	Unclear. Perhaps £6.8–21.25 million	£6.1–8.2 million	£0.65–0.95 million	Fell from £10 million to £4 million as prices fell	Not given
Organization structure	Respondent and friends hired drivers for £750 per kg	~6 people; entire lorry company was a front	Ten people who hired the driver	Six people, including respondent who was the driver (and owned his lorry)	Respondent owned firm; one partner in Spain and one who distributed drugs in UK	Unknown (respondent was just the 'driver')
Organization vulnerable to a driver's arrest?	Unclear	Nine drivers arrested between 2002 and 2005 without killing organization	Not given	Respondent was lorry owner/driver but others had worked with another driver before	Organization collapsed when driver's wife called Customs in a love triangle spat	Yes. Respondent was the 'driver' and plane owner
Sentence length (years)	15	7	8	19	12	25

[a] Based on Singleton et al. (2006) and assumption that cocaine and heroin are 50–75% pure at import.
[b] Respondent paid £370,000 for 30 kg, but he was just a driver who was allowed to buy a small stake at a compromise between export and import price; value to partners was £10,000 per kg.

in the conspiracy), except for the greater costs and skill requirements of using cargo planes rather than lorries.[19]

The largest lorry organization was led by the owner of a large trucking firm with warehouses throughout Europe. He sent dozens of 'wagons' per day with legitimate commerce along the same routes he used for smuggling and invested £1 million building and stocking a phony warehouse in Spain to provide cover for his operation. He paid drivers £200 per kilo of cannabis imported from Spain. Thus drivers earned an average of £20,000 per load, comparable to a £30,000 per year annual legitimate lorry driver salary.

Another organization used even more elaborate ruses, including sending a caravan of trucks with several dummy trucks to distract Customs. The dummy trucks would contain no drugs but were driven by known dealers and so would attract the bulk of the Customs officials' attention. This respondent claimed that sometimes their Turkish suppliers would tip off Customs to some smaller shipments to distract them from the trucks containing the larger shipments.

A testimony to the sophistication employed in hiding the drugs comes from the following bizarre anecdote. On one run the supplier hijacked the convoy after the deal had taken place to steal back the drugs. They shot up the trucks and the drivers fled, but the suppliers could not find the drugs. Even the police investigating the shooting did not notice the drugs, and shipped the trucks back to the respondent in the UK with the load of drugs intact.

Decker and Chapman's respondents primarily came from smuggling organizations who sold their services on a fee-for-service basis to other people who retained ownership of the drugs being transported.[20] In our sample, fee-for-service providers were typically employees or individuals, while organizations usually owned the drugs they transported. However, three of our respondents gave hints of being the sort of professional smuggling/broker organizations Decker and Chapman describe as the norm in their sample. One head of a lorry operation, who imported 100 kg loads of cocaine and 120 kg loads of amphetamine, stressed that he never owned the drugs. He charged £2000 per kilo regardless of substance and netted £500 per kilo after expenses. In contrast with other respondents, he said he kept his personnel on a fixed salary of £500 per week regardless of whether they were making deliveries, and made a practice of having a trained 'understudy' ready to step in whenever one of his people was arrested.

Another described himself as a cannabis broker who organized the import of shipments of 0.5–20 tons of cannabis for suppliers who grew the cannabis abroad and transshipped through the Netherlands. He was paid £10,000–250,000 per deal (apparently £12.5–20 per kg) to organize the transport via bent lorry drivers, who charged £200–250 per kg, or by shipping in cargo containers, which cost £100–200 per kg.

---

19. The pilot had been operating a legitimate air transportation business when he became involved with the Irish Republican Army (IRA). The respondent claimed initially to have been coerced by the IRA, but also said he was paid £70,000 for the first trip, and continued to receive money from the IRA throughout his drug trafficking career. The respondent hauled drugs and guns from various European locations into the UK through the Liverpool and Birmingham Airports. The largest single load of cannabis he reported was 2.5 metric tons and the largest payment he received was £250,000, suggesting a rate of £100 per kg. The respondent said actual transport costs were only £6500–7000 per trip, suggesting that skilled labour (pilot) wages dominated other expenses. He was caught when, as part of a training program for new Customs officers, Customs was searching incoming planes.
20. Decker and Chapman, *Drug Smugglers on Drug Smuggling*.

Although the respondent could describe the purchase and selling prices of the cannabis, apparently he never owned any of the cannabis shipments he arranged. The organization was only stopped when it shifted both its drug and route by attempting to import 5 tons of cocaine from Colombia to Spain, with portions intended to go on to the UK and The Netherlands. The respondent claimed to have corrupted government officials in London, Manchester and Scotland.

Finally, a third respondent reported importing 200 kg of cocaine per year, typically by paying a transport operator £1500–2000 per kilo, with his 2–10 kg being just part of the load. That is, the smuggling was outsourced to a transport operator who pooled loads from multiple drug enterprises.

Hiding drugs among unaccompanied legitimate commercial shipments

Bent lorry drivers carried drugs along with legitimate commerce as camouflage. However, the driver was a willing participant, so the drugs only needed to be hidden from customs inspection, not from discovery by the vehicle operator.

Another technology is hiding drugs in legitimate commerce and sending the combined cargo via a standard commercial shipper who is not complicit in the smuggling scheme. In this strategy no criminal accompanies the drugs as they cross the border, reducing the risk that drug seizure will lead to arrest and, hence, interrogation of someone who might provide useful information to law enforcement. On the other hand, a company, not just a private individual, has to be set up to receive commercial cargo.

This approach appears with some frequency in media descriptions of smuggling operations into various countries. Only two respondents in our sample employed this technology. However, after describing these two, we mention some circumstantial evidence from four other interviews suggesting that this may actually be an important smuggling strategy in the UK.

The more successful of the two tried this technology twice. The first time (1995) he and a partner created a company that purchased electrical transformers from around Europe and sent them to Morocco to be renovated by a legitimate firm. The renovated devices were then sent to a warehouse he and his partner created in Morocco where the oil coolant was replaced with 150 kg of cannabis. The operation took a year to create (using money he made from VAT fraud), but after setup, shipping and other costs of £60–80,000 they would make £100,000 per shipment, split two ways. The respondent claimed that, when arrested in 1995 on weapons offences, threatening to kill and drug charges, he had already been under surveillance for 6 months by Customs, so it is not clear how long the scheme operated undetected.

The respondent was arrested again in 2005 for possession of 200 kg of ketamine, 140,000 LSD hits and 600 Viagra tablets. The ketamine was imported from India in 50 kg containers of a chemical that physically resembled ketamine, enjoying a mark-up from £1500 per kg in India to £4000 per kg in the UK. The interviewer thought this activity began shortly after the respondent's 2002 release from prison, and that the respondent implied he was only admitting to what the police already knew about. Furthermore, the arrest stemmed from domestic distribution not detection of the importation. Hence, it seems plausible that the respondent's operation was successful at importing considerable quantities of drugs over several years, although the respondent never said that explicitly.

The second respondent claimed to have attempted importation only once, yet managed to be turned in by his own brother. The respondent was a sales manager at a printing machinery manufacturer. An acquaintance offered him £20,000 to import three crates containing 52 kg of ecstasy (250,000 tablets) and 5 kg of amphetamine alongside his company's legitimate cargo. His brother came across the drugs in the shipping container, and not thinking the respondent could be responsible, called the police.

In addition, there were four people who made at least passing reference to importation of drugs mixed with legitimate commerce. One was a domestic transporter for an organization that imported drugs. He reported picking drugs up at UK ports in containers that also had legitimate goods (e.g. Tables and chairs, oranges, etc.) shipped in from Amsterdam. Interestingly, the other half of his job was exporting the drugs to places where the prices were higher than in England (Jersey, Guernsey, Isle of Man, Tenerife). He reported that it was very easy to ship drugs out of the UK because no one expected it.

Another reported picking up 100–350 kg shipments of 75% pure heroin from various docks around England for a large importer for £5000 per job. He also bought 5 kg loads from this importer and employed four or five people to sell that on to multi-ounce customers. The respondent claimed the importer brought in a shipment every three weeks until the September 11th attack and Iraq War brought heightened security. If true, this one organization was responsible for importing on the order of 1.7–6 metric tons of heroin per year, or between one-sixth and one-half of total estimated UK heroin consumption at 75% purity.[21]

Finally, there were two individuals convicted of importing drugs mixed with legitimate commerce who claimed to be innocent victims of association. One said his partner used their company details (address, accounts, etc.) to set up a company that imported fruit from Brazil within which cocaine was concealed. The second imported furniture from Pakistan with a partner who arranged for 14 kg of heroin to be hidden in the furniture container.

Smuggling via commercial air by corrupting people

Three individuals used corruption, not couriers, to take advantage of commercial air flights to import drugs, two into the UK and one into the Netherlands. The corrupted individuals were a foreign diplomat, an airplane cleaner and airport baggage handlers, not Customs or police officers.

A common view is that drug traffickers in developed nations do not generally resort to corruption, possibly due to the difficulty of corrupting officials in these countries. Indeed, one respondent reported offering a police officer friend £150,000 for information, but the

21. Two details offered by this respondent are unique among the interviews we read. First, he claimed that the importer cut each kilogram of 75% pure heroin with 4.5 ounces of manitol, cutting the purity from 75 to 65%. Other respondents described more substantial cutting, or none at all. Second, he described each pick-up being made by a group of people divided over three cars, one to carry the drugs and two others to run interference with the police if there was trouble. Paying a team of people £5000 each per pick up is far more than most organizations pay staff, suggesting the importers were large enough to pay an 'efficiency wage' to ensure high-quality staff (e.g. the respondent was arrested along with 36 others from low-level sellers up to people at his level, but no one above him was arrested). The respondent also described getting a very good price for the 5 kg purchases (£15,000 per kg). A last possibly confirmatory observation is that another respondent reported buying quantities of heroin – up to 60 kg per purchase for 15 + purchases per year – that, if true, suggest the existence of an importer of this scale. Those tidbits lend some credence to what otherwise would seem to be an account of an organization with an implausibly large throughput capacity.

friend refused, although the officer did not turn the respondent in and they remained friends. These three respondents show, however, that it is not only integrity of government officials that matters; corrupting others may be an alternative way to create porous borders.

The first scheme took advantage of a corrupt Indian diplomat. The respondent had organized twelve 100 kg heroin lorry trips from Belgium to the UK, working with Turkish suppliers. To move up the supply chain, the respondent visited exporters from India and Pakistan. His contacts told him they could give 8 kg of heroin to an individual who worked at the Indian consulate in the UK, and whose usual and legitimate role was to get high-ranking consulate officials through Customs quickly. This man carried the heroin in his briefcase, and made two trips carrying 8 kg each trip.

The second respondent facilitated 10–15 kg cocaine shipments roughly every other month into England between the late 1990s and 2003. He was working at Heathrow Airport as a plane cleaner when a South American drug cartel representative asked him to supply information about where on the plane cocaine could be stored undetected. Subsequently the respondent would tell his contact which flights leaving Rio de Janeiro, Bogota, Caracas and Jamaica would be arriving during his shift hours in England. He and another corrupt Heathrow employee would unload the cocaine and pass it to the buyer, who was also in direct contact with the South American contact.

The third corrupted airline baggage handlers at Schipol airport in the Netherlands. The cocaine was placed in checked luggage associated with a courier who had tickets to fly through Schipol airport. The respondent claimed that the Venezuelan army loaded the cocaine on the plane for him and provided security for the operation. Corrupt baggage handlers at Schipol removed the cocaine, before the courier flew on to his or her final destination. Hence, the courier did not actually carry the drugs through Customs. A shipment was seized in Schipol less than one year after operations began, and the operations subsequently dissolved.

Mailing drugs to individuals in the UK

Three respondents described mailing drugs into the UK from abroad. A successful but small-scale scheme was devised by an individual who concealed 50 g of heroin in thin sheets between the pages of a law journal, which he sent by legitimate next-day courier from the Netherlands to the law office where his girlfriend worked, timed to arrive when she would be the only one in the office. The plan was never discovered, but was only capable of importing a small quantity of heroin.

Another respondent worked for an organization that imported 20–30 kg of cannabis per week. The organization paid growers £1800 per kg and drivers £200 per kg to move the cannabis to Belgium, where it was mailed to Post Office boxes in England, 1 kg at a time in A4-sized padded envelopes. The organization sold the cannabis for £3000–3100 per kg, suggesting annual revenues net of product purchase and driver costs of about £1–1.7 million per year. The organization appeared to consist of a boss, an investor and three or four employees.

The largest of these organizations shipped cocaine and cannabis to the UK from Ghana by DHL. The two bosses lived in Ghana, and came to the UK only to collect money. Their organization transported drugs from suppliers to a ‘factory’ where the drugs were packaged, suggesting there was a legitimate front for the DHL shipping. There were three or four ‘receivers’ in the UK, including the respondent, who collected the packages from 20 people who were employed just to provide an address to which the packages could be shipped and signed for.[22] It is precisely because the addressees were private citizens receiving individually addressed boxes, not commercial container shipments, that we view this operation as posting drugs, not intermingling them with legitimate commercial shipments.

The respondent suggested the organization shipped eight boxes a week containing an average weekly total of 20 kg of cocaine and 20 kg of cannabis. If true, that implies one metric ton of cocaine per year, the largest throughput for cocaine described in concrete terms by any respondent. Given the markups described (£5000–25,000 per kg of cocaine and £300–1000 per kg of cannabis), revenues net of product purchase costs were £350,000–425,000 per week or £18–22 million per year, with a UK payroll of £6.24 million per year.

Classic smuggling by boat

Several individuals took the classic approach to smuggling by stealthily landing a boat between ports of entry to avoid customs altogether, albeit on substantially different scales of operation. One used a speedboat to make three trips between Holland and the UK between 1990 and 1991, carrying 16, 27 and 22 kg of cannabis, respectively. The respondent and a friend met a contact on a dock in Holland, where they would collect the load and speed across the English Channel and into the River Medway, hiding the cannabis in a bush, to return later and retrieve it by car. Expenses were modest, at £200–300 per trip, but so were the organization's profits of £800–900 per kilo. The smuggling went undetected, as the arrest and subsequent incarceration stemmed from a customer down the distribution chain who cooperated with police. (Note: this respondent's long sentence seems to reflect his involvement in domestic ecstasy manufacture more than the cannabis importation; he also had previous imprisonment for drug law violations.)

The second example involved a respondent who was an expert mariner for an organization that bought and repaired sailboats in Florida. An individual with the plan to sail across the Atlantic Ocean convinced the respondent to join his crew. Off the Grenadine Islands they were met by a speedboat, whose Colombian crew transferred 500 kg of cocaine to the sailboat. (The respondent claims to have been surprised by this development and forced at gunpoint to continue the trip.) They sailed across the ocean and landed on a private beach on the Isle of Wight that had been purchased for £1 million the year before for the purpose of providing a safe landing spot in the UK for the shipment. (Nevertheless, they were arrested immediately.)

A third respondent was part of a three-person conspiracy to smuggle 400 kg of cocaine from the Caribbean by sailing a yacht, also to the Isle of Wight. The yacht entered a harbour, not a deserted beach, and those involved were immediately caught by Customs. It is unclear whether they planned to clear Customs but mistakenly believed the drugs were so well hidden they would not be detected, or whether they expected to be able to berth without entering Customs by blending in with day-trippers.

---

22. Receivers were paid £10,000 per box, and people to whom the box was addressed received £5000 per box, apparently without knowing for sure the boxes contained drugs. The only other cost mentioned was £600 per month to rent a house where the drugs were stored before being distributed to the 50–200 lower-level dealers they supplied. The respondent was arrested when DHL called the police about a suspicious box, and the police made a controlled delivery. That arrest did not stop the organization.

Importers' motivations and means of entrée

Not surprisingly, the allure of easy money was a common motivator, but more than a few couriers reported being coerced and/or tricked into carrying drugs. Others described spur of the moment choices and/or urgent extenuating circumstances. In particular, 60 of the 66 individuals involved in plane courier operations explained why they got involved in smuggling. Money was the modal (44 of the 60) but not the universal explanation, and 18 of the 44 mentioned a specific reason for needing the money beyond lifestyle aspirations.[23]

The second most frequently reported motivation was coercion, with eight of the 60 reporting being coerced into trafficking under threat of death. Several claimed to have been coerced by threats of violence against their families if they refused to cooperate. Several reported being unwitting participants, some with more plausible stories than others.

Some couriers sought out their role; one from the Dominican Republic announced publicly at a bar that he was looking for a courier manager for whom he could carry drugs. In contrast, several European residents were in Latin America on vacation (Venezuela) or to attend a family funeral (Brazil), when they were approached by dealers. One even described his motivation as 'doing a favour for' a local dealer who befriended him while he was in St Lucia on vacation. He said it was 'like someone saying, 'Can you watch my pint while I go to the loo?' – a favor for which he was sentenced to 11 years in prison.

Among the respondents who were not plane couriers, the majority mentioned money explicitly, and only one (a courier, but not on a plane) mentioned extenuating circumstances such as financial difficulty, endangered loved ones, or extreme poverty. For the 43 importers not involved in plane courier operations we tried to distinguish those who took advantage of an opportunity that more or less fell into their lap ('opportunistic') from those who made a long-term lifestyle commitment to drug trafficking ('entrepreneurs'). By these criteria, roughly one-third were opportunistic, one-third were entrepreneurs and one-third did not neatly fall into either category.

Eight of the 14 entrepreneurs had previous involvement in black market activity, including money laundering (a profit of £16,000 per £100,000 laundered), gun smuggling and selling explosives. Four had smuggled to evade paying taxes, and two by importing cigarettes. One cigarette importer purchased a lorry load at a time in Dubai for £600,000, selling them for £1.2 million in the UK. He commented that there was more money to be made in cigarette importation than in cannabis smuggling via the simple trick of shutting down the shadow import company after making the sales and before paying taxes.

Distinct from motivation is the issue of means. For the full sample of 222 interviewees, including domestic dealers, Matrix reached the same conclusion as Reuter and Haaga, namely that there are not many obvious barriers to entry.[24] We agree with that for domestic distributors, but note that many importers were invited by someone already in the business, rather than starting entirely on their own. So even if smuggling does not require

23. Six to repay a debt, two to support their drug habits, four for common expenses associated with low-income families such as feeding children and paying a mortgage, two each to cover expenses with illness in the family (sister's HIV treatment and sick mother), financial difficulties associated with their business in Africa, and travel costs to return to Africa from Europe.

24. Knowledge Group, 'The Illicit Drug Trade in the United Kingdom'; and Reuter and Haaga, *The Organization of High-Level Drug Markets*.

unusual skill, it may still benefit from obtaining tacit know-how and/or connections from someone already in the business.[25]

This is important because smuggling capacity may be the choke point for the drug distribution system. If importers get started by being invited in by other importers, then growth in drug distribution throughput capacity may have a positive feedback loop similar to that governing the early spread of drug demand, with existing importers stimulating recruitment of others into drug importation either intentionally (expanding their own organization's capacity) or unintentionally (when an employee strikes out on his or her own, using knowledge and connections gained while an employee).

Discussion

This section attempts to explore economic implications of some of the insights discussed above via rough calculations. Specific numbers are used because they make the logic of the analysis transparent, but none of the arithmetic is at all precise, even to within a factor of 2 or 4.

Since price per unit weight and other cost considerations are roughly comparable for heroin and cocaine, the calculations are intended to be reflective of operations importing either of those two drugs, which account for the great majority of the respondents. Cannabis smuggling is different, and in this data set was done predominantly via one technology (bent lorry drivers), so there is not much point in trying to compare returns across modalities. Smuggling of ecstasy and other amphetamine-type stimulants was too rare, too diverse and subject to too much price variation to support such calculations.

Does crime pay?

Various researchers have asked, 'Does crime pay?', both generally and for drug dealing in particular.[26] The data examined here are insufficient to determine whether crime pays for drug importers, but profit per expected year in prison appears to be substantially higher for operations employing corrupt truck drivers ('bent lorry driver' operations) than for couriers.

Consider a self-employed courier who successfully imports 2 kg of cocaine per trip from the Caribbean on three trips before being arrested on the fourth. With the selection biases inherent in working with data derived from people who have been incarcerated, there is no way to claim that three successful trips before getting arrested

25. Forty-seven of 66 plane couriers, seven out of 13 confessed non-plane couriers and 10 out of 30 non-couriers got involved with drug trafficking by being invited by someone they knew, rather than a stranger, a recruiter or self-starting. Prison, prior smuggling or criminal involvement, and family smuggling businesses were also mentioned as ways respondents got started in drug distribution, but comprised a smaller part of the sample. On the other hand, nine of the 66 plane couriers, two of 13 non-plane couriers and 10 of the 30 non-courier respondents were clearly self-initiating. For the others there was insufficient information to make a determination.

26. James Wilson and Allan Abrahamse, 'Does Crime Pay?', *Justice Quarterly* 9 (1992): 359–97; Pierre Tremblay and Carlo Morselli, 'Patterns in Criminal Achievement: Wilson and Abrahamse Revisited', *Criminology* 38 (2000): 663–69; and Peter Reuter and Robert MacCoun, 'Are the Wages of Sin $30 an Hour? Economic Aspects of Street-level Drug Dealing', *Crime and Delinquency* 38 (1992): 477–92.

is a reasonable let alone representative career length, but given that over 80% of incarcerated couriers report being caught on their first trip, it may be generous. Markups of £15,000 per kg are typical of such operations, suggesting net revenues before arrest of £90,000. Subtracting £10,000 for expenses (e.g. plane tickets) and assuming 3–4 years served in prison would suggest profits on the order of £20,000–25,000 per year of incarceration.

The 3–4 year figure is just a guess. The average sentence length for self-employed couriers in this sample is 8 years. Dividing by two to account for early release for good behavior would suggest an average of 4 years served. However, this might be biased upwards since our sample comes from people in prison. Green et al. (1994) study a large conviction-based rather than incarceration-based sample of couriers. Their table 2 implies an average sentence of 7 years for Class A drug couriers, or 3.5 years if half of sentenced time is served.

In contrast, our typical bent lorry driver operation might import 50 kg per load, 10 loads per year, for 4 years with a mark-up of £7500 per kg before being caught. Expenses are usually modest, so most of the resulting £15,000,000 in net revenues are profits. Even after dividing across six co-conspirators each serving 7 years in prison (again, half the sentence length of relevant respondents in our sample), profit could be on the order of £350,000 per year in prison.

There is no way to know how much compensation dealers would, could or should demand per year of incarceration. Probably few think about the calculus in such terms. Nevertheless, it seems plausible that for a potential offender in the UK who could instead achieve a middle-class lifestyle legitimately (e.g. by driving trucks without carrying contraband), £20,000–25,000 would not be enough to compensate for the pain of spending a year in prison, whereas £350,000 might be. Perhaps not coincidentally, those convicted in bent lorry driver operations came from all walks of life, while most couriers who were UK residents were unemployed or otherwise under financial distress and/or made spur of the moment decisions. An income of £20,000–25,000 per prison-year might look relatively better for someone living in a poorer country, and not surprisingly many couriers were non-residents or recent immigrants. Furthermore, even among foreign couriers, quite a few reported being duped or coerced into carrying the drugs, suggesting that £20,000–25,000 per kg may not always be adequate compensation even when legitimate labour market prospects are limited.

Evidence is scarcer concerning organizers of multi-person courier operations. The hands-on managers who accompany couriers on planes appear to suffer a non-negligible risk of arrest and may not have an ownership stake in the drugs. However, at least some courier operations have another, higher layer of management that never enters the UK and so may have considerably lower risk of incarceration. Several respondents described operations that might import 20 kg per operation, 10 times per year, while sacrificing one courier per trip to Customs so the others could get through. Expenses (plane tickets, paying managers, bribes in the UK and source country, etc.) were reported to be considerable, but the 'owner' might make £100,000 per trip or £1,000,000 a year, with apparently modest personal risk.

Likewise, a number of respondents reported involvement with importation of very large loads of heroin (perhaps on the order of 500 kg up to 10 times per year) in shipping containers. Their statements suggest that the owners stayed out of the UK, which might explain why none were represented directly in our data set.

Are prison resources being used efficiently?

Reuter and Kleiman's 'risks & prices' theory posits that enforcement drives up prices by increasing risks for dealers who must be compensated for these risks with higher income.[27] A corollary is that enforcement ought to be most cost-effective when it allocates expensive prison cells to the participants in drug dealing who demand the highest compensation for prison risk. Caulkins et al. criticize US mandatory minimum sentences because they are keyed to the quantity possessed at the time of arrest, and often the people physically possessing the drugs are mere employees (couriers, mules, etc.), who do not own, control or have a profit stake in the drugs they possess.[28]

The UK's imprisonment of drug importers might suffer from a similar problem. Selection biases could be significant, but among our respondents, the great majority were simple couriers. A substantial minority ran larger operations (importing say 50 kg at a time), but none were owners (as opposed to managers) of large courier operations or individuals who owned multi-hundred kilogram shipments secreted within containers.

If the interview subjects were representative of the total population of incarcerated importers – which they well might not be – then the UK's incarceration of drug importers would appear to be focused exactly backwards. The most prison space would be allocated to the types of individuals who have the lowest criminal incomes, and, hence, one would expect, who demand the least compensation per unit of prison risk. Likewise, the great majority of respondents came from the smuggling technology for which participants are most easily replaced (couriers), and the next biggest group of respondents used a technology which also had relatively low barrier to entry (bent lorry driver operations).

Are smuggling organizations efficient with respect to prison risk?

One can also ask how 'efficient' are smuggling organizations in terms of kilograms delivered per year spent in prison. Of course the smugglers do not care about this sort of efficiency, since they do not pay for the prisons. Nevertheless, differences across technologies in this sort of efficiency have policy implications in terms of demand for prison cells generated per kilogram consumed in the UK.

The descriptions above of self-employed couriers, courier organizations and bent lorry driver operations are sufficient to support these calculations. We have no way to guess how many of the big importers' workers get arrested per year, but for the sake of argument, suppose that it is one per year.

The first half of Table 7 shows the results. In brief, unsophisticated courier operations could be something like an order of magnitude less efficient than bent lorry driver and sophisticated courier operations, which in turn could be a factor of 3–10 times less efficient than the big importers in terms of kilograms delivered per year spent in prison.

27. Peter Reuter and Mark Kleiman, 'Risks and Prices: An Economic Analysis of Drug Enforcement?', in N. Morris and M. Tonry (eds) *Crime and Justice: An Annual Review of Research* 7 (1986): 289–340.

28. Jonathan Caulkins, C.P. Rydell, William Schwabe and James Chiesa, *Mandatory Minimum Drug Sentences: Throwing Away the Key or the Taxpayers' Money?* (Santa Monica, CA: RAND 1997).

Table 7. Some speculations about contrasts across types of importing organizations.

Line		Source	Courier-Based Operations		Other Operations	
			Self-employed (including non-plane)	Courier Organi-zati ons	Lorry Driver Operations	Big Importers
1	Load Size (kgs/load)	Assumption	2	20	50	500
2	Loads/Year	Assumption	3	10	10	10
3	Throughput Capacity per Org per Yr	Line 1 * Line 2	6	200	500	5000
4	Convictions/Org/Yr.	Guesstimate	1	10	1.5	1
5	Time Served/Conviction	Assumption	5	5	10	10
6	# in Sample	Data	20	60	25	5
7	Share of Prisoners	Strong Assumption	18%	55%	23%	5%
8	Share of Organizations in Operation	Scaled Line7/(Line4 * Line 5)	54%	16%	23%	7%
9	Share of Throughput Capacity	Scaled Line 8 * Line 3	0.7%	7%	23%	69%
	Projected Totals, assuming 45 mt delivered per year					
10	Collective Throughput Capacity (mt/yr.)	45 * Line 9	03	3	10	31
11	Organizations in operation	1000 * Line 10 /Line 3	50	15	21	6

Note: All entries are at best guesstimates; highlighted entries are essentially just place holders for what-if analysis.

Does the Pareto rule apply to drug importation?

Italian economist Wilfredo Pareto observed that the majority of the income in Italy went to a minority of the people. Since then skewed distributions are often referred to as following a 'Pareto rule' or an '80/20' rule (e.g. if 20% of the population received 80% of the income).

Here we might ask whether a minority of the importing organizations seem to be responsible for importing the majority of the drugs. This is similar to the more familiar question of asking if a modest number of high-rate offenders account for a disproportionate share of conventional street crime.[29] Our sample cannot answer this question directly because there is no reason to think that incarcerated importers are representative of active importers. Nevertheless, we can do some calculations that many people find thought-provoking, and do them in a way that makes clear the underlying assumptions and limitations.

We want to be very clear. The calculations above made strong assumptions. Some of these assumptions had a connection to the data and/or could vary quite a bit without changing the basic tenor of the discussion. Others, such as the idea that large importers lose one person per year to enforcement, are based on almost no data and matter quite a bit more. So already the calculations above are best thought of as illustrating ways of thinking quantitatively about the data, not derivations. However, the Pareto rule calculations require still one more set of heroic assumptions. Their value lies in making clear and transparent what is truly a qualitative argument, not in bringing any precision to the resulting figures. Readers who are sceptical of the value of such exercises are encouraged to skip the remainder of this section.

In particular, if we thought that the proportions of respondents by smuggling technology in our sample bore some relation to the proportions by technology of all UK inmates incarcerated for importation, then we can estimate the 'market share' of each smuggling technology in terms of proportions of throughput capacity that utilizes that technology. For simplicity, we lump the various miscellaneous categories (corrupting airport employees, smuggling by boats between ports of entry, and mailing drugs in) together with the more numerous bent lorry driver operations.

The second half of Table 7 carries through the calculations, scaling to 45 metric tons per year, the quantity Singleton et al. estimate for heroin plus cocaine (including crack); recall that cannabis is not included in these calculations.[30] Just to clarify how the table should be read, if all the many assumptions above held, then at any given time there would be 50 self-employed couriers in business. Combined, they would represent just 0.7% of the drug deliveries to the UK, while accounting for 18% of those incarcerated for importation. Adding in 15 large courier-based operations (that bring in 20 kg per trip, 10 times per year by sacrificing one courier per trip), collectively all courier-based technologies would account for three-quarters of the inmates but less than 8% of the drug deliveries. In other words, courier operations would be greatly over-represented in prison relative to the volume of drugs they deliver.

In this illustrative calculation, the bent lorry operations are neither over- nor under-represented. They represent 23% of smuggling operations, 23% of drugs smuggled and 23% of incarcerated importers.

29. A. Blumstein, J.A. Canela-Cacho and J. Cohen, 'Filtered Sampling from Populations with Heterogeneous Event Frequencies', *Management Science* 39, no. 7 (1993): 886–99.
30. Singleton et al., 'Measuring Different Aspects of Problem Drug Use'.

Hence, the last category (importers of large quantities intermingled with legitimate commerce) are under-represented in prison. If the numbers above were taken literally, the under-representation would be extreme, with perhaps 70% of the throughput capacity but just 5% of the inmates.

Now that it is clear how to read Table 7, it is important to explain what numbers are and are not robust, with respect to the many assumptions. What is least robust is the number and importance of the big importers. If they produced five convictions per organization per year of operation instead of one (which is an equally plausible number), their market share falls from 69 to 31%, and the other three modalities grow in relative importance, with bent lorry driver operations accounting for just over half (52%) of throughput capacity.

What is much more robust is the relative magnitude and over- vs under-representation of the couriers vs lorry driver operations. Even if we erase the column for big importers altogether, the courier-based operations still account for less than one-quarter of import capacity, with the remainder in the bent lorry driver column. Likewise, the 10 to 1 ratio of capacity of courier organizations vs individual couriers is not sensitive to assumptions made about the big transporters. So it seems likely that some version of the Pareto rule applies, as has been suggested by the work of Farrell et al. (1996) and others, although limitations in the data preclude hazarding a guess as to the specific magnitudes.[31]

Conclusions

One overall conclusion of this analysis is that interviews with incarcerated drug importers can yield fascinating insights. Which specific insights are most interesting depends greatly on one's prior knowledge and expectations.

Relative to the existing literature, an important observation is that our UK importers' organizational structures differ from those described by Decker and Chapman's sample of 34 smugglers incarcerated in US prisons.[32] Decker and Chapman describe a structure in which specialized smuggling organizations sell importation services. The smugglers' customers (e.g. Colombian cocaine organizations) generally either receive the drugs in the United States or arrange for their customers to meet the smugglers to receive the drugs. The smuggling operations may be responsible for the drugs while the drugs are in their possession, but the smugglers' revenue model is fee-for-service; they never own the drugs or profit directly from the drugs' increase in value as they move across the border.

In our sample two other financial models predominate. In the first, individuals were paid on a fee-for-service basis (e.g. £1000 per kg), but they were not responsible for drugs lost en route, presumably because loss was usually part and parcel of being arrested. Among those directly involved in the importation itself (as opposed to providing ancillary services), only one (a pilot) had a specialized skill. Some were lorry drivers, but most were couriers, who were more like cannon fodder than professional service providers. In the second model, the organization moving the drugs across the border owned the drugs in the same sense that a mid-level domestic distributor does. Indeed, they almost always broke

---

31. G. Farrell, K. Mansur and M. Tullis, 'Cocaine and Heroin in Europe 1983–1993: A Cross-national Comparison of Trafficking and Prices', *British Journal of Criminology*, 36 (1996): 255–81.
32. Decker and Chapman, *Drug Smugglers on Drug Smuggling*.

down the drugs into smaller quantities (e.g. bought 10 kg lots abroad and sold it in 1 kg lots within the UK). Hence, they looked like any other wholesale drug distributor, buying from higher-level suppliers and selling at lower market levels, except that their supplier happened to be on the other side of an international border. Only a few of the bent lorry driver operations had hints of being the sort of specialized smuggling operations akin to what Decker and Chapman describe.[33]

We cannot exclude the possibility that these apparent differences are mere artifacts of differences in sampling. However, one can speculate about ways geography and related factors could matter, as has already been suggested by Farrell et al. (1996). From the UK perspective, the Netherlands, as well as Spain, France and Belgium, serve as convenient transshipment countries for UK-based wholesalers to locate high-level suppliers. Even though the UK is literally an island, these countries are only a drive away (via ferry or tunnel), and UK drug wholesalers can operate in these other European Union countries relatively inconspicuously. Therefore a high-level domestic wholesale operation within the UK may not believe it needs the specialized skills of a professional smuggling firm to get the drugs from Continental Europe into the UK.

Superficially, Mexico would seem to be a similarly convenient, transshipment country for Colombian drugs entering the United States. However, a variety of institutional factors might make it harder for US-based wholesalers to meet up with Colombian exporters in Mexico City than it is for UK-based wholesalers to meet up with Turkish heroin suppliers in Amsterdam. And shipping directly from Colombia to the United States or via any transshipment country is a greater logistical challenge, involving small planes, go-fast boats, etc., not just driving a truck. By this line of reasoning, one would expect that organizations that can comfortably operate on either side of the US–Mexican border might, like their UK counterparts, be less likely to employ the services of professional smuggling organizations.

With respect to smuggling methods, the majority of respondents were involved in operations that used couriers on commercial plane flights, but that technology may account for only a modest share of all importation. Tied for second in terms of numbers of respondents were two technologies that involved other routine forms of crossing the border: couriers who used other types of transport that are available to anyone (e.g. ferries or the Euro-tunnel) and operations that employed corrupt truck drivers, who would knowingly hide the drugs within the cargo in their truck. Several other modalities were represented by just a handful of respondents. For one of those, secreting drugs within containers of legitimate commerce entering via ports or entry, there were hints that it might account for a large share of all drug imports. Even if such ‘big importers’ do not account for a substantial share of imports, it still appears that a form of Pareto rule applies, with modalities that generate more modest numbers of inmates perhaps accounting for the bulk of imports.

A principal insight concerning courier operations is that enforcement risk already makes it an unpalatable business for the couriers. However, the main driver behind ongoing courier activity may not be the couriers themselves so much as the organizers and owners of operations that employ multiple couriers. These higher-level operatives can receive significant income relative to their personal risk while resorting to various tactics other than high pay to recruit a steady stream of couriers. Those tactics include coercion,

33. Ibid.

deception and recruitment of people who are under unusual financial duress and/or who are making spur of the moment decisions.

For non-plane couriers and bent lorry driver operations the data on duration of successful operation suggest that smuggling is not like a Bernoulli or 'Coin-Toss' process, in which each border crossing carries an independent and equi-probable risk of detection. Rather, accounts seem to be divided between people who report being arrested within the first few attempts and operations that continued for multiple years until they caught a bad break or were shut down for other reasons. Indeed, a number of respondents described operations that were never detected by law enforcement. Furthermore, some people who enjoyed ongoing success with one smuggling modality failed immediately or soon after changing routes or tactics. So perhaps a better model of enforcement risk would involve tossing two coins. The first coin toss determines whether the smuggling strategy is a good one or not. If it is not, e.g., because Customs are already wise to that trick, the importers will be caught within the first few events. If the smuggling strategy is a sound one, the operation will probably continue for quite some time, but it will still not be entirely risk free. A second coin with a lower probability of coming up 'tails' would model the bad luck or unusual circumstances that can lead to arrest from any given importation, even for smugglers with extensive experience.

Note that it was hard to see how the basic smuggling concept differed between operations that failed from the outset and those that enjoyed an extended period of success. Likewise, no obvious patterns emerged to suggest that successful smugglers were systematically smarter, better educated, stronger, more violent or more experienced with criminal offending than were those who were less successful. So these interviews did not necessarily support an image that limited access to a brilliant idea or skill was a key barrier to entry into successful dealing. For many, entering the business was simply a matter of responding affirmatively to an invitation from a friend or family member.

This does not mean that anyone could start an operation employing these technologies on any given day. It would be easier for a lorry driver or the friend or relative of a lorry driver to start importing via a bent lorry driver operation than it would be for the average person. Similarly, it would be easier for someone who owned an existing business to start importing drugs comingled with legitimate commerce than for the general public. However, given the opportunity created by being in the right 'place' professionally (being a lorry driver) or socially (having a friend who is already importing), no special talent seems to be required.

Acknowledgements

This work was funded in part by the Qatar Foundation and Qatar National Research Program and is based on data collected by Matrix Knowledge Group for its project *The Illicit Drug Trade in the United Kingdom*, conducted for the UK Home Office. We thank many colleagues, notably Peter Reuter and Laura Wilson, for their insightful comments and suggestions.

Economic analysis of drug transaction 'cycles' described by incarcerated UK drug dealers

Jonathan P. Caulkins, Benjamin Gurga and Christopher Little

Qatar Campus and H. John Heinz III School of Public Policy and Management, Carnegie Mellon University

Introduction

In 2006, Matrix Knowledge Group and the London School of Economics conducted interviews with 222 drug-law violators mostly serving 7 + year sentences in 22 prisons throughout the UK.[1] This paper reports on the 65 of those interviews that contained sufficient information to deduce an economic description of the interviewees' operations.

The emphasis is on 'cycles'. A dealer executes a drug dealing cycle each time he or she purchases illicit drugs, breaks them down into smaller quantities (if applicable) and subsequently resells them. A typical dealer in this data set might complete one cycle per week; some retail sellers complete a cycle each day. Drug users do not usually buy directly from producers; rather, they are connected to producers through a distribution chain with multiple layers. Consequently, any given dose of drugs may have passed through a half dozen or more cycles, one for each layer in the distribution chain.

This focus on cycles stands in contrast to much of the literature that takes the deal, dealer or dealing career as the unit of analysis, but a cycle perspective has proved useful in the past when examining retail drug sellers in New York City.[2] Furthermore, not much processing or refinement of drugs occurs between their export from the source country and final sale to the user. Usually the only 'processing' is when cocaine powder is converted into crack, but that is easily done with inexpensive materials and there is little evidence it increases the price per unit.[3] Likewise, diluting and/or adulterating drugs ('cutting')

1. Matrix Knowledge Group, 'The Illicit Drug Trade in the United Kingdom', *Home Office Online Report* 20/07 (2007).
2. Jonathan P. Caulkins, Bruce Johnson, Angela Taylor and Lowell Taylor, 'What Drug Dealers Tell Us About Their Costs of Doing Business', *The Journal of Drug Issues* 29, no. 2 (1999): 323–40.
3. Jonathan P. Caulkins, 'Is Crack Cheaper than (Powder) Cocaine?', *Addiction* 92, no. 11 (1997): 1437–43.

is an inexpensive process and Coomber argues it is not very common in the UK in any event.[4] Hence, these drug dealing cycles are the very essence of the drug distribution supply chain.

The 65 interviews yielded information on 116 cycles, including 182 reports of price and quantity bought or sold and 55 cycles with 'complete' information, meaning price and transaction size at both purchase and sale(s). The respondents were mostly high-level dealers, but some cycles pertain to retail dealing (e.g. respondents' descriptions of activities earlier in their career). Hence, these data offer a valuable window into how price markups vary – or do not vary – across drugs, time and market levels, and also into associated variables such as cycle frequency and branching factor. (The cycle frequency is the number of cycles completed per unit time. The branching factor is the number of sales a dealer makes per purchase from the higher-level supplier, i.e. sales per cycle.[5])

Understanding these variables has policy implications. Knowing how much prices are marked up from one distribution level to the next is key to understanding where the monetary profits from drug dealing go both physically (to dealers within the UK or upstream) and organizationally (how much dealers at different market levels make). Likewise, cycle frequency dictates how quickly disruptions at one market level will manifest at lower market levels, and how branching factors determine the fundamental architecture of the distribution network.

However, we do not organize this paper around specific policy questions. Rather, we take as given that understanding drug distribution networks better would be useful and so investigate what these incarcerated dealers tell us about their dealing cycles. The next section defines the particular niche we seek to fill within the larger literature on drug markets. The third section describes the data and coding. Results are summarized in the fourth section, while the fifth concludes.

Literature review

There is a growing body of research on the illicit drug trade.[6] Much is descriptive or ethnographic.[7] However, an important subset focuses on economic variables. Data on price and purity provide insights about drug markets, but data regarding business revenues, costs and profits above the retail level remain scarce.[8] That is understandable given the difficulty in gathering quantitative data on criminal activities.

Important contributions have been made by scholars who obtained access to drug gangs' financial records, wire tap logs and prosecution files.[9] This paper mines another

4. R. Coomber, 'The Adulteration of Drugs – What Dealers Do, What Dealers Think', *Addiction Research* 5 (1997): 297–306.

5. The term 'branching factor' comes from recognizing that the distribution network looks like an (upside down) 'tree', with a node (individual dealer or dealing organization) at one level usually supplying multiple nodes at the next lower level. The number of branches coming out of a node is called its branching factor.

6. Mangai Natarajan and Mike Hough (eds), *Illegal Drug Markets: From Research to Prevention Policy, Crime Prevention Studies Volume 11* (New York: Criminal Justice Press, 2000).

7. Damian Zaitch, *Trafficking Cocaine: Colombian Drug Entrepreneurs in the Netherlands* (The Hague: Kluwer Law International, 2002).

8. Jonathan P. Caulkins and Peter Reuter, 'What Price Data Tell Us About Drug Markets', *Journal of Drug Issues* 28, no. 3 (1998): 593–612; and Frederick Desroches, 'Research on Upper Level Drug Trafficking: A Review', *Journal of Drug Issues*, 37 (2007): 827–44.

9. Financial records: Steven Levitt and Sudhir A. Venkatesh, 'An Economic Analysis of a Drug-selling Gang's Finances', *Quarterly Journal of Economics* 115, no. 3 (2000): 755–89. Wire taps:

source: interviews with incarcerated dealers. Perhaps the most common subjects are drug smugglers in US prisons, ranging from Reuter and Haaga's initial exploration through Decker and Chapman's recent work with 34 such individuals, but there have also been international efforts, such as Desroches's study of 70 high-level Canadian traffickers.[10] Studies of drug dealers in the UK represent a large subset of this literature, with important work by Pearson and Hobbes and Dorn et al.[11]

Given this excellent foundation, we do not attempt a comprehensive description of the dealers' activities.[12] Instead, our focus on drug dealing cycles attempts to bridge the operational literature and complementary literature on drug prices.

The singular observation about illegal drug prices is how high they are in affluent final market countries. Heroin and cocaine sold at retail in developed countries are quite literally worth many times their weight in gold. Since they are essentially just semi-processed agricultural commodities, like coffee or sugar, it is clear that prices get marked up enormously as the drugs move through their multi-layered distribution chain. The majority of that value addition occurs within the final market country. In very rough terms, cocaine and heroin that cost 1000 dollars or pounds in the source country are typically still worth 'only' 15,000 dollars or pounds on import into the United States or UK, but sell for 100,000 dollars or pounds on the street.[13]

It is well established that drug initiation and use are inversely related to retail prices.[14] In economists' jargon, the 'elasticity of demand' (percentage change in use caused by a 1% increase in price) is not zero. While demand may or may not be 'elastic' (meaning the percentage change in consumption exceeds the percentage change in price in absolute terms), demand is clearly not 'perfectly inelastic' (meaning, not at all responsive to price). This inverse relationship with price pertains not only to first-time use of so-called 'soft drugs' such as cannabis; it is also observed among needle exchange clients, overdose records and other indicators of use associated primarily with established or dependent users.[15]

(Footnote 9 continued)
Mangai Natarajan, 'Understanding the Structure of a Large Heroin Distribution Network: A Quantitative Analysis of Qualitative Data', *Quantitative Journal of Criminology* 22, no. 2 (2006): 171–92. Prosecution files: Joseph R. Fuentes, 'Life of a Cell: Managerial Practice and Strategy in Colombian Cocaine Distribution in the United States' (PhD diss., City University of New York, 1998).

10. Peter Reuter and John Haaga, *The Organization of High-Level Drug Markets: An Exploratory Study* (Santa Monica, CA: RAND 1989); Frederick Desroches, *The Crime that Pays: Drug Trafficking and Organized Crime in Canada* (Toronto: Canadian Scholars' Press 2005); and Scott Decker and Margaret Chapman, *Drug Smugglers on Drug Smuggling: Lessons from the Inside* (Philadelphia, PA: Temple University Press, 2008).

11. Geoffrey Pearson and Dick Hobbs, 'Middle Market Drug Distribution', *Home Office Research Study, 227* (London: Home Office, 2001), http://www.homeoffice.gov.uk/rds/pdfs/hors227.pdf; Geoffrey Pearson and Dick Hobbs, 'King Pin? A Case Study of a Middle Market Drug Broker', *The Howard Journal of Criminal Justice* 42, no. 4, (2003): 335–47; Nicholas Dorn, O. Lutz and S. White, 'Drug Importation and the Bifurcation of Risk', *The British Journal of Criminology* 38 (1998): 537–60; and Nicholas Dorn, Michael Levi and Leslie King, 'Literature Review on Upper Level Drug Trafficking', *The Home Office of the United Kingdom Online Report* 22/05 (2005), http://www.homeoffice.gov.uk/rds/pdfs05/rdsolr2205.pdf.

12. Matrix Knowledge Group, 'The Illicit Drug Trade in the United Kingdom'.

13. Caulkins and Reuter, 'What Price Data Tell Us About Drug Markets'.

14. Michael Grossman, 'Individual Behaviors and Substance Use: The Role of Price', in *Substance Use: Individual Behaviors, Social Interactions, Markets and Politics*, ed. Bjorn Lindgren and Michael Grossman (Amsterdam: Elsevier, 2005).

15. Rosalie Pacula et al., 'Marijuana and Youth', in Jonathan Gruber (ed.), *An Economic Analysis of Risky Behavior Among Youth* (Chicago, IL: University of Chicago Press, 2001), 183–91; Jenny

Hence, understanding drug price markups is of great interest. Caulkins and Padman showed that, if drugs are marked up by $100(\delta - 1)\%$ when moved through a transaction layer with branching factor ϕ, then the total price (value) P of a transaction of size Q obeys a power law:

$$P(Q) = \alpha Q^{\beta} \quad (1)$$

where α is a proportionality constant and $\beta = 1 - \ln(\delta)/\ln(\phi)$. They then showed that this relationship describes prices at different market levels as reported by enforcement agencies for a wide range of substances.[16] Empirically the coefficient β is less than 1.0.[17] So the total value of a drug transaction increases less than proportionally in transaction size, implying there are quantity discounts. Price markups as one moves down the distribution chain are just the flip side of the quantity discounts obtained by purchasers who cut out the middleman by buying further up the distribution chain.

Caulkins showed that this power law relationship holds not only for enforcement agencies' judgmental assessments of prices, but also with actual transaction-level data derived from undercover purchases.[18] Caulkins and Crane et al. gave theoretical explanations for why a power function might be expected from a drug distribution network in which dealers at one level sell to multiple dealers at the next level, and Clements derived the same relationship taking a complementary perspective that focused on packaging costs and economies of scale.[19] Clements also confirmed the relationship holds for marijuana prices in Australia, with the unit price falling by 2.5% for every 10% increase in transaction size.[20]

While the power function describes drug price markups, it does not explain why the markups are so large. Some have suggested that enormous markups are the norm, e.g. observing that the wholesale value of the corn or wheat in breakfast cereal represents a tiny share of the retail price.[21] However, that misses the point that the great majority of the

---

(Footnote 15 continued)
Williams, 'The Effects of Price and Policy on Marijuana Use: What can be Learned from the Australian Experience?', *Health Economics* 13 (2004): 123–37; Anne Bretteville-Jensen, 'Drug Demand-initiation, Continuation and Quitting', *De Economist* 154, no. 4 (2006): 491–516; Raymond Hyatt and William Rhodes, 'The Price and Purity of Cocaine: The Relationship to Emergency Room Visits and Deaths, and to Drug Use Among Arrestees', *Statistics in Medicine* 14 (1995): 655–68; Jonathan P. Caulkins, 'The Relationship Between Prices and Emergency Department Mentions for Cocaine and Heroin', *American Journal of Public Health* 91, no. 9 (2001):1446–8; Timothy Moore et al., *Heroin Markets in Australia: Current Understanding and Future Possibilities*. DPMP Monograph Series (Fitzroy, Australia: Turning Point Alcohol and Drug Centre 2005); Dhaval Dave, 'The Effects of Cocaine and Heroin Price on Drug-Related Emergency Department Visits', *Journal of Health Economics* 25, no. 2 (2006): 311–33; and Dhaval Dave, 'Illicit Drug Use Among Arrestees, Prices and Policy', *Journal of Urban Economics* 63, no. 2 (2008): 694–714.

16. Jonathan P. Caulkins and Rema Padman, 'Quantity Discounts and Quality Premia for Illicit Drugs', *Journal of the American Statistical Association*, 88, no. 423 (1993): 748–57.

17. Ibid; and Jonathan P. Caulkins et al., *The Price and Purity of Illicit Drugs: 1981 Through the Second Quarter of 2003*. Report prepared by RAND and published by the Office of National Drug Control Policy as Publication no. NCJ 207768, 2004.

18. Jonathan P. Caulkins, *Developing Price Series for Cocaine* (Santa Monica, CA: RAND 1994).

19. Jonathan P. Caulkins, 'Modeling the Domestic Distribution Network for Illicit Drugs', *Management Science* 43, no. 10 (1997): 1363–71; Barry Crane, Rex Rivolo and Gary Comfort, *An Empirical Examination of Counterdrug Interdiction Program Effectiveness* (Virginia: Institute for Defense Analysis, 1997); and Kenneth W. Clements, 'Pricing and Packaging: The Case of Marijuana', *Journal of Business* 79, no. 4 (2006): 2019–44.

20. Clements, 'Pricing and Packaging'.

21. Jeffrey A. Miron, 'The Effect of Drug Prohibition on Drug Prices: Evidence from the Markets for Cocaine and Heroin', *The Review of Economics and Statistics,* 85, no. 3 (2003): 522–30.

markup in illegal drug prices occurs after they have been processed into their final form. Some legal goods may be marked up enormously as they move down the distribution chain in more or less final form (e.g. plastic toys), but only in percentage terms. Illegal drugs are unique among physical goods in having price markups that are so large in both percentage terms and in terms of absolute value per unit weight, without being refined, processed or improved in any noticeable way.[22]

An old-fashioned explanation was that drug markups were rents extracted by monopolists who could exclude competition, perhaps forcibly. However, studies repeatedly show that, at least in countries like the United States and UK, drug distribution is dominated by small, highly competitive organizations operating within networks, and that barriers to entry are relatively low.[23] Matrix's analysis of these interviews observed that few special skills or talents are required to be a successful drug distributor.[24]

Reuter and Kleiman offer the more plausible explanation that price markups represent compensation for non-monetary costs of doing business, notably risks from violence and law enforcement, including arrest, incarceration, and seizure of drugs and other assets.[25] Caulkins and Reuter add to this list compensation for dealers' own time, which could account for a nontrivial proportion of retail prices (~13% for US cocaine at that time).[26]

Risks and prices theory seems to be contradicted by long-run market trends inasmuch as cocaine and heroin prices fell sharply both in the United States and Europe during the 1980s even as drug enforcement intensified in the United States. However, Claudia Storti and De Grauwe suggest that globalization may have been the force driving prices down over time.[27] Consistent with this, Kuziemko and Levitt estimate an empirical model that suggests that increasing enforcement partially offset what would have otherwise been even more precipitous declines. Also, Caulkins and MacCoun argue that psychological factors could explain a weaker coupling between enforcement and prices than classical economic models predict, without negating the basic logic that, all other things being equal, tougher enforcement against suppliers should drive prices up.[28]

This paper does not offer any new or better theory for why price markups are so large. Its goal is simply to describe them in a novel way, by looking at cycles rather than transactions. Also, although not entirely novel, studies using data from outside the United States and for several different types of drugs are still relatively rare. Good theories need to be built upon accurate descriptions of empirical regularities, and the goal of this paper is to improve the knowledge base concerning these empirical regularities.

22. Caulkins and Reuter, 'What Price Data Tell Us About Drug Markets'.
23. Natarajan and Hough (eds), *Illegal Drug Markets;* and Reuter and Haaga, *The Organization of High-Level Drug Markets.*
24. Matrix Knowledge Group, 'The Illicit Drug Trade in the United Kingdom'.
25. Peter Reuter and M.A.R. Kleiman, 'Risks and Prices: An Economic Analysis of Drug Enforcement', *Crime and Justice: An Annual Review* 7, (1986): 289–340.
26. Caulkins and Reuter, 'What Price Data Tell Us About Drug Markets'.
27. Cláudia Costa Storti and Paul De Grauwe, 'Globalization and the Price Decline of Illicit Drugs', *International Journal of Drug Policy*, 20(1) (2009): 48–61.
28. Ilyana Kuziemko and Steven D. Levitt, 'An Empirical Analysis of Imprisoning Drug Offenders', *Journal of Public Economics* (2004): 2043–66; and Jonathan P. Caulkins and Robert MacCoun. 'Limited Rationality and the Limits of Supply Reduction', *Journal of Drug Issues*, 33, no. 2 (2003): 433–464.

Data

Data collection process

The data are extensive notes and in some cases full transcripts stemming from a subset of interviews of convicted drug law violators conducted by Matrix Knowledge Group in 22 prisons in the United Kingdom. These interviews in no way represent a random sample of incarcerated drug law violators, let alone of operating drug dealers, so it is important to understand the interview process, which is described in full by Matrix.[29] Matrix contacted prison managers seeking cooperation. In the 22 cooperating prisons, a total of 1390 prisoners were invited to participate, with 263 volunteering to do so. Some interviews were not completed because of scheduling problems. A few were aborted out of safety concerns. In the end, 230 interview records were created, deriving from interviews with 222 individuals. (A few interviews generated multiple interview records if the respondent was categorized as having served multiple roles in an organization.)

Matrix followed an informed consent approach and provided a letter to each respondent in advance outlining the project and its confidentiality protocols. The interviews were conducted in private rooms, and the data were documented in a manner that maintained anonymity. Matrix worked with the prisons to minimize disruption to their operations. This caused some variation in interview length, with the majority being 1–1.5 hours long but some lasting 3 or 4 hours.

Data were partially validated by consulting professionals with a background in the field, including prison staff, law enforcement personnel, customs agents, asset recovery staff and academics. However, Matrix was not given access to law enforcement debriefs nor Crown Prosecution Service summary case files. This inhibited validation and could only be partially compensated via internet searches of media reporting and public domain court reports.

Matrix identified four primary limitations concerning the data:[30]

- *Sampling* – the sample was self-selected inasmuch as respondents had to volunteer to be interviewed and only 263 of 1390 (19%) did so.
- *Sample size* – the 222 interviews were diverse, covering a range of drugs, time periods, market levels and methods, leaving small sample sizes when interviews were grouped by these characteristics.
- *Gaps* – the interview protocol was semi-structured, interview duration varied and some subjects had more to discuss than others (e.g. a long time leader of a large organization vs a first time courier). Hence, the same questions were not always asked of every interviewee, so the absence of response cannot be interpreted as a negative response. This is a particular issue for us with respect to descriptions of business costs other than the cost of acquiring the drugs.
- *False reporting* – it is possible that some information provided by the interviewees is not genuine. Our subjective impression is that the greater risk is exaggeration (e.g. boasting about skill or success) not outright fabrication, although there were occasional incredible statements.

On the positive side, the Matrix data are based on a large number of detailed interviews, conducted consistently and with an emphasis on business and organizational

29. Matrix Knowledge Group, 'The Illicit Drug Trade in the United Kingdom'.
30. Matrix Knowledge Group, 'The Illicit Drug Trade in the United Kingdom'.

aspects of drug dealing. They offer a unique opportunity to look behind the scenes at why drug dealing is a 'crime that pays'.[31]

Analysis of the 65 interview records used here

Matrix provided the 65 of the 230 interview records which they believed might have information about a complete 'cycle' of selling. Many of the others were obtained from couriers, runners, drivers or other employees (e.g. money launderers) who did not necessarily have complete information about both the purchase and sales prices of the drugs they helped to distribute. Note, the interview protocol asked how the drugs were obtained and who the customers were, but cost and transaction size information was only requested explicitly for a typical transaction, not a complete cycle.

Not all of the 65 interviews turned out to be usable. Sometimes detailed information was provided about both acquisition and sale, but not for the same drugs or the same time periods, or both purchase and sale occurred outside the UK (e.g. from dealing activity earlier in the individual's career). Sometimes the information was too vague or implausible, e.g. citing very broad ranges for numbers of customers or prices well below the average.

Even usable interviews posed coding challenges. Prices and weights of several transactions might be described at different points in the interview, and some judgment was required to connect those quantities. To reduce the risk of error, each interview was coded separately by two people, without consultation and then reconciled.

Analysis

It proved useful to distinguish three types of respondents: (1) typical domestic wholesalers who sell to multiple customers per cycle; (2) 'brokers' who sell the entire lot of drugs to a single customer; and (3) importers who purchase drugs outside the UK. Brokers profit by moving drugs laterally within the distribution network. Importers likewise profit by moving the drugs laterally – specifically across the international border – but in this data set they also profit by breaking the drug lots down into smaller units and selling them at a lower market level. Distinguishing the three groups avoid conflating profits from arbitrage (i.e. moving drugs from where prices are low to where they are higher) with profits from the price markups that are the flip side of quantity discounts.

We describe the cycle data for each of these three groups after two preliminary sections, one which describes a typical sequence of cycles connecting importation to the end user and a second which verifies that the power function relationship (equation (1)) holds for these data.

Snapshot of distribution chain from import to street

Table 1 illustrates a typical sequence of transactions connecting drug users to importers using information drawn primarily from a single respondent (Respondent A) who describes buying kilograms or half-kilograms of heroin then selling 1–9 ounces (~0.03–0.25 kg) at a time. Respondent A's customers were lower-level dealers who sold fractions of an ounce to dependent users (sometimes known as 'jugglers'), who used some but sold

31. Pierre Tremblay and Carlo Morselli, 'Patterns in Criminal Achievement: Wilson and Abrahamse Revisited', *Criminology* 38, no. 2 (2006): 633–57; and Desroches, *The Crime that Pays.*

Table 1. Heroin price (in £) at different market levels in the UK circa 2003: Observations between 1/8 ounce and 1 kg all reported by a single respondent (respondent A).

Transaction level	Seller	Buyer	Amount	Price (per transaction)	Price/kg
4th Level wholesale	Importer	Respondent B	10–60 kg	£437,500	£12,500
3rd Level wholesale	Respondent B	Respondent A	1 kg	£15,000	£15,000
			0.5 kg	£8000	£16,000
2nd Level wholesale	Respondent A	A's Customers	9 oz	£6750	£27,000
			1 oz	£900	£32,400
			0.5 oz	£625	£45,000
1st Level wholesale	A's customers	Retail Sellers	0.25 oz	£350	£50,400
			0.125 oz	£187.50	£54,000
Retail	Retail Sellers	Users	1 g	£60	£60,000
			0.1 g	£10	£100,000

Note: Transaction prices given in table for 0.5 and 0.125 oz are mid-points of ranges reported (£600–650 and £175–200, respectively).

the rest to other users in smaller bags. From other interviewees, we surmise that these smaller quantities might have sold for £60 for a gram and £10 for a 0.1 gram bag.

Respondent A (who lived in Brighton) believed that his supplier (in Liverpool) worked directly for a large organization that imported as much as 100 kg at a time from Turkey. Respondent A did not know any further details. However, there was another respondent in the sample (Respondent B) who sold kilograms of heroin at this time in Liverpool for £15,000, so we extend the table upward by one row using information from that individual's interview. In particular, Respondent B reported buying first 10–20 kg and then eventually 30–60 kg at a time for £12,500 per kilogram from a Kurdish man based in Turkey that Respondent B had met while in a UK prison. The Kurdish man arranged the shipping and even introduced Respondent B to customers who bought kilograms for £15,000 per kg. Apparently, the Kurdish exporter wanted Respondent B to operate as a somewhat separate entity, rather than directly employing him as a runner to move the heroin from the docks to a customer who would only buy a kilogram at a time.[32]

The power function confirmed in these data

As noted above, drug price markups can be well described by a simple power function. Taking the log of either side of equation (1) yields a linear relationship between ln(Price)

32. Two other respondents with Liverpool connections at this market level operated somewhat earlier in time, when prices were higher, but they had at least roughly the same markup as respondent B. Respondent C bought 10–15 kg at a time for £16,000/kg from an organization that brought 100 kg shipments from Pakistan or Turkey into British ports (London, Liverpool and Dover) via Europe in hidden compartments in transport trucks (apparently good ones, costing £20,000–30,000 to make). Respondent C would sell on in units of 0.5, 2–3 and 4–5 kg for £18,500 per kg. Respondent C helped the importing operation by referring a trustworthy truck driver to them and called the importer his 'supplier/partner', but otherwise had no involvement in importing. Finally, respondent D bought 50 kg at a time from Turkish suppliers in Liverpool for £14,000 per kg and re-sold for £18,000 per kg. Interestingly, respondent D quit that business twice. After three years operating at these levels he was arrested and took a 10 month break from dealing to buy legitimate companies and doctor their books in a (successful) attempt to look legitimate and avoid conviction. Then, after a few more years he quit to focus on spending the money he had made. Some years later he was convicted for attempting to import cocaine from South America.

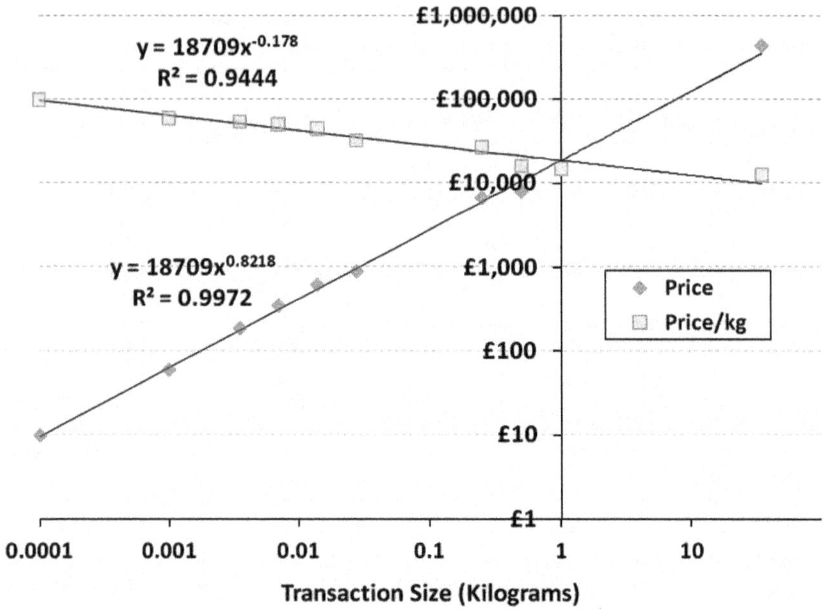

Figure 1. Transaction price and price per kilogram for UK heroin sales in 2003 Plotted vs transaction size (in kg). (Observations from 1/8 ounce to 1 kg all reported by one respondent; the larger and two smaller observations are based on other respondents.)

and ln(Transaction Quantity). The upward sloping line in Figure 1 shows this price markup relationship for the price–quantity pairs in Table 1. The second line provides equivalent information in terms of quantity discounts by plotting ln(Price per unit) vs ln(Transaction Quantity); it is included because it is sometimes more useful to think in terms of the price per unit, not the total value of a transaction.

Across all respondents, there were a total of 62 heroin price observations. If we plotted them all on the same axes, we would expect to see the same basic log–linear relationship but with greater variability because the observations would come from different years, organizations and cities around the UK. Figure 2 shows that is exactly what we observe.

Note: while we can adjust for dilution/adulteration reported within a cycle, most dealers did not report purity in absolute terms, so no adjustment for purity is made in Figure 2. Since omitting purity did not do more to undermine the overall log–linear relationship, this can be seen as consistent with Coomber's finding that dilution or 'cutting' is uncommon within the UK. Indeed, cutting was scarcely reported by these respondents, and when reported,[33] the cutting was typically immediately after import, before the first sale within UK borders.

The exponent β is a useful summary of how large the price markups (equivalently, quantity discounts) are. The smaller β is, the more extensive are the price markups.

For the 62 heroin price observations in Figure 2, some covariates were related to price, so we regressed ln(Price per kg) on ln(Transaction Size) with dummy variables for before/after 1995, whether the sale was on credit (vs for cash), whether the sale occurred in London and whether it occurred in Liverpool (two dummy variables, one for each city). Controlling for these covariates changed the β estimate very little relative to the bivariate

33. Coomber, 'The Adulteration of Drugs'.

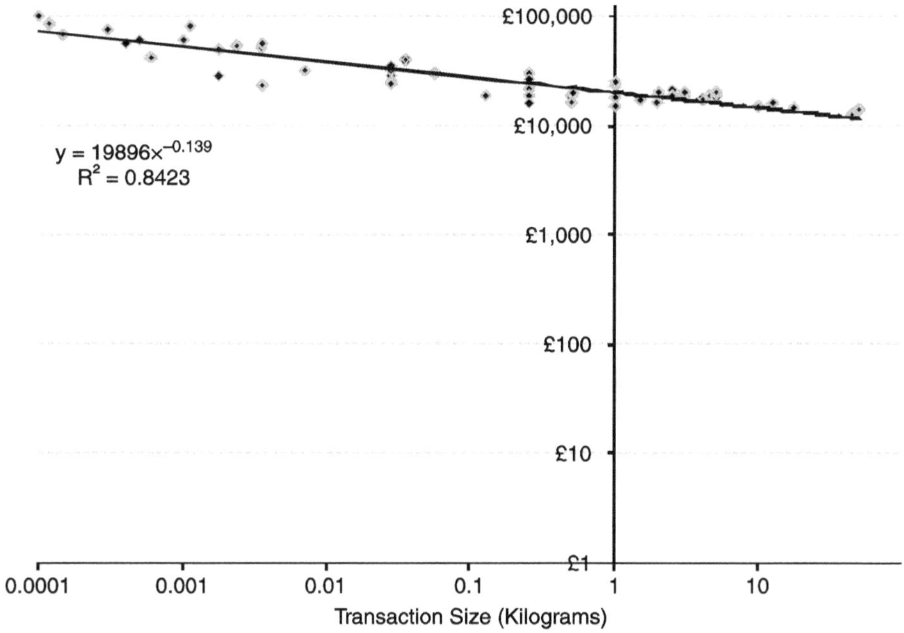

Figure 2. Price per kilogram plotted vs transaction size on log–log axes for all 62 observations of heroin price in the UK that were associated with a cycle.

relation in Figure 2 ($\beta = 0.87$ vs 0.86). So price markups in the market overall appear to be slightly smaller than those described in Table 1. A few of the other regression coefficients were statistically significant. In particular, prices after 1995 averaged 15% lower, and prices in Liverpool averaged 23% lower than in the rest of the UK. The coefficient for transactions conducted% on credit is not significant but has the expected sign (customers who were advanced credit had to pay more).

Parallel analyses were conducted with other substances, but they involved smaller samples and are not reported here in the interest of space. Perhaps the most interesting, albeit tentative, finding is that the price markups for cocaine seemed to be more substantial at the lower end of the distribution chain (below about 0.125 kg) than at higher market levels. Also a non-finding worth mentioning is no evidence suggesting that crack was any more or less expensive than powder cocaine, after adjusting for transaction size.

Price markups for conventional domestic drug dealers

We now turn to describing the cycle data for the three groups of dealers, starting with conventional domestic dealers who sell to more than one customer. Usually these dealers sold in the same city where they obtained the drug and never carried the drugs across an international border, so their profits come almost entirely from repackaging drugs for sale at a lower market level.

For these dealers the β measure for price markup within a particular dealing cycle can be computed directly using equation (1). For example, one respondent purchased 1 kg for £18,000 and sold it in 1 ounce amounts for £900 per package. Since there are 35.27 ounces in a kg, the β for that cycle is: $\beta = \ln(£18{,}000/£900)/\ln(1/35.27) = 0.841$.

Table 2. Price markup coefficients β estimated from complete selling cycle data, by drug.

	Number of cycles	Average	Minimum	Maximum	Standard deviation
Cannabis	5	0.817	0.674	0.966	0.116
Cannabis resin	4	0.851	0.775	0.932	0.076
Cocaine	7	0.869	0.792	0.920	0.040
Crack	5	0.827	0.731	0.886	0.058
Ecstasy	6	0.754	0.547	0.937	0.129
Heroin	28	0.834	0.253	0.975	0.142
Heroin (w/o outlier)	27	0.855	0.620	0.975	0.086

Note: when the respondent reported consuming some of the drugs, the cycle calculations were conducted as if the respondent had sold all of the drugs. Also, dealers did not always sell all of the drugs in similar sized lots. For example, a respondent might sell a single ounce for £900, while 9-ounce blocks would sell for £6750. This was addressed by calculating the value of the product at various price levels based on each reported lot size. Therefore the 9 ounces would be valued at £8100 when calculating by individual ounces, but only £6750 when treated as a 9-ounce lot. The average of these values was then used in the final analysis.

These calculations were done for all 55 instances in which information about a domestic dealing cycle was complete. Table 2 shows descriptive statistics for these β estimates for each drug. For heroin, statistics are given both with and without the one apparent outlier, a very low estimate of $\beta = 0.253$ that comes from the respondent highlighted in Table 1 above, specifically the cycle reported as buying 0.5 kg for £8000 and selling nine ounces (essentially 0.25 kg) for £6750.

The primary result is that there do not appear to be large differences in the price markup parameter across drugs. With respect to a simple (unequal variances) *t*-test for differences in means, no pair of drugs had a significantly different average value of β. The value of ecstasy was borderline to being lower in a one-tailed test with $\alpha = 0.05$, but there was no prior reason to predict higher markups for ecstasy, so a two-tailed test is preferred. Possible trends in β over time were investigated with plots and simple regression, but no clear trends were evident.

Table 3. Price markup coefficients β compared with earlier estimates in the literature.

	UK		US			
			Arkes et al. (2004)			
	Matrix Data (Avg.)	Caulkins & Padman (1993)	Retail	Level	Mid-Level	Top-Level
Cannabis	0.817	0.72 imported 0.76 domestic	0.573		0.802	0.783
Sinsemilla		0.850				
Cannabis Resin	0.851					
Hashish		0.770				
Cocaine	0.869	0.830	0.716	0.751	0.787	0.813
Crack	0.827	0.790	0.731		0.661	0.833
Heroin	0.834	0.83 brown 0.84 white	0.531		0.718	0.764

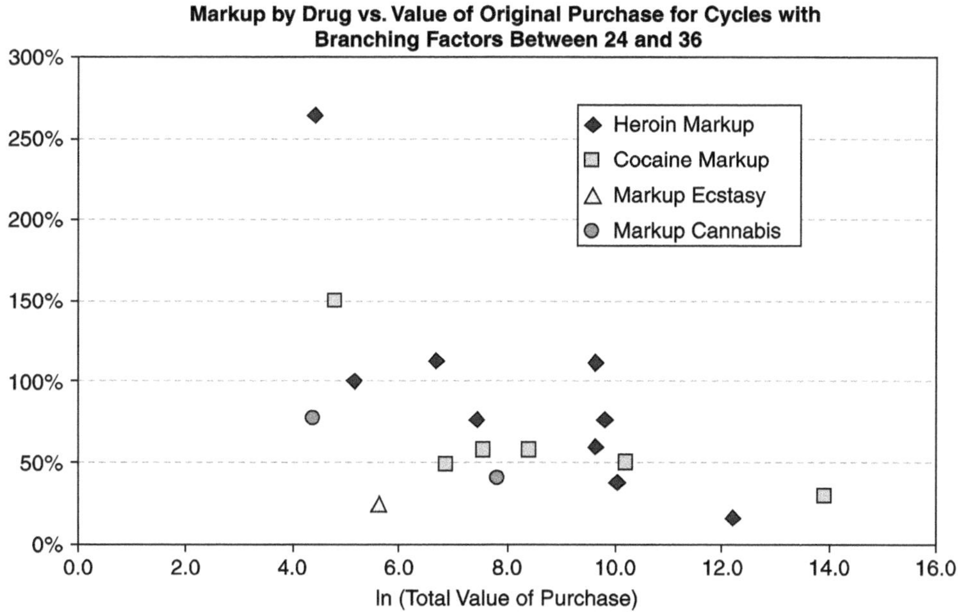

Figure 3. Dealers at higher market levels achieve a lower markup in percentage terms.

Table 3 compares these estimates with United States-based estimates by Caulkins and Padman and Arkes et al.[34] Overall there is some tendency for the United States-based estimates to be lower, meaning that price markups (and, hence, quantity discounts) are greater in the United States than in the UK. That is what one would expect from risks and prices theory given that drug enforcement is particularly stringent in the United States.

The Arkes et al. β estimates tend to be higher at higher market levels, and there are suggestions that the same may be true in the Matrix data, although the limited number of data points preclude stronger statements. In various regressions of β, larger purchases were associated with larger values of β. (We proxy market level by value not weight because of the differences in dose size across substances.) However, given how β is defined, this is to be expected; random shocks that increase how much a dealer paid for the drugs directly reduce markups. That is, they directly increase the value of β.

Still, the relationship may not be mere statistical artefact. If dealers at higher levels can amortize fixed costs over greater volumes sold, then the markup per unit could be smaller. It is hard to observe this directly without controlling for the branching factor. For any given purchase size, larger branching factors imply selling in smaller unit volumes. Because price per unit is higher for smaller transaction sizes, that in turn implies achieving a greater markup. Indeed, that is exactly what the formula for β recognizes. However, Figure 3 shows that, among the 18 cycles with a branching factor between 24 and 36 (a range narrow enough not to affect markups much), the actual markup (i.e. price per unit sold divided by price per unit at purchase, minus one) is negatively related to the market

34. Caulkins and Padman, 'Quantity Discounts and Quality Premia for Illicit Drugs'; and Jeremy Arkes, Rosalie Liccardo Pacula, Susan Paddock, Jonathan P. Caulkins and Peter Reuter, *Technical Report for the Price and Purity of Illicit Drugs Through 2003*. RAND Technical Report prepared for the ONDCP (Santa Monica, CA: RAND, 2004).

Table 4. Average number of cycles reported per week (with associated sample size), by drug and value of purchase from supplier.

	Value purchased		
Drug	<£5000	>£5000	Total
Cocaine	1.0 ($n = 3$)	1.2 ($n = 4$)	1.1 ($n = 7$)
Ecstasy	1.5 ($n = 4$)	0.6 ($n = 2$)	1.2 ($n = 6$)
Cannabis	2.0 ($n = 4$)	0.4 ($n = 4$)	1.2 ($n = 8$)
Heroin	4.6 ($n = 4$)	1.0 ($n = 9$)	2.1 ($n = 13$)
Crack	5.3 ($n = 3$)	1.8 ($n = 2$)	3.9 ($n = 5$)
Total	2.8 ($n = 18$)	1.0 ($n = 21$)	1.8 ($n = 39$)

level as reflected in the dollar value of the purchase. Thus, these data are consistent with the idea that dealers at higher levels can get by with smaller percentage markups because they are dealing larger volumes.

Forty-four of the 55 domestic cycles included information about the frequency with which the dealing cycle was executed, but five were dropped because they were redundant (same dealer, same drug, and same purchase value – differing only in sales value/branching factor). Table 4 shows that 19 of the remaining 39 reported executing the cycles ‘weekly’, with 13 of the other 20 reporting cycles frequencies faster than once per week.

Cycle frequency was related to both drug and transaction size. Cycles involving the purchase of smaller quantities were more frequent, as were cycles involving heroin and crack. Larger purchases of cannabis and ecstasy were the least frequent.

One aspect of dealing that is not well understood is how much inventory exists at different levels of the distribution chain. These cycle frequency data suggest that not much is held within the UK, except perhaps at the highest levels. Cycle frequency was weekly or faster for the majority of even the larger transactions (seven of 11 cycles with purchases of £10,000–100,000 and three of five of over £100,000). Hence, even dealers several levels above retail make purchases from their suppliers with great frequency. Furthermore, dealers do not maintain inventory throughout the entire cycle. The dealer reporting the largest purchases (50 kg of cocaine at £22,000 per kg, or £1.1 million) reported purchasing monthly but keeping drugs in stock for only 3–5 days after purchase.

Price markups for pure brokers

There were six instances in which we had full information about purely domestic brokerage activity, where the dealer sold the entire quantity in one lot. Table 5 summarizes the markups in these cases. Some of these transactions have complexities that cannot be fully reflected in a simple table. For example, the cannabis transaction was conducted by a cocaine dealer who assisted his supplier when the supplier wanted to get rid of some cannabis. So the deal was something of a favour embedded within an ongoing relationship.

Given these complications and the small number of brokerage cycles, there is no way to analyse the markups with respect to any covariate. However, the data tentatively support two conjectures. First, markups for pure brokerage appear modest; no one ‘doubled their money’. Second, in all cases the transaction values were at least £30,000. It may be that customers at lower market levels have an easier time finding suppliers, so there is less room for profiting purely from being a go-between.

Table 5. Domestic brokerage transactions.

Drug	Year	Quantity purchased (kg or pill)	Purchase price (£/kg or pill)	Total purchase value (£)	Sale price (£/kg or pill)	Total revenues (£)	Markup	Repeated?
Cannabis	2000	50	650	32,500	750	37,500	15.4%	Repeated
Cocaine	2003	2	25,000	50,000	27,000	54,000	8.0%	Repeated
Cocaine	2005	1	28,000	28,000	31,000	31,000	10.7%	One-off
Cocaine	2005	1	30,000	30,000	32,000	32,000	6.7%	One-off
Ecstasy	1990	20,000	5.75	115,000	6.25	125,000	8.7%	Repeated
Heroin	1995	3	18,500	55,500	20,000	60,000	8.1%	One-off

Price markups for importation

For importers, we attempted to differentiate between value added by importation and value added by breaking down the drugs within the UK and selling them in smaller lot sizes. The basic finding is that importers do not necessarily generate the majority of their net revenues from importing. It is not possible to be more precise because importers' organizational and operational structures are more diverse and more complicated than those of solely domestic dealers, so there are more grey areas in coding these data.

The general principle underpinning this analysis is simple enough. Where there is full information about a cycle with a purchase made overseas or made at an overseas price and the selling was done in the UK, we can use equation (1) to impute what the 'import price' would have been had the entire imported load been sold within the UK as a single lot. That is, we project what the selling price would have been had the importers' branching factor been one. We then split the observed markup between the international purchase price and the actual selling price into (1) the increment between the international purchase price and this imputed import price and (2) the increment between the imputed import price and the actual selling price.

Algebraically, if we use the subscripts B and S to denote the transactions when the drugs were actually bought abroad and sold in the UK, respectively, then the imputed price of a hypothetical transaction with the drugs sold as a single lot within UK borders would be:

$$P_{\mathrm{I}} = P_{\mathrm{S}}(Q_{\mathrm{B}}/Q_{\mathrm{S}})^{\beta} \tag{2}$$

Dividing each of the transaction prices by the corresponding quantities give the price per unit weight, so the two price increments are

$$\begin{aligned} &(P_{\mathrm{I}}/Q_{\mathrm{B}}) - (P_{\mathrm{B}}/Q_{\mathrm{B}}) \text{ and} \\ &(P_{\mathrm{S}}/Q_{\mathrm{S}}) - (P_{\mathrm{I}}/Q_{\mathrm{B}}) \end{aligned} \tag{3}$$

It is perhaps useful to illustrate the formulas with a specific example. One respondent bought 3.5 kg of cocaine in Holland for £52,500 (£15,000/kg) and sold it in the UK as 0.25 kg quantities for £7,500 each when paid in cash (£30,000/kg). Using the $\beta = 0.869$ in Tables 2 and 3 for cocaine,[35] that selling price and quantity suggests that the estimated total price if the entire 3.5 kg had been sold in a single lot within the UK is $£7500 \times (3.5/0.25)^{0.869} = £74{,}310$, and the imputed import price per kilogram is £74,310/3.5 = £21,231. So we attribute (£21,231/kg − £15,000/kg)/(£30,000/kg − £15,000/kg) = 41.5% of this importer's revenues net of product purchase to importation, and 58.5% to breaking the 3.5 kg down into 0.25 kg lot sizes within the UK. That is, if one views this dealer's activity as a vertically integrated combination of both importation and high-level domestic distribution, then the high-level domestic distribution accounts for the majority of its net revenues. The same respondent also described selling 0.5 kg loads for the same price per kilogram, which generates a lower imputed import price and a larger (55%) proportion of net revenues due to importation.

The calculations were straightforward for this respondent, but in other cases things were murkier. For example, one respondent partnered with a Turkish organization. He had a functional role as 'coordinator' of importation across the English Channel, and also was allowed to finance and profit from 30 kg out of each 100 kg load. As a further

35. We use $\beta = 0.817$ for cannabis and 0.85 for heroin for these calculations.

complication, the Turkish organization allowed him to buy 10 kg at the Belgian price of £10,000 per kg, but the other 20 kg were purchased at the 'UK price' of £13,000–14,000 per kg. We coded the respondent as purchasing 30 kg shipments abroad for (10 × £10,000 + 20 × £13,500)/30 = £12,333 per kg, but other interpretations might be equally reasonable.

Whereas that respondent got something of a 'raw deal' from his Turkish partners, the other heroin importer got what might be called a 'sweetheart deal'. He describes his two uncles as being drug lords who owned poppy fields in Kandahar and Peshawar. They transported the heroin into the UK (via Turkey, Dubai, India and/or Pakistan), but still charged the respondent only the Afghani price of £800–1100 per kg. Such largess is consistent with their earlier practice of sending the respondent £15,000 per year in 'spending money' even before he started dealing, ostensibly to get the respondent used to such a lavish lifestyle that he would want to be involved in dealing. Apparently, even though the sellers underneath the respondent were primarily Afghanis from the same community, the uncles still valued having a blood relative in the UK to connect those sellers to the incoming shipments. At any rate, although that respondent appeared to generate the majority (75%) of his revenues from importation, that large share is partly attributable to his international purchase price being in some sense partially subsidized.[36]

Space constraints preclude describing all such idiosyncratic circumstances, but the essential point is that the figures in Table 6 are even less precise than are other figures in the paper. They serve only to make the general points that (1) all importers for which we had full cycle information broke down the drugs they imported for resale at smaller quantities and (2) if the price markup parameter estimated from purely domestic cycles is applied to these highest levels of distribution within the UK, then many importers derive as much of their net revenues from high level domestic distribution as they do from the importation *per se*.

We stress the importance of this second caveat. The specific proportions listed in the far right-hand column of Table 6 do clearly depend on the assumed value of β. In the extreme, if $\beta = 1.0$, then there would be no markups and so no profits to be made from moving drugs down to lower market levels, implying that all net revenues derive from importation. Hence, while it is clear that the UK importers are vertically integrated and derive some of their net revenues from high-level domestic distribution, we avoid drawing specific conclusions about the breakdown.

Discussion

The analysis above generated a range of specific findings. It confirmed some prior expectations based on research in other countries, including the facts that drug dealing cycles are short (often a week or less) and that price as a function of transaction size is well described by a power function. It documented empirical regularities that call out for theoretical analysis and explanation, such as the apparent stability in price markup coefficients over drugs and time. It generated new insights such as evidence that UK importers may be vertically integrated into high-level domestic distribution and derive much of their net revenues from the domestic distribution, not solely from importation

36. The first dealer in Table 6, who seems to derive negative net revenues relative to the imputed import price, might have been quoting the price per kilogram for a multi-kilogram sale when he gave the price for which he sold a kilogram. If so, that would artificially inflate the imputed import price and depress the imputed share of net revenues attributable to importation.

Table 6. Imputed import price and proportion of the revenues of importers that is attributable to importation, given that imputed import price.

Drug	Person	Source	Quantity Purchase d	Purchase Price (£/kg)	Branching Factor	Sales Quantity	Reported Sale Price (£/kg)	Imputed Import Price (£/kg)	Revenues Due to Importing
Cannabis	#1	Holland	30	£1,800	30	1	£3,050	£1,637	−13%
	#2	Belgium	60	£475	60	1	£2,125	£1,005	32%
	#3	Morocco	3,000	£350	30.0	100	£1,600	£859	41%
		Morocco	3,000	£350	7.5	400	£1,600	£1,107	61%
		Spain	3,000	£800	30.0	100	£1,600	£859	7%
		Spain	3,000	£800	7.5	400	£1,600	£1,107	38%
Skunk		Spain	3,000	£1,800	30.0	100	£3,500	£1,878	5%
		Spain	3,000	£1,800	7.5	400	£3,500	£2,421	37%
Cocaine	#4	Holland	3.5	£15,000	7	0.5	£30,000	£23,249	55%
		Holland	3.5	£15,000	14	0.25	£30,000	£21,231	42%
	#5	Colombia	10	£1,000	20	0.5	£40,000	£27,016	67%
		Jamaica	10	£4,000	20	0.5	£40,000	£27,016	64%
	#6	Jamaica	23	£4,000	22.5	1	£25,000	£16,627	60%
	#7	West Indies	2	£5,000	7.5	0.27	£28,000	£21,504	72%
	#8	Venezuela	3	£2,500	3	1	£30,000	£25,979	85%
	#9	Ghana	20	£5,000	20	1	£25,000	£16,885	59%
		Ghana	20	£5,000	2	10	£22,000	£20,090	89%
	#10	Ghana	4	£1,400	144	0.028	£9,000	£4,694	43%
	#11	Spain	10	£17,500	7.5	1.33	£25,500	£19,584	26%
Heroin	#12	Belgium	30	£12,333	7.5	4	£17,000	£12,566	5%
	#13	Afghanistan	12	£950	6.2	1.95	£19,000	£14,467	75%
		Afghanistan	12	£950	6.2	1.95	£16,000	£12,183	75%

per se. Finally, it prompted some modest methodological innovation; to the best of our knowledge, this is the first paper to seek to impute import prices or even to recognize the difference between the actual first domestic sale price and a theoretical import price.

The analysis also raised questions that cannot be addressed by this data set. For example, there were relatively few pure brokerage observations (in which a dealer sells the entire quantity of drugs purchased to a single buyer), and all involved transactions of at least £30,000. Perhaps such brokerage is in fact rare, but various biases in the data collection and coding mean that no such inferences can be drawn from this data set; they would have to be investigated in another manner.

Beyond these specific insights, the analysis supports at least two general observations. First, quantitative variables coded from summaries of interviews with incarcerated drug dealers can show consistent patterns with sensible interpretation. To the extent that documenting empirical regularities of drug markets provides a scientific foundation upon which policy analysis can build, further investments in interviewing incarcerated drug dealers may be warranted. Such optimism was not necessarily warranted at the outset. For various reasons (selection bias, false reporting, innumeracy of respondents, etc.), the results of such quantitative analysis could have turned out to be gibberish.

Second, if incarcerated dealers are interviewed in the future, it would be useful to ask respondents about drug dealing 'cycles' explicitly, not just about individual transactions. Some respondents in the present data set described their dealing cycles, but the interview protocol was not designed explicitly to elicit information on cycles. Had it been so designed, we likely would have obtained a larger sample size and been confronted with fewer instances where the coding was ambiguous. Likewise, an interview protocol with more detailed information regarding fixed costs, operating costs, and extra costs would be of value for developing a more encompassing economic model of drug dealing, one that focuses more on profits rather than just revenues net of product purchases costs.

We are hesitant to attempt to draw even tentative policy conclusions, both because we do not want to distract from the value of providing simple descriptive information and because of the many limitations in the data. However, to the extent one were willing to speculate about implications, it is hard not to note that the β coefficients estimated here suggest that price markups moving from one distribution level to the next within the UK appear to be more modest than those previously estimated for the United States. Reuter and Kleiman's risks and prices theory might attribute such a difference to the relatively more stringent enforcement of drug laws within the United States.

It is important to note, however, that any enforcement-differential induced differences, even to the extent that they exist, are subtle. Table 1 shows that heroin prices can increase eight-fold within the UK as the drug passes through five distinct layers of transactions that separate the importer from the user. That suggests that enforcement within the UK is stringent enough to make UK heroin distribution networks adopt the same basic structure as those in the United States.

Likewise, the consistency within the UK of price markups across drugs that are subject to quite different levels of enforcement stringency seems inconsistent with the predictions of risks and prices theory. Roughly speaking, the prices per unit weight of cannabis, cocaine and heroin all triple as those drugs move down the distribution chain from the 1 kg to 1 g sales levels.

Of course, tripling the value of a kilogram of cannabis only generates one-tenth as much net income as does tripling the value of a kilogram of cocaine, and an even smaller fraction than for heroin. So if there is even a modest fixed cost of drug distribution – independent of drug type and enforcement risk – then the residual increase in value that can be attributed to compensation for enforcement risks does behave as risks and prices theory would predict, with bigger risk compensation increments for heroin and cocaine, than for cannabis. For instance, a fixed cost of £2 per transaction (e.g. compensating sellers at £12 per hour for making 6 sales per hour) would eat up more than half of the net revenue produced by selling cannabis at the gram rather than kilogram level, but less than 10% of the corresponding markup when distributing cocaine and heroin. This suggests that further thought and data collection on the question of compensation for dealers' time may be useful.

Acknowledgements

This work was funded in part by the Qatar Foundation and the Qatar National Research Program, and it would not have been possible without access to data provided by Matrix Knowledge Group. We thank Martin Bouchard, Honora Burnett, Claudia Costa Storti, Jamie Drysdale, Ted Leslie, Kevin Marsh, Peter Reuter, Laura Wilson and several anonymous referees for helpful comments and complementary analysis of these data.

The market for crystalline methamphetamine in Sydney, Australia

Rebecca McKetin, Jennifer McLaren, Erin Kelly and Jenny Chalmers

National Drug and Alcohol Research Centre, University of New South Wales

Introduction

An estimated 15–16 million people worldwide use methamphetamine each year and the global retail market for this drug is estimated to be worth around US$28 billion per annum.[1] The estimated production of methamphetamine has stabilized at around 290 metric tons per annum since 2001, but over this time there has been a 58% increase in the number of countries affected by supply,[1] increased involvement of organized crime groups and the development of more sophisticated manufacturing and trafficking operations.[2] These changes in supply have been mirrored in a more diverse retail market for the drug, which has complicated efforts to monitor and respond to the methamphetamine situation.[3]

---

1. *2007 World Drug Report* (Vienna: United Nations Office on Drugs and Crime, 2007). *Amphetamines and Ecstasy: 2008 Global ATS Assessment* (Vienna: United Nations Office on Drugs and Crime, 2008).
2. *Amphetamines and Ecstasy*: *2008 Global ATS Assessment* (Vienna: United Nations Office on Drugs and Crime, 2008).
3. N. Kozel, J. Lund, J. Douglas and R. McKetin, *Patterns and Trends in Amphetamine-type Stimulants in East Asia and the Pacific 2006* (Bangkok: United Nations Office on Drugs and Crime Regional Centre for East Asia and the Pacific, 2007).

This global trend toward a more dynamic market for methamphetamine has been mirrored in Australia, where organized crime groups dominate the illicit drug trade.[4] Up until recently, most methamphetamine available in Australia was domestically produced. Domestic methamphetamine supply is believed to be the strong-hold of Outlaw Motor Cycle Gangs (OMCGs) and/or their associates, who reportedly control its production and distribution.[5] Over the past few years this domestic methamphetamine supply has been supplemented with crystalline methamphetamine imported by organized Southeast Asian crime groups.[6] The first significant detection of crystalline methamphetamine at the Australian border occurred in 2000, and this was followed by several subsequent large-scale seizures.[7] This trend toward methamphetamine importation does not appear to have dented domestic production efforts, with the number of clandestine laboratory detections increasing throughout this period (from 95 in 1997–8 to 249 in 2006–07).[8]

These shifts in methamphetamine supply have been accompanied by dramatic changes in the retail market for the drug.[9] The most notable change has been the increased availability and use of crystalline methamphetamine. Reports of 'crystal' or 'ice' first emerged on the illicit drug retail market in Sydney in the late 1990s. Unlike it predecessor 'speed', which was sold in half-grams and grams as a low-purity powder, high-purity crystalline methamphetamine was being purchased in small quantities (approx. 0.1 g) called 'points'.[10] The emergence of crystalline methamphetamine was accompanied by reports of a damp or oily form of methamphetamine that users called 'base' or 'base meth'. Base was thought to be domestically produced, but it was marketed in a similar way to crystalline methamphetamine, in that it was also sold in points and reported to be more potent that the traditional powder form of the drug.[11]

---

4. *The Parliamentary Joint Committee on the Australian Crime Commission Inquiry into the Future Impact of Serious and Organized Crime on Australian Society, 2007* (Australian Crime Commission), http://www.crimecommission.gov.au/html/pg_publications.html, 4 (accessed December 16, 2008).
5. *Parliamentary Joint Committee on the Australian Crime Commission Inquiry into the Manufacture, Importation and Use of Amphetamines and Other Synthetic Drugs (AOSD) in Australia, 2007* (The Parliament of the Commonwealth of Australia), http://www.aph.gov.au/Senate/committee/acc_ctte/completed_inquiries/2004-07/aosd/report/report.pdf (accessed December 16, 2008). R. McKetin and V. Murtagh, 'Importation and Domestic Production of Methamphetamine', in *The Sydney Methamphetamine Market: Patterns of supply, Use, Personal Harms and Social Consequence.* NDLERF Monograph Series no. 13, ed. R. McKetin, J. McLaren and E. Kelly (National Drug Law Enforcement Research Fund, Commonwealth of Australia, 2005), 25–37. C. Ovenden, W. Loxley and C. McDonald, *The West Australian Drug Market: Descriptions from Convicted Drug Dealers, 1992* (Perth: National Centre for Research into the Prevention of Drug Abuse, 1995).
6. *Organised Crime in Australia* (Australian Crime Commission, 2007), http://www.crimecommission.gov.au/content/publications/Other_Publications/080117_Organised_Crime_In_Australia.pdf (accessed December 16, 2008). McKetin and Murtagh, 'Importation and Domestic Production of Methamphetamine'.
7. *Australian Illicit Drug Data Report* (Australian Crime Commission, 2007), http://www.crimecommission.gov.au/html/pg_publications.html (accessed December 16, 2008). McKetin and Murtagh, 'Importation and Domestic Production of Methamphetamine'.
8. *Australian Illicit Drug Data Report* (Australian Crime Commission, 2007), http://www.crimecommission.gov.au/html/pg_publications.html (accessed December 16, 2008).
9. L. Topp, L. Degenhardt, S. Kaye and S. Darke, 'The Emergence of Potent Forms of Methamphetamine in Sydney, Australia: A Case Study of the IDRS as a Strategic Early Warning System', *Drug and Alcohol Review* 21 (2002): 341–8.
10. Ibid.
11. Ibid.

The variation in the supply and sale of methamphetamine in Australia suggests that there may be distinct retail markets for the drug. This phenomenon has been found in cannabis markets in New York, where the retail markets for imported cannabis and domestically produced hydroponic cannabis were found to be associated with different consumers, different purchase venues and different prices.[12] The existence of such division in the retail market for a drug has important implications for policing of drug markets and public health campaigns, because both rely on identifying and targeting affected 'populations' (types of drug users) or areas (e.g. street markets, venues). Such segregation (or commonality) of markets can also affect how buyers and sellers will respond if one market is constrained (e.g. through policing or reduced drug availability). Finally, the segregation of retail markets has important implications for monitoring and understanding the drug situation. Considerable resources have been invested in identifying and monitoring the market for various forms of methamphetamine (i.e. speed, base and crystalline methamphetamine);[13,14] however, estimating their cumulative impact depends on the extent to which these three markets overlap, if indeed they do.

The aim of this study was to determine whether there was evidence of a separate retail market for crystalline methamphetamine and other domestically produced forms of the drug, namely speed and base. The analysis was based on a survey of 309 regular methamphetamine users in Sydney, and it involved comparing various aspects of the market (consumption, price, purchase units, perceived purity, availability, purchase location and sale by dealers) for crystalline methamphetamine with that for the other forms of the drug.

Method

Participants

Participants were 309 regular methamphetamine users, who were recruited in Sydney through advertisements in free press publications ($n = 131$), word of mouth ($n = 91$), needle and syringe programmes ($n = 34$), flyers ($n = 21$), websites ($n = 17$) and various other means (newspapers, health services and direct approach, $n = 16$). Inclusion criteria for participation were being at least 16 years of age and having used methamphetamine at least monthly in the past year. A structured questionnaire was administered face-to-face by researchers at a mutually convenient location (e.g. cafes, parks and health centres). All participants were volunteers who completed informed consent prior to the interview and were reimbursed AU$30 for their time and travel expenses.

---

12. S. Sifaneck, G. Ream, B. Johnson and E. Dunlap, 'Retail Marijuana Purchases in Designer and Commercial Markets in New York City: Sales Units, Weights, and Prices per Gram', *Drug and Alcohol Dependence* 90 (2007): S40–S51.
13. E. Black, A. Roxburgh, L. Degenhardt, R. Bruno, G. Campbell, B. de Graaff, J. Fetherston, S. Kinner, C. Moon, B. Quinn, M. Richardon, N. Sindicich and N. White, *Australian Drug Trends 2007: Findings from the Illicit Drug Reporting System (IDRS)*. Australian Drug Trends Series no. 1 (Sydney: National Drug and Alcohol Research Centre, 2008).
14. E. Black, M. Dunn, L. Degenhardt, G. Campbell, J. George, S. Kinner, A. Matthews, B. Quinn, A. Roxburgh, A. Urbancic-Kenny and N. White, *Australian Trends in Ecstasy and Related Drug Markets 2007: Findings from the Ecstasy and Related Drugs Reporting System (EDRS)*. Australian Drug Trends Series no. 10 (Sydney: National Drug and Alcohol Research Centre, 2008).

Measures

Demographics

Demographics measured included age, sex, employment status, income in the past week (AU$), completed years of schooling, prison and arrest history, main language spoken and country of birth.

Drug use

Drug use measures included lifetime, past year and past month prevalence, and days of drug use in the past month, for each drug class (methamphetamine, heroin, other opioids, ecstasy, hallucinogens, cocaine, benzodiazepines, antidepressants, alcohol, cannabis, inhalants and tobacco). The same measures were obtained for each form of methamphetamine, which were based on the categories developed by Topp et al.:[15] (a) 'powder/speed', (b) 'base', (c) 'ice/crystal'and (d) other or don't know. These categories are referred to here as 'speed' 'base', 'crystal' and 'other', respectively. A photographic identification sheet was used to aid the identification of these forms of methamphetamine, the details of which are documented elsewhere.[16] Age of first methamphetamine use, frequency of methamphetamine use in the past year (less than weekly, weekly, more than weekly and daily) and main route of administration in the past year were also recorded for methamphetamine.

Price, weight and form of most recent methamphetamine purchase

Participants were asked the price (AU$), weight and form of their most recent methamphetamine purchase, and how they usually paid for methamphetamine. Weight was coded by the interviewer against common local street level purchase units, these being 'points' (approximately 0.1 g), half-grams, full-grams, 'eight-balls' (one-eighth of an ounce) or other quantities.[17]

Perceived purity, availability and purchase location

For each form of methamphetamine that the participant had purchased within the past year, they were asked to rate its purity (high, medium, low, fluctuating), availability (very easy, easy, difficult, very difficult) and to nominate the main place of purchase (street dealer, dealer's home, mobile dealer or home delivery, pub, nightclub, other entertainment venue, from a friend, as a gift, other). Participants were also asked 'what forms of methamphetamine can your main dealer supply?'

---

15. L. Topp, L. Degenhardt, S. Kaye and S. Darke, 'The Emergence of Potent Forms of Methamphetamine in Sydney, Australia: A Case Study of the IDRS as a Strategic Early Warning System', *Drug and Alcohol Review* 21(2002): 341–348.
16. R. McKetin, C. Quinn, G. Groves, J. McLaren and E. Kelly, 'Methamphetamine: Physical Forms, Purity and Terminology', in *The Sydney Methamphetamine Market: Patterns of Supply, Use, Personal Harms and Social Consequence*. NDLERF Monograph Series no. 13, ed. R. McKetin, J. McLaren and E. Kelly (National Drug Law Enforcement Research Fund, Commonwealth of Australia, 2005), 16–24.
17. L. Topp, L. Degenhardt, S. Kaye and S. Darke, 'The Emergence of Potent Forms of Methamphetamine in Sydney, Australia: A Case Study of the IDRS as a Strategic Early Warning System', *Drug and Alcohol Review* 21(2002): 341–348.

Statistical analysis

Data were analysed using STATA SE version 10.0. Medians and ranges were calculated where continuous data were not normally distributed. Statistical comparisons between the lifetime, past year and past month use of the various methamphetamine forms were made using the McNemar test of symmetry, and comparisons of days of use in the past month were made using the Wilcoxon signed-rank test. All of these tests were two sided. Statistical comparisons were not made between the price, purity, availability and purchase location of the various methamphetamine forms because participants were only asked these questions if they had purchased the relevant form of methamphetamine in the past year, and not all of these participants could comment on purity and availability (purity: speed $n = 226$, base $n = 235$, crystal $n = 206$; availability: speed $n = 217$, base $n = 224$, crystal $n = 195$).

Results

Participant characteristics

Participants had a median age of 28 years (range 16–60 years), 59% were male, 61% were currently unemployed, and they had a median net income in the past week (including government benefits) of $240 (range $0–5120). The majority were Australian born (80%) and nominated English as their main language (96%). Most participants had an arrest history (68%) and one-third had been to prison. Participants had been using methamphetamine for a median of 10 years (range <1–38 years); the majority (82%) had used the drug weekly or more often in the past year and they had used it on a median of 8 days in the past month (range 0–30). Most injected methamphetamine (64%), 8% smoked and 28% used other non-injecting routes of administration. Polydrug use was common, with participants having used a median of seven drug classes in the past year (range 2–11): during this time most had used tobacco, alcohol and cannabis (88, 77 and 76% respectively), around half had used other stimulants (ecstasy 59%, cocaine 45%) and 40% had used heroin.

Methamphetamine use

The use of all forms of methamphetamine was high within the past year (Table 1), although participants were less likely to have used crystal than base (χ^2 (d.f. $= 1) = 7.0, p = 0.008$). It was typical for participants to have used either two or three forms of the drug during this time (89%, Figure 1). The exclusive use of crystal was uncommon (3%) and the same was true for speed and base (5 and 2% respectively). Participants who used crystal in the past year also had similar demographic characteristics to those who did not.[18] There was no significant difference in the days of use for each form of the drug in the past month ($p > 0.05$).

Price and purchase weight

Transactions for methamphetamine almost exclusively involved cash (94%), with only 3% of participants being provided drugs on credit or in return for goods/services, and the

18. Our previous research on this sample found that crystalline methamphetamine users were more likely to be female (62 vs 49%), but did not differ in their age, employment status, ethnicity, schooling or prison history. R. McKetin, J. McLaren and E. Kelly, 'The Relationship Between Crystalline Methamphetamine Use and Dependence', *Drug and Alcohol Dependence*, 58 (2006): 198–204.

Table 1. The characteristics of the retail market for each form of methamphetamine.

	Form of methamphetamine		
	Speed	Base	Crystal
Use			
Past year (%)	83	85	77[a]
Past month (%)	55	59	49[a]
Days in past month (median)[b]	3	4	5
Median price of last purchase (range)[c]	50 (15–1200)	50 (20–5000)	50 (20–1000)
Purchase unit[c] (%)			
Point (0.1g)	13	55	66
Half-gram	28	8	13
Gram	32	19	12
Other	28	18	9
Perceived purity[d] (%, 95% CI)			
High	14	47	57
Medium	41	38	28
Low	36	9	11
Fluctuating	9	6	4
Availability[d] (%, 95% CI)			
Very easy	39	31	32
Easy	44	54	45
Difficult	17	16	24
Location of purchase[d] (%)			
Don't know	2	1	<1
Dealer's home	36	37	37
Mobile dealer	19	23	19
Friend	18	17	16
Street	8	7	13
Venue	3	2	1
Other	15	14	14
Available from main dealer[e] (%)	60	69	66

[a] Base use was significantly more common than crystal use in both the past month and the past year ($p < 0.05$). There were no other significant differences in exposure to each form of methamphetamine in the past month or year.
[b] Among participants who had used each form during this time. Days of use in the past month in the total sample did not differ by methamphetamine form ($p > 0.05$).
[c] Most recent purchase occasion: speed ($n = 83$), base ($n = 102$), crystal ($n = 106$).
[d] Among participants who had used the form in the past year and could comment on its purity and/or availability (purity: speed $n = 226$, base $n = 235$, crystal $n = 206$; availability: speed $n = 217$, base $n = 224$, crystal $n = 195$).
[e] Among participants who knew what forms of methamphetamine their main dealer supplied ($n = 285$).

remaining participants reporting that they received it for free. Similar numbers of participants reported that their most recent methamphetamine purchase was speed ($n = 83$), base ($n = 102$) or crystal ($n = 106$), while 15 participants reported purchasing another form of the drug and four participants had not purchased the drug. The median price of participants' most recent methamphetamine purchase was AU$50 irrespective of the form of methamphetamine purchased (Table 1). The modal purchase unit for crystal and base was 'points', whereas speed was purchased in half-grams and gram quantities and was thought to be less pure than either base or crystal (Table 1).

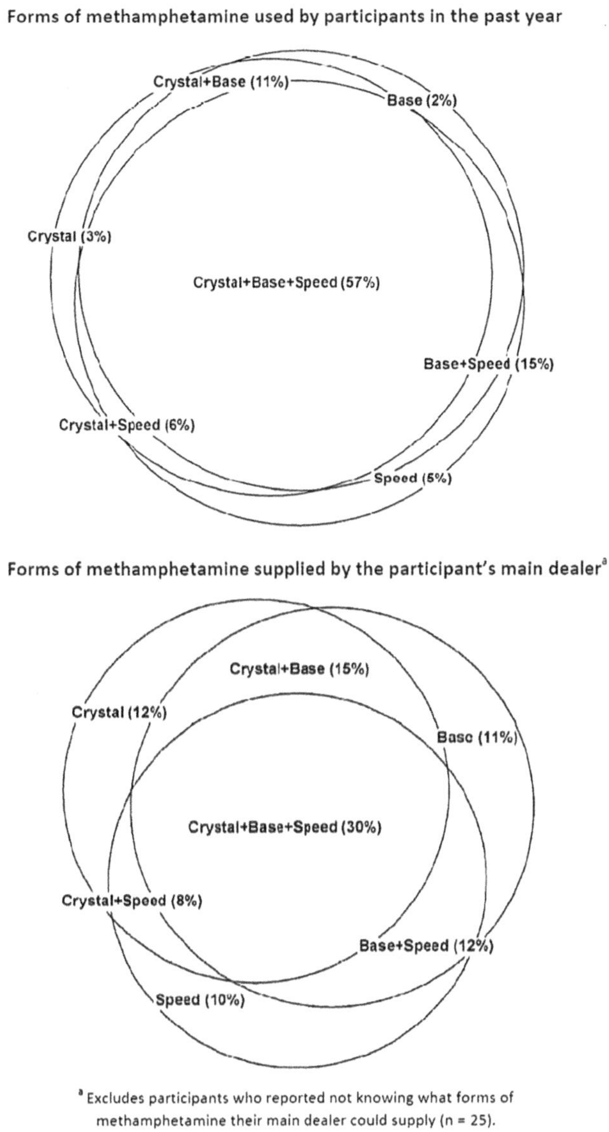

Figure 1. The various forms of methamphetamine used by participants and supplied by their main dealer.

Availability, perceived purity and purchase location

All forms of methamphetamine were rated as easy or very easy to obtain by the majority of participants (Table 1), although slightly more participants rated crystal as difficult to obtain. The purchase locations typically reflected a 'closed' market[19] for the drug (e.g. dealer's home, mobile dealer or friend) with a comparatively small street market, and this did not vary by the form of methamphetamine being purchased (Table 1). The majority

19. M. Natarajan and M. Hough, *Illegal Drug Markets, From Research to Policy* (Monsey, NY: Criminal Justice Press, 2000).

of participants reported that their main dealer was either a close friend or an acquaintance (91%), with only 2% of participants reporting that their main dealer was a stranger.

Although the majority of participants (68%) reported that their main dealer could supply more than one form of methamphetamine, dealers appeared to be somewhat more specialized than consumers (Figure 1). Specifically, 30% reportedly sold all three forms of the drug, compared with 57% of participants having used all three forms within the past year. However, there was no clear separation in the market between the supply of crystal and other forms of the drug. While a third of the main dealers did not usually supply crystal, over a half supplied crystal in concert with at least one other form of the drug and few supplied crystal alone (Figure 1). Participants reported that they had purchased methamphetamine from a median of two different dealers in the past month (range 1–8), suggesting that some participants may purchase different forms of the drug from different dealers.

Discussion

The current study did not find evidence of a segregated market for crystalline methamphetamine in Sydney, Australia. Based on annual consumption patterns, only 3% of methamphetamine consumers in our sample were exclusive crystalline methamphetamine users, and the vast majority of methamphetamine users took at least two different forms of the drug, if not all three. While dealers were more specialized, there was no clear pattern suggesting that crystalline methamphetamine was sold by a different set of retail-level dealers than other forms of the drug. The retail market for crystalline methamphetamine and that for other forms of the drug was remarkably uniform: their consumption levels were similar, they were purchased from the same dealers, from the same locations, and consumers paid the same price irrespective of which form they bought.

The retail market for methamphetamine in Sydney was predominantly a closed drug market,[20] with most participants buying the drug from a friend, either at their friend's home, or by phoning their friend to arrange a meeting place. While these types of social supply networks have a less visible impact on the community than 'open' markets (i.e. street-based drug markets), their fluidity and hidden nature makes them particularly resilient to interdiction efforts.[21] The resilience of supply would be further enhanced by the number of dealers through which consumers purchased the drug (most had purchased methamphetamine from two or more dealers within the past month).

Not only were participants typically able to access methamphetamine from more than one dealer, but they could also access various forms of the drug from a given dealer. This arrangement would provide consumers with information about the relative availability, quality and price, of the various forms of methamphetamine from different dealers, and thereby potentially increase competition in the market. This is a possible explanation for the apparent price equivalence for 'units'[22] of methamphetamine despite the market being closed in nature. Other factors contributing to competition may include the social-interconnectedness of the market, the presence of mobile dealers, and a small

---

20. Ibid.
21. *Organised Crime in Australia* (Australian Crime Commission, 2007), http://www.crimecommission.gov.au/content/publications/Other_Publications/080117_Organised_Crime_In_Australia.pdf (accessed December 16, 2008).
22. Assumes dose equivalence between a point of base/crystal and the larger purchase amounts of the low purity powder form of the drug (speed). While this inference is generally consistent with consumer reports, it needs to be confirmed using data on the purity and weight of purchases.

street market scene, all of which would increase knowledge among consumers about the availability, quality and price of methamphetamine.

A peculiar aspect of this drug market was that consumers paid the same amount regardless of what form of methamphetamine they purchased, while variation occurred in the quantity and perceived purity of purchases. This phenomenon has been observed in other illicit drug markets,[23] and it may simply reflect the convenience of charging customers round sums of money. However, it has important implications for monitoring the retail market for methamphetamine. Most drug monitoring systems rely heavily on tracking the street price of drugs as an indicator of street-level availability. Our data suggests that stability in price alone may mask shifts in the drug market, which, as Caulkins explains,[24] are more likely to appear as changes in the purity and/or quantity of the drug supplied for a given price.

While it is not possible to draw inferences about high-level methamphetamine supply from these data, the relatively integrated retail market for imported and domestic methamphetamine does suggest that these supply chains converge at the retail level. This convergence could reflect either a homogeneous supply of methamphetamine above the retail level of the market (e.g. a monopoly over methamphetamine distribution within Australia or collaboration between syndicates involved in importation and domestic production) or that there is sufficient fluidity and inter-connectedness among drug dealers that various supply channels readily converge into a single retail market (e.g. dealers know enough other drug dealers that they can access whatever drugs they wish to sell).

The relatively tight-knit retail market for various methamphetamine forms has important implications for policy around controlling the Sydney methamphetamine market. The ready availability of all forms of methamphetamine to consumers suggests that strategies which reduce the supply of one form of methamphetamine (e.g. border controls to reduce methamphetamine importation) may result in users substituting with other forms of the drug (e.g. domestically produced speed and base). In response to the resultant increase in demand for domestically produced methamphetamine, suppliers might increase its price, which would in turn increase profitability, and potentially drive up supply. This is important because law enforcement strategies are necessarily different for domestically produced and imported methamphetamine. For example, in Australia there have been a series of initiatives to reduce the diversion of over-the-counter cold-and-flu medications, which are the major source of precursor chemicals used in domestic methamphetamine manufacture. Such initiatives may reduce the supply of domestically produced methamphetamine, but they could have the unintended consequence of increasing the supply of imported methamphetamine (in so far as other costs and regulatory constraints permit this to occur). The factors that influence the supply and demand for methamphetamine are undoubtedly far more complex than portrayed in this example, but it highlights the need to consider the potential for reactive changes in a drug market when controlling its supply channels.

The overlap between the market for crystalline methamphetamine and other forms of methamphetamine also has implications for research and public health policy.

---

23. S. Sifaneck, G. Ream, B. Johnson, E. Dunlap, 'Retail Marijuana Purchases in Designer and Commercial Markets in New York City: Sales Units, Weights, and Prices per Gram', *Drug and Alcohol Dependence* 90 (2007): S40–S51.
24. J. Caulkins, 'Price and Purity Analysis for Illicit Drugs: Data and Conceptual Issues', *Drug and Alcohol Dependence* 90 (2007): S61–S68.

Pharmacologically, the effect of methamphetamine is the same irrespective of how it is marketed, and therefore research and policy strategies that focus solely on crystalline methamphetamine at the exclusion of other forms of the drug[25] are likely to underestimate the true extent of methamphetamine use and related harm. Any associations between crystalline methamphetamine use and harms found in such circumstances would also be confounded by the use of other forms of the drug. Obtaining an accurate picture of the public health implications of methamphetamine must consider the composite of its consumer market.

Methodological considerations

While we found convergence of the market for various forms of methamphetamine, this does not negate individual variation in consumer preferences for different forms of the drug. Moreover, there are likely to be a range of factors that influence availability, price and other aspects of the retail market, which may vary across geographic location, between individuals and over time. There are a number of further limitations to keep in mind. First, we were unable to corroborate participant's reports of what their dealers could supply with objective evidence of drug-dealing behaviour, and there are a number of validity and reliability issues around self-reported price and transaction data.[26] Second, we cannot assume that participants in the current study, or their main dealers, are representative of all methamphetamine users or dealers. Finally, drug markets tend to be specific to geographic locations,[27] and therefore the current results may not generalize to other methamphetamine markets in Australia or elsewhere. However, the findings of the current study are very consistent with those from sentinel drug monitoring systems in Australia. These systems show the same retail price of AU$50 per unit, the same ready availability, and the same relative perceived purity, for the various forms of methamphetamine, in most major Australia cities.[28]

Conclusion

The involvement of various organized crime groups in methamphetamine supply, and the various forms of the drug they are suspected to be involved in trafficking, is not necessarily reflected as distinct retail markets for methamphetamine in Sydney, Australia. Variations in the marketing of methamphetamine may provide tell-tale signs of its high-level supply, but these markets converge at a retail level, such that they are accessed by a common group of consumers. In particular, we found that the consumer market for crystalline methamphetamine almost completely overlapped with that for other forms of the drug and

25. L. Degenhardt and L. Topp, 'Crystal Meth Use Among Polydrug Users in Sydney's Dance Party Subculture: Characteristics, Use Patterns and Associated Harms', *International Journal of Drug Policy* 14 (2003): 17–24. S.A. Kinner and L. Degenhardt, 'Crystal Methamphetamine Smoking Among Regular Ecstasy Users in Australia: Increases in Use and Associations with Harm', *Drug and Alcohol Review* 27 (2008): 292–300. *National Leadership Forum on Ice*. NSW Health, http://www.druginfo.nsw.gov.au/national_leadership_forum_on_ice (accessed 2 October 2008).
26. Caulkins, 'Price and Purity Analysis for Illicit Drug'. P. Reuter, 'The First Agenda for Drug Enforcement Research', *Addiction* 97 (2002): 653–64.
27. R. Curtis and T. Wendel, 'Toward the Development of a Typology of Illegal Drug Markets', in *Illegal Drug Markets: From Research to Policy*, ed. M. Natarajan and M. Hough (Monsey, NY: Criminal Justice Press, 2000), 121–52.
28. E. Black, A. Roxburgh, L. Degenhardt, R. Bruno, G. Campbell, B. de Graaff, J. Fetherston, S. Kinner, C. Moon, B. Quinn, M. Richardon, N. Sindicich and N. White, *Australian Drug Trends 2007: Findings from the Illicit Drug Reporting System (IDRS), Australian Drug Trends Series No. 1* (Sydney: National Drug and Alcohol Research Centre, 2008).

that the characteristics of their retail markets were almost identical. Perhaps the inclination to focus on the market for each form of methamphetamine as a separate entity[29] has been a 'red herring' and has shifted our focus from the more important issue of overall consumption and harm from methamphetamine. Future efforts to characterize and monitor the market for methamphetamine need to be cautious about the implications of attempting to segregate this market into its various components, particularly if this should occur at the expense of understanding the composite market for the drug.

Acknowledgement

This research was funded by the National Drug Law Enforcement Research Fund, Commonwealth of Australia, and was also supported by the Australian Government Department of Health and Ageing. Thanks go to the staff associated with the Central Sydney, South Eastern Sydney and Wentworth Area Health Services for assistance with the recruitment of participants for the study.

29. L. Topp, L. Degenhardt, S. Kaye and S. Darke, 'The Emergence of Potent forms of Methamphetamine in Sydney, Australia: A Case Study of the IDRS as a Strategic Early Warning System', *Drug and Alcohol Review* 21 (2002): 341–348. N. Kozel, J. Lund, J. Douglas and R. McKetin, *Patterns and trends in Amphetamine-Type Stimulants in East Asia and the Pacific 2006* (Bangkok: United Nations Office on Drugs and Crime Regional Centre for East Asia and the Pacific, 2007). L. Degenhardt, A. Roxburgh, E. Black, R. Bruno, G. Campbell, S. Kinner and J. Fetherston, 'The Epidemiology of Methamphetamine Use and Harm in Australia', *Drug and Alcohol Review* 27 (2008): 243–252.

The black market in China for tiger products

Brendan Moyle

Department of Commerce, Massey University

Introduction

This paper is focused on the Chinese black market for tiger products. The motivation for this work is that wild tigers in Asia are facing an elevated extinction threat. One of the significant extinction pressures is poaching. It is obvious that poaching occurs because it is profitable. It must also be the case that the organizations able to procure, transport and sell tiger products over thousands of miles and international borders also exist. It is the nature of these organizations that will be discussed in this paper.

The main issues this research will attempt to address are as follows. First, it will identify which tiger parts are smuggled into China. Second, it will discuss which factors influence consumer demand. Third, it will discuss whether the black market is homogeneous or in some sense separated by product-type and geography. Fourth, it will try to identify the relevant costs along the supply chain and the responses to these costs by criminal organizations. A transaction-cost economics methodology will be employed.

The illegal trade in wildlife is large in scope and importance.[1] It has been estimated as one of the largest illegal international trades in global terms, behind illegal narcotics and weapons.[2] A caveat is that such estimates cannot be calculated with either much accuracy or confidence.[3] Wildlife is a very heterogeneous good as it takes in a wide variety of

---

1. Jacqueline L. Schneider, 'Reducing the Illicit Trade in Endangered Wildlife: The Market Reduction Approach', *Journal of Contemporary Criminal Justice*, 3 (2008): 274–95.
2. Steven Broad, Teresa Mulliken and Dilys Roe, 'The Nature and Extent of Legal and Illegal Trade in Wildlife', in *The Trade in Wildlife: Regulation for Conservation*, ed. Sara Oldfield (London: Earthscan Publications, 2003), 3–22.
3. Schneider, 'Reducing the Illicit Trade in Endangered Wildlife', 282.

species. Wildlife products are used for food (e.g. bush-meat), for medicine (e.g. musk-deer oil), as collectable goods (e.g. butterflies) and in the manufacture of other goods (e.g. crocodile leather). Wildlife and their products are not produced to a uniform standard and considerable price variation can occur. This heterogeneity makes valuing traded wildlife products very challenging. Nonetheless, the trade in wildlife is apparently valuable to its participants and with fewer risks of apprehension than for illegal narcotics.[4]

Wildlife crime, however, frequently attracts low enforcement effort and offenders often receive weak sanctions. It is also not a trade that has attracted significant attention by criminologists or economists.[5] One of the major concerns of this trade is that it puts many endangered species under elevated extinction pressure.

Tigers are a species that is subject to severe poaching pressure. The research here is necessarily preliminary. It is currently difficult to supply definitive answers on this particular wildlife black market. This relates to the rather invisible way it operates, combined with infrequent arrest data. This is not actually unusual for wildlife black markets.[6] Nonetheless the tiger black market remains surprisingly poorly researched given the high profile of the species. For tigers however, policies are being proposed (such as education in China or more interdiction effort at international borders) to reduce poaching. The current international policy framework is based on assumptions about the market that have never been properly tested or analysed. A critical assumption is that the dominant effect of the Chinese domestic ban has been on the demand for tiger parts rather than the supply. A better understanding of the black market, even if incomplete, may increase the effectiveness of measures to reduce poaching.

This paper is also a result of several trips to China to investigate their black market in tiger products. It included a covert investigation of Traditional Chinese Medicine (TCM) shops in Hekeu (Yunnan) and Xi'an (Shaanxi). Chinese citizens were employed to inquire about purchasing genuine tiger-bone medicine from these shops. This research also makes use of the Chinese arrest data of black-market offenders. This data has not been used by other researchers. This data set dates back to 1999 but is unlikely to be exhaustive. There remain significant challenges to collating data in a large country like China, where wildlife crime is policed by several different enforcement agencies (e.g. Customs, Forest Rangers and Police). An important consequence of this is that the information in each case was not consistent. Prices were not usually recorded. Bones were reported either in weights or in terms of the number of pieces. Linking the seizure data to the sanctions was also rarely possible. This meant that any robust statistical testing of this data was not possible. As a consequence, only very general statements could be made about the location of the arrests, number of offenders, types of tiger products seized and the subspecies of the tiger involved.

Background

Tigers (*Pantheris tigris*) are a large cat species endemic to Asia. There are six remaining extant sub-species.[7] These are the Amur (or Siberian), Bengali, Indo-Chinese, Malayan,

4. Ibid.
5. Ibid.
6. Ibid.
7. Eric Dinerstein, Colby Loucks, Eric Wikramanayake, Joshua Ginsberg, Eric Sanderson, John Seidensticker, Jessica Forrest, Gosia Bryja, Andrea Heydlauff, Sybille Klenzendorf, Peter Leimgruber, Judey Mills, Timothy G. O'Brien, Mahenddra Shrestha, Ross Simons and Melissa Songer, 'The Fate of Wild Tigers', *Bioscience* 57 (2004): 508–14.

Sumatran and South China. The three extinct sub-species are the Javan, Balinese and Caspian. Tigers face a range of extinction threats. These include habitat loss, genetic depression and illegal hunting.[8] The most numerous sub-species is the Bengali but recent Indian population estimates indicate serious declines. The Siberian population is currently the most stable, and its range includes Russia, northern China and possibly North Korea. The South China population is possibly the most imperiled, as no wild population remains. A relic population of South China tigers exists in captivity in China.

In the recent past tiger populations were larger and more widely spread. Declines, however, were very rapid during the twentieth century.[9] The latest extinctions all occurred in the twentieth century. Some of this decline was a product of government policies. Tigers for many years were seen as a threat to livestock and rural human populations. Hence policies to reduce tiger densities have actually been the norm. This culminated in Chinese efforts in the 1960s to severely cull the South China tiger populations.[10] Tigers have also struggled to maintain viable populations in Asia, as they require large areas with plenty of prey items to hunt. Large wilderness areas that are free of human impact are increasingly rare in Asia. Even where tigers receive legal protection, the loss of prey items to forest-dwelling human hunters can generate an ongoing survival threat.

The concern about the speed and scale of the decline in tigers has led to measures to avert extinction. The scale of these efforts is possibly indicated by reports that about US$100 million are being spent annually throughout Asia to prevent decline.[11] It is not clear that these conservation efforts are making an impact on the rate of decline.[12] Disagreements about the appropriate policies have emerged following two initiatives from China. The first initiative is to restore habitat for the South China tiger and embark upon an ambitious re-wilding trial of this sub-species. The second initiative is a proposal to resume tiger farming. This is motivated by the hypothesis that farmed tiger products may reduce demand for wild tigers, hence poaching. This is a much more controversial proposal and has secured little support outside of China.

The current policy stance towards tigers is characterized by a total ban on the trade in tiger products. The international ban on the trade in tiger products was initiated soon after CITES (Convention on the International Trade in Endangered Species) was signed in 1973. Tigers were listed in 1975 as an Appendix I species. This meant that no commercial trade was permitted under any circumstances. An unfortunate consequence of the Appendix I listing is that no population monitoring need occur. This differs from an Appendix II listing where some trade is permitted (under quotas and a permit system). An Appendix II listing requires population monitoring. This Appendix I listing means that population estimates for tigers in their various range states are attendant with much uncertainty. Ironically (given the decline in tiger populations), participants of the first CITES meeting recall that one of the intended beneficiaries of the treaty was in fact, the tiger.[13]

8. Ibid., 508, 510.
9. Ibid., 509.
10. Ronald Tilson, Hu Defu, Jeff Muntifering and Philip J. Nyhus, 'Dramatic Decline of Wild South China Tigers *Panthera tigris amoyensis*: Field Survery of Priority Tiger Reserves', *Oryx* 38 (2004): 40–47.
11. *The International Workshop on Strategy for Tiger Conservation*, Harbin, China, 6 July 2007.
12. Dinerstein et al., 'The Fate of Wild Tigers', 508–509.
13. Eugene Lapointe, personal communication, 6 July 2007.

China, however, still had a domestic market in tiger parts. CITES only placed a ban on the international trade in tiger parts. Within China, tiger products were still being traded. By the early 1990s, China was using about 4 tons of bone per year. A mature tiger yields between 10 and 12 kg of dry weight bone. Hence 4 tons represents about 330–400 tigers. This was well in excess of the wild tiger population within China. This was possibly only 50 animals, occurring as three small populations of Indo-Chinese, Bengali and Siberians. This situation generated concern amongst China's Asian neighbors that their tigers were being poached to meet this supply. China banned the domestic trade in tiger parts in 1993 in response to these concerns. To reinforce this ban, the description of tiger medicines was purged from published medical texts. The goals of this domestic ban were to suppress or reduce demand for tiger products. Penalties for trading in tiger products are also severe, and typically have a strong punitive component.

The difficulty of obtaining tiger products in China also led to a supply response. This was to embark upon tiger farming within China to meet the domestic demand for tiger products. China had given permission for two such large farms to begin operations before the ban. One of these is in Harbin in the very north (Heilongjiang) and one is further south in Guilin. The situation is further complicated by the subsidy the State Forestry Administration provides to the Harbin farm, in contrast to the lack of subsidy to the Guilin farm. Both farms are, however, are in a parlous financial state. They have been able to capture some revenue through tourism but by all accounts are losing money. The two farms mentioned have about half China's captive tiger population, which is estimated at 4000–5000 animals. It could expand rapidly because breeding has been restrained for cost reasons.

Nonetheless, the domestic and international ban has not been associated with marked declines in poaching in Asia. Indeed, poaching in India following the Chinese ban is believed to have increased.[14] While various strategies have been proposed to reduce this poaching, these strategies have not been well-informed by knowledge of the Chinese black market.

The lack of information about the Chinese black market is not surprising. Collecting market data on illegal activity is always challenging. This is complicated by the geographical scale of the problem. China's southern border stretches from Vietnam to Pakistan. This covers a large area often characterized by mountains and forests. This border also includes many ethnic communities on either side that have historically traded with each other and continue to do so. On the sea-board, China has three of the five busiest ports in Asia. Shanghai, Hong Kong and Shenzhen handle very high volumes of containers and freight. On the Siberian border, numerous large rivers and rail networks exist to move contraband. Concealing illegal activity from government agencies is aided by the problems of policing and inspecting the large volume of trade occurring. In effect, in the post-CITES period smugglers had an existing endowment of a distribution network between China and key range states. With such opportunities for concealment, opportunities to observe black-market activity are limited.

Developing an understanding of this market is reliant on having a model or framework to account for our observations. Given the lack of actual observations on this market, an appropriate model becomes a powerful analytical tool. The discussion in this paper is motivated by two main economic themes. The first is that the criminal organizations involved in this traffic are motivated by profit. They are not poaching tigers because they wish to see tigers become extinct. They are poaching and smuggling tiger-products in order

---

14. Belinda Wright, personal communication, 6 July 2007.

to make money. The second theme is that the limited observations we have can be fitted into a transaction-cost economics framework.[15] The fundamental argument of transaction-cost economics is that organizations are arranged so as to minimize production and transaction costs.

Economic issues

The supply chain from the individual poacher to the final consumer in China is long and involves transactions between different parties at different nodes. This international dimension is often true of other wildlife products.[16] The criminal organization has to make economic decisions at each node of the chain. Such decisions ought to reflect the production and transaction costs faced by the organization at these nodes.

In transaction-cost economics, there are two prevalent types of costs. The first are the *coordination costs*. In order for a sale to be completed, prices have to be negotiated and both buyers and sellers need to make their existence and location known to the other. Finally, buyers and sellers have to come together to complete the transaction. The second are the *motivation costs*. Both parties may be deterred from the transaction if they suspect the motivation of the other party. For instance, buyers may suffer from informational incompleteness (e.g. are not sure that the product being offered is tiger or a fake). This may discourage them from making a purchase, even if the product is real. In legal markets there are regulations and the possibility of court action to enforce contracts. In illegal markets recourse to such mechanisms are not possible.

In illegal markets it is useful to introduce a third type of transaction cost. This will be termed *evasion costs*. Tiger parts are an illegal product both domestically and internationally. This means that participants in this black market face costs associated with evading arrest or prosecution. Such costs may include the loss of the product to law enforcement agencies and any associated criminal sanctions. Smugglers may modify their transport methods or the size of their shipments to compensate. Explicit costs such as bribes might be incurred to avoid arrest. The higher the evasion costs facing the conspiracy the more difficult it will be to complete the transaction. In many illegal markets these evasion costs are a significant burden to the criminal organization. For instance, in the international illegal narcotics market, the procurement costs are largely insignificant compared with the evasion costs.[17]

Evasion costs relate to economic theories of optimal deterrence. The economic theory of crime was first outlined by Becker.[18] This theory holds that criminal acts are rational, economic decisions.[19] Crime will occur more frequently when the benefit to the criminal is relatively high. It occurs less frequently when the benefit is low. One of the main policy tools to reduce crime is through law enforcement activity. This influences the cost to the criminal through the probability of arrest, the probability of conviction and the sanctions

15. Oliver E. Williamson, 'The New Institutional Economics: Taking Stock, looking Ahead', *Journal of Economic Literature* 38, no. 3 (2000): 595–613.
16. Schneider. 'Reducing the Illicit Trade in Endangered Wildlife'.
17. Peter Reuter and Mark Kleiman, 'Risks and Prices: An Economic Analysis of Drug Enforcement', *Crime and Justice* 7 (1986): 289–340.
18. Gary S. Becker, 'Crime and Punishment: An Economic Approach', *Journal of Political Economy*, 169 (1968): 176–77.
19. Bill McCarthy, 'New Economics of Sociological Criminology', *Annual Review of Sociology* 28 (2002): 417–42.

that apply if convicted.[20] For instance, the harsher penalties normally imposed on heroin traffickers causes a shift in behaviour to evade some of these costs. This includes more discrete behaviour, smaller shipments and fewer intermediaries.[21]

The factors that influence the demand for tiger products also need to be elaborated. The first issue is that tigers generate multiple products. The list of products includes bones, skins, teeth, claws, meat and penises. Poaching occurs to satisfy demand for these different products. Seizures and interdictions by law enforcement agencies show that the most important products for the Chinese market are skins and bones (see below). Skins have been used by many Asian communities for centuries. Within China the Tibetan community retains a large cultural attachment to the skins. One conspicuous use of these skins is as decoration on traditional costumes (*chupas*).

Tiger bones were also used in TCM and have been employed since the Han dynasty (about 2000 years ago). Tiger bone is believed to have a unique pharmacological effect. This is in the treatment of severe bone diseases. The closest substitute to tiger bone is leopard bone, but more leopard bone is needed to achieve this effect. It is the demand for the treatment of bone diseases that continues to drive the demand for tiger parts on China. People with severe bone diseases are frequently in pain. The desire to find an effective treatment for the disease motivates people to obtain the bone. It is alleged that there are 25 million people in China with bone diseases severe enough to benefit from tiger-bone medicine. In response to the 1993 ban, the Chinese TCM community has tried to develop alternatives to tiger bone. The two most common substitutes are leopard or sailong-rat bones. Neither of these is believed to be as effective (albeit they are not ineffective).

The demand for tiger penises and other parts (teeth, claws) is very weak in comparison. This is backed up by the arrest data from China. Such arrest data is based almost exclusively on bones and skins. Only one of the 22 seizures of genuine tiger parts in China involved anything other than skin or bone. This was in Qing Dao (Shan Dong province) in 2006. A similar situation exists in India, where only two of 26 seizures of tiger parts recorded by EIA included anything other than skin or bone.[22] The reason may well rest on the alleged unique medicinal effect of tiger bone. There are however, many substitutes for tiger penises, for instance (seal penises or viagra).

Another factor influencing demand is uncertainty about future supply. This is leading to some *option demand*. Some consumers are buying tiger bones even if they have no current medicinal demand. Rather they are storing bones in case the will need them for the treatment of bone diseases later in life. This option demand has been identified in a Chinese market survey. The two main sources of uncertainty are the possible extinction of tigers and the inability to find a seller when the need arises in the future.

There are two possible moderating influences on demand. The first is that the product is illegal and this may stigmatize its use. It is not clear, however, whether this stigmatizing effect exists, how strong it is, and even how to measure it. The second is that tigers are an endangered species. In a study of attitudes towards TCM products in Hong Kong, the vast majority of customers were motivated to avoid using endangered wildlife products.[23]

---

20. Ibid.
21. Reuter and Kleiman, 'Risks and Prices'.
22. Environmental Investigation Agency (EIA), *Skinning the Cat: Crime and Politics of the Big Cat Skin Trade*, September 2006. Environmental Investigation Agency, *The Tiger Skin Trail*, October 2004.
23. Broad et al., ' The Nature and Extent of Legal and Illegal Trade in Wildlife'. The authors discuss a study on the TCM market in Hong Kong conducted by TRAFFIC.

About 2% of these customers, however, said they would continue to use products from endangered species despite the conservation consequences.

Analysis

The supply chain into China begins with procurement or poaching in neighbouring states. Tigers have to be killed for their parts. An important source of these wild tigers are those that live in natural habitat (often wildlife reserves). The procurement stage involves several production costs. The poachers need to have traps or firearms to kill the tigers. Poachers are also likely to need some knowledge of where tigers are, and possess some hunting skills. There will also be a coordination problem, as the poacher must find a buyer and arrange a physical transfer of the product. The poacher also faces an apprehension risk, as forest rangers, police or members of the public could discover the poached animals.

The other relevant aspects of this transaction are its complexity (which impacts on the ability to evaluate the performance of the involved parties) and its interconnectedness. That is, how does the procurement of tiger parts connect to other wildlife products or other illegal products? Information on the procurement stage has three possible sources. The first is the arrest data. The second is information obtained from covert observations. The third is implicit knowledge about poaching possessed by local inhabitants or law enforcement agencies. The main problem with the last source is that as it is implicit, i.e. it is not codified. Some locals may have knowledge of how much poaching is in their areas and what is being poached, but lack the motivation to ability to make this explicit. Covert observations are also rare. This means that currently the arrest data is the primary sources of information on procurement. Unfortunately relevant economic details are not recorded on a consistent basis.

At the outset, tiger poaching could be something requiring specialized search and hunting skills, or be an activity accessible to many. For many wildlife products, some specialized hunting skills are required. This is true in both legal and illegal harvest. Most of the butterflies harvested in Papua New Guinea, for instance, come from a minority of the more skilled harvesters.

The requirement for local specialists seems to be the case for tigers as well. Tigers have a secretive, largely solitary lifestyle. They occur in low densities in reserves of limited accessibility. An obvious way to reduce these search costs is to employ people with either local knowledge or hunting skills. Hence indigenous communities that have a strong hunting culture are often ideal candidates to recruit as poachers. Examples in India include the Bawariya and Behliya tribes.[24] Many well-known poachers in Asia, such as Sansar Chand and the Cambodian Yor Ngun, came from hunting cultures. Similarly a 1997 study on tiger poaching in Sumatra found that this was dominated by local inhabitants rather than exogenous poachers.[25]

This dependence on poachers with hunting skills or local knowledge has an implication for the connectedness to other illegal traffic. There is likely to be a higher connectedness to other wildlife crime. The skills required to poach tigers are broadly similar to those required to poach leopards and other protected animals. There is likely

24. Navin Singh Khadka, 'Double Trouble for Nepal's Tigers', *BBC News*, http://news.bbc.co.uk/go/pr/fr/-/2/hi/science/nature/7607203.stm (accessed 20 September 2008).
25. Campell Plowden and David Bowles, 'The Illegal Market in Tiger Parts in Northern Sumatra, Indonesia', *Oryx* 31 (1997): 59–66.

to be a low connectedness to other illegal traffic, such as drugs, as the skill sets do not match. The need to have access to specialized hunters may also create barriers to other criminal organizations (such as drug traffickers) entering this trade.[26]

The coordination problem of making poacher and buyer known to each other can be tackled in two ways. The first is for the poacher to attempt to find buyers. The second is for the buyer to try to locate the poacher. In legal wildlife markets, buyers typically seek out harvesters. Harvesters generally lack capital and knowledge of prices and the distribution network. This implies they lack the capacity to find buyers on their own initiative. The illegal market for tiger-parts appears to follow the same pattern. In addition the use of market mechanisms like advertising is not feasible for illegal activity. Poachers are essentially offered cash for tigers by middlemen. Presumably successful hunters can be identified and employed by these middlemen relatively easily.

Such cash transactions have the advantage of being simple to undertake. Both parties can easily evaluate each other's performance. Cash and tiger parts are uncomplicated goods. The reported payments for tigers also help motivate the poacher. In effect, they are offered cash sums very large relative to their current income.[27] This also makes them less willing to defect to law enforcement agencies. Such defections would mean forgoing very lucrative illegal payments.

Seizure data generally shows that poachers are not found further along the supply chain. This mirrors legal wildlife markets where harvesters transfer their products at initial nodes.[28] This use of a market-based transaction approach probably reflects the simplicity of the contracts and the unwillingness of the participants to be observed in each other's company. Such meetings may alert others to the illegal activity. It also ensures that the poacher has little knowledge of the other members of the organization. This is likely to lower the evasion costs for the criminal organization.

The cost of employing poachers from outside the organization still leaves the conspiracy with a defection risk by poachers. Poachers may owe little loyalty to the organization and behave with less discretion. For instance, the arrest of Yor Ngun followed an earlier amnesty in 2001.[29] He had undertaken to stop poaching during this amnesty, but was convicted of poaching over 600 animals afterwards. In this period his hunts ranged over 10 Cambodian provinces.[30] This is not consistent with discrete behaviour. If caught, poachers may also be more willing to defect to authorities and inform on other participants. This defection risk could be overcome if it was internalized in the organization. This could be accomplished if the poachers also occupied nodes further up the supply chain. For instance, if they have the capacity they may be able to also undertake the distribution and transport of tiger parts. This appears to be the organizational form adopted by Sansar Chand's conspiracy.[31]

---

26. Schneider, 'Reducing the Illicit Trade in Endangered Wildlife'.
27. Biswajeet Banerjee, 'Tiger Poaching Ring Busted by Indian Police', National Geographic News, http://news.nationalgeographic.com/news/pf/47620673.html (accessed 2 November 2008). Cash offers of between $1400 and 1500 for each tiger are common. In rural communities living in or proximate to forests, this is typically well above average wages.
28. Broad et al., 'The Nature and Extent of Legal and Illegal Trade in Wildlife'.
29. BBC News, 'Cambodia Tiger Hunter Gets jail', http://news.bbc.co.uk/go/em/fr/-/2/hi/asia-pacific/4211506.stm/ (accessed 19 September 2008).
30. TRAFFIC, *TRAFFIC Bulletin Seizures and Prosecutions* 6, no. 3 (1997) to 21, no. 3 (2008), 91.
31. EIA, *Skinning the Cat*, 16–17. Sansar Chand began as a poacher and expanded his operations to eventually smuggle thousands of skins into Kashmir and Nepal.

The organizational form adopted at the poaching node appears to be influenced by coordination costs and search costs for tigers. There is little evidence that poachers are influenced by evasion costs. The risk of detection appears trivial. Law enforcement agencies manifest low detection, arrest and conviction rates of poachers. There are conspicuous examples of poachers operating for decades without getting caught. These include Sansar Chand, who was active for almost 30 years in India, and the Cambodian Yor Ngun, who began his poaching in the 1970s. Plowden and Bowles note that no poachers were arrested in connection to any of the poached tigers in their 1997 study.[32] A Sumatran conspiracy that was later convicted in Indonesia had operated for 10 years. In this period it had trafficked at least 60 tigers. Notably, this was the first case of its kind to be fully prosecuted in Indonesia. Conviction rates are low in other Asian countries. EIA notes that, of 1898 people accused or implicated in the illegal trade of otter, leopard and tiger in India, only 30 convictions resulted.

The black market is also supplied by two other sources. These sources are symptomatic of the high search costs for tigers and the coordination costs of bringing poachers and buyers together. One (likely) source is captive tigers. China has a large population of tigers distributed over a number of farms and zoos. Thailand also has a significant number of captive tigers. An important example is Sriracha Zoo, which exported 100 bengali tigers to Hainian in China.[33] Vietnam has recently recognized that the illegal breeding of tigers is occurring.[34] Finding evidence of these tiger populations supplying the black market is, however, difficult. The arrest in 2007 in China of someone trading a South China tiger skin shows that such supply has occurred.[35] South China tigers are only found in captivity so the skin would not have come from a wild population.

The tracing and verification of tiger numbers is not straightforward. Nonetheless tigers have been stolen and butchered from Chinese zoos.[36] There are persistent reports that the Chinese farm in Guilin and the Sriracha Zoo in Thailand has made tiger products for sale.[37] There is strong evidence that the Guilin farm has made tiger meat available for sale.[38] Given the financial pressure facing tiger farms in China, selling tiger products into a black market would certainly be attractive. Wildlife regulations typically do not enjoy a 100% compliance rate.

Another source of tiger products is fakes. Tiger bone can be faked by using the bones of other animals, such as cows (Figure 1). The bones may be embellished to add veracity to the claims that they are genuine. This includes gluing on fur dyed to resemble tiger and adding claws carved out of horn to the fake phalanges. Naturally this greatly lowers the search and production costs for tiger bone. It also lowers the transport costs. Hence it is undertaken by local Chinese who lack the resources and organization to import the bones themselves. Arrest data from China show that, to date, there is no overlap between those

32. Plowden and Bowles, 'The Illegal Market in Tiger Parts in Northern Sumatra'.
33. Han McGirk and Annabel Fallon, *Scandal of Zoo's Missing Tigers*, http://www.independent.co.uk/news/world/asia/scandal-of-zoos-missing-tigers-562656.html (accessed 19 September 2008).
34. Anh Tuan and Ha Nguyen, *Extinction Threatens Viet Nam Tigers*, http://vietnamnews.vnagency.com.vn/showarticle.php?num=02SUN250508 (accessed 18 September 2008).
35. TRAFFIC, *TRAFFIC Bulletin Seizures and Prosecutions*, 108.
36. China Wildlife Conservation Agency, 'Second Zoo Tiger Killed in Xchina', http://www.cwca.org.cn/Article/Showarticle.asp?ArtilceID=9493 (accessed 25 September 2008).
37. McGirk and Fallon, *Scandal of Zoo's Missing Tigers*.
38. CITES, *DNA Confirms Tiger Meat for Sale at Chinese Farm*, http://www.traffic.org/home/2007/6/12/cites-dna-test-confirms-tiger-mat-for-sale-at-chinese-farm.html (accessed 18 September 2008).

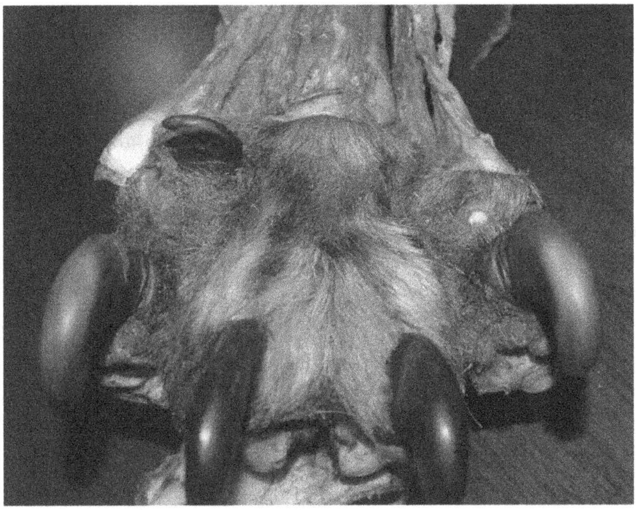

Figure 1. Fake Black-Market Tiger Foot (Harbin).

criminals that sell real bone (international in scope) and those that sell fakes (domestic in scope). Fakes are often sold alongside other wildlife fakes, in clusters of shops all participating in the same fraud. Prices also differ dramatically between fakes and real tiger products.[39] This confirms that the real and fake suppliers operate in completely different markets.

From the conservation perspective, the most important black-market segment is that of wild tigers sourced from range states. This is also the most relevant for international crime. Once tiger parts have been collected the next step is to transport the tiger products up to international borders. The primary data we have for this stage comes from interception data and covert observations in Siberia, India and Nepal.

The organization of the products within range states does not use the same market mechanism as recruiting poachers. Rather, the transport and storage of the wildlife products are done by a single domestic organization. Transport and warehousing are not subcontracted to other agents. This would be influenced by both the motivation costs and evasion costs. Wildlife products have to be gathered at hubs where transport is available. This typically means organizing this activity in proximity to people (cities rather than forests). The risk of being observed and tip-offs provided to authorities will need to be reduced. If a single organization undertakes all these transport and warehousing tasks then it reduces this risk. It may also be more difficult or expensive to motivate agents outside the organization to remain loyal. There may also be increased difficulty preventing law enforcement agents infiltrating the firm.

39. One arrest in Nan Chang (Jiangxi) province involved a trader offering a piece of fake bone for 80 Yuan. The customer negotiated the price down to 20 Yuan. In Guan Zhou province another arrest involved fake tiger bone being sold for 5 Yuan a gram. By way of contrast, a seizure of one skin and 41 pieces of bone in Hai Lin (Heilongjiang province) had a value of 1.5 million Yuan. Given that a recent seizure of skin established a black market price of 500,000 Yuan, each of these pieces of bone would have had an average value of 24,000 Yuan.

This loyalty or motivation cost is inflated in criminal organizations. These organizations are unable to rely upon legal sanctions to enforce loyalty. Another approach is to rely upon family or ethnic community links to increase loyalty (reduce defections) and insulate the organization from infiltration. The family connections of the Indian poacher Sansar Chand for instance, pervaded his organization.[40]

The primary market transaction is between a foreign buying agent and the domestic criminal organization in the range state. For instance, Sansar Chand sold initially to Kashmirian buyers and then Nepalese buyers within India. Meetings were organized in New Delhi. In the Russian Far East, a Chinese national using several passports organized purchase of a number of wildlife products in Siberia. Evasion costs are the likely explanation for this preference for travel to range states. It is more difficult for foreign nationals to move freely through China and legal sanctions are quite punitive. Evasion costs (bribes, transport) are thus likely to be lower in range states than for China.

The criminal organizations show a high level of connectedness to other wildlife products. Tigers are in fact a minority product.[41] In 2007 Tibetan officials intercepted 32 tiger, 579 leopard and 665 otter skins in one shipment. Sansar Chand claimed to have sold 300 tiger skins, 2000 leopard skins, 6000 fox skins and 4000 cat skins to the Nepalese buyer Tsering Tamang. There is no evidence from seizure data in Russia, India and China that other illegal products (drugs, weapons) are being smuggled.[42] This point implies that poaching rings have specialized knowledge and skills that emphasized wildlife. Evidence that tiger poaching is done by larger criminal conspiracies with a large portfolio of illegal activities is lacking. This indicates that there are significant organizational barriers to other criminal firms engaging in this trade.

The use of vehicles to transport large volumes (hundreds of skins) of different animals implies that there are large coordination costs. That is, the cost of physically bringing the product to a node to transfer to Chinese-based conspirators is high. By transporting large volumes at a time, the criminal organization can exploit some economies of scale to reduce their transport costs. The evasion costs do not appear to be influencing these transport decisions. The risk of detection and apprehension is has not prompted a shift to more covert techniques.

The next stage in the supply chain is crossing the international border. Crossing the international border involves an increased detection risk. Law enforcement agencies like Customs concentrate interdiction efforts on these borders. In many illegal markets like narcotics or parrots, low-wealth people are corrupted and employed to take on this risk. Such couriers have little knowledge of the network and are unable to provide much information to law enforcement agencies. This has also occurred with tigers. Border crossings in Russia have been associated with the bribery of train or truck drivers and sometimes police. The courier is typically unaware of the identity of the main conspirators.

Outside of Tibet the trade is about two tiger products – bones and skins. Other potential products (teeth, claws) are not being exported this route. The other minor tiger products of teeth (Figure 2) and claws are still available in domestic markets in range states. These are sometimes sold to tourists who are often unaware that this trade is illegal.

40. EIA, *Skinning the Cat.*
41. EIA, *Skinning the Cat*, 23.
42. Schneider, 'Reducing the Illicit Trade in Endangered Wildlife'. Schneider also makes the point that it is rare for other illicit products to be distributed by organizations that specialize in wildlife.

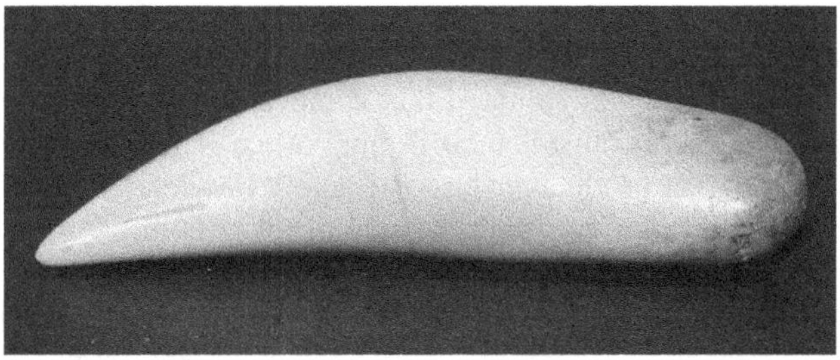

Figure 2. Sumatran Tiger Canine (Indonesia).

Nonetheless, the main point remains. The black-market trade of wild tigers into China is being sustained largely by demand for two products. Criminal organizations are opting to specialize in the distribution of skins and bones. Hence while poachers and smugglers outside Asia are multi-species and multi-product, smugglers in China are single species and bi-product.

The use of trucks and other land routes is not the only way tiger products get across the border. China also has busy airports and seaports. The arrest data, however, is very sparse here. Illegal wildlife shipments are occasionally detected in Hong Kong, but there is only one instance of tiger. In 2000 a Chinese woman travelling from Bangkok was caught with pills worth 12,000 Yuan at Hong Kong airport. The pills contained tiger-bone and had been obviously manufactured prior to this trade. The ability to purchase tiger medicine in Thailand has been previously attributed to the Sriracha Zoo. If the practice of making tiger-bone medicines in range states like Thailand is more common then realized, then this has to be of concern. Detecting a tiger bone in a pill or bottle of wine is not straightforward. If air and sea routes into China have much lower detection rates than land routes, then it makes it difficult to infer that the land routes are the most common approach. The evidence from the entry of skins from Nepal into Tibet is that it has exclusively been via land routes.

There is comparatively little data on the organization of the tiger-part black market within China. There have been a number of recent investigations that have targeted TCM shops or surveyed TCM customers. There is also arrest data from China that has been collated by the Chinese State Forest Administration.

The arrest data has the following properties. In terms of the distribution of real tiger products, there is a strong geographical bias. About two-thirds of the arrests of conspiracies are concentrated in two provinces. These are Heilongjiang (seven arrests) in the far north and Yunnan (eight arrests) in the far south. The shared characteristic of these provinces is that they border range states. Heilongjiang borders Russia and the Siberian sub-population distribution (Heilongjiang also has a small population of wild Siberian tigers). Yunnan borders Vietnam, Laos and Burma. This geographic concentration is matched by the sub-species distribution. Most arrests in Heilongjiang involve Siberian tigers. Most arrests in Yunnan are for Bengali or Indo-Chinese sub-species (the Bengali is found in Burma). Heilongjiang also has the Harbin farm. Yunnan does not have any tiger farms. There have been no arrests in the Guangxi province, which has the Guilin farm. Hence, it is not possible to infer any effect caused by the proximity of farms to tiger-part consumption. There was one arrest of three conspirators in Tibet (Xizang) in this period.

The data on arrests for fakes (18 instances) has a different pattern. Only one arrest for a fake occurred in Yunnan or Heilongjiang. This was a case involving the sale of fake tiger meat in Harbin (Heilongjiang). Most of the arrests thus occur outside of the most important

Chinese provinces for black-market arrests. As alluded to above, the sale of fakes is often done more openly in clusters of shops all participating in the same fraud. State Forestry Administration (SFA) officials have noted that some vendors have been bold enough to attempt to sell fake tiger-skins outside their Beijing office. The culprits were not arrested. The price of such fake tiger products is also extremely low relative to value of real tiger products in the black market. Given that the sale of fakes is in practice not treated very seriously, the risks of selling fakes are much lower.

There have been covert attempts to find tiger bone for sale in TCM shops or markets in China. This was undertaken by TRAFFIC. Another smaller attempt was made by me with the Chinese SFA in March 2008. The goal of this latter visit was, however, primarily to scope out viable sources of information on the Chinese black market. The TCM shop and market visits were one of the sampling approaches taken. The other data sources that were examined were the un-codified knowledge local wildlife authorities have on smuggling and the level of detail accompanying the arrest data.

Both covert attempts used Chinese citizens to make inquiries about the availability of tiger-bone medicine. Both investigations concur on two main findings. The first is that there is very high knowledge of the illegality of selling tiger products and further that the reason the trade is illegal is because tigers are endangered. The second point is that an extremely small percentage of shops claimed to have real tiger bone medicine for sale. The veracity of these claims could not be tested. The TRAFFIC study found that 3% of the shops claimed to have tiger medicine for sale.[43] This means that most potential customers would not in fact, be able to find tiger bone medicine if they relied upon the shops and the time spent searching would be very high. For instance, Xi'an had 24 TCM shops during our survey. At an approximate 3% stocking rate (if true), the coordination costs for a customer would be very high. They would have to spend a lot of time searching for the product. Indeed, there would be a reasonable expectation that many potential customers would not find any tiger bone for sale. A city would need 30–33 TCM shops in order to average at least one TCM seller stocking illegal tiger bone.

There has also been a recent attempt to examine the end-user market for tiger products in China.[44] This surveyed households in seven major Chinese cities (1880 respondents). A key result was that 43% of the respondents said that they had used tiger products (most often tiger bone plasters), and most since the 1993 ban. Tests on tiger-plasters from 518 TCM stores in China (tigers appear as brand-images as per Figure 3), however, showed no evidence of tiger bone.[45] It was not stated whether consumers were using tiger products procured after the ban or consumed from product stockpiled in anticipation of the ban.

Other key results were that household income had no statistically measurable effect on consumption and that the geographical concentration of consumption (away from Heilongjiang and Yunnan) did not match Chinese arrests of 'real' tiger product. The lack of a household income effect seems difficult to sustain if prices are for genuine tiger-products. The ability of poorer households to obtain tiger products is far more likely at the prices at which fakes are traded. There was no attempt to verify that sales were

43. Kristin Nowell and Xu Ling. *Taming the Tiger Trade: China's Market for Wild and Captive Tiger Products since the 1993 Domestic Trade Ban* (TRAFFIC, March 2007).
44. Ibid.
45. Brian Gratwicke, Judy Mills, Adam Dutton, Grace Gabriel, Barney Long, John Seidensticker, Belina Wright, Wang You and Li Zhang. 'Attitudes Toward Consumption and Conservation of Tigers in China', *PLos ONE*, 3, no. 7 (2008): 1–7.

Figure 3. Tiger Plaster (TCM Shop, Hekeu).

of fakes or real. The geographical centres of consumption reported in this survey also conformed the pattern of arrests for the sale of fakes.

The distribution of tiger products in Tibet, however, is not consistent with the rest of China. Tiger skins have been observed openly available for sale in Tibet and out west to Gansu. The high visibility of tiger skins in markets suggests that the enforcement effort has been low and provides little deterrence. As a crude measure of law enforcement activity, SFA record only one arrest 1999–2007 period. This was from 2003 when three Tibetans were arrested when smuggling 31 Bengali tiger skins (but no bone). In an attempt to reduce demand, the Daili Lami called upon Tibetans to stop purchasing tiger skins in 2005.[46] The lack of enforcement effort may have a political basis. The trade in tiger skins in Tibet is influenced by Tibetan cultural practices. It is possible that Chinese authorities have accommodated this illegal trade rather than risk higher enforcement provoking the Tibetan population. There is certainly a striking difference between the arrest data in provinces like Yunnan and Heilongjiang (eight and seven cases) compared with Tibet (one case).

The geographical concentration of arrests, coincident with range-state proximity, implies that smugglers face significant transaction costs distributing their products.

46. EIA, *Skinning the Cat*, 23, reports three instances of seizures in the Tibetan Autonomous Region in the same period.

While smugglers apparently began the ban-period with an existing network, this endowment appeared to be based on local connections. An example of this is the Tibetan involvement with Sansar Chand's network. In fact the Tibetan community within China appears to be a broad transmission path of tiger products through Qinghai and Gansu. Increases in transaction costs to less proximate provinces are likely to need a new organizational form.

Getting black-market products to more distant provinces incurs two major transaction costs. The first is reducing the risk of detection (evasion costs are high). The smuggling of threatened wildlife (those that merit the highest protection under Chinese law) receives heavy sanctions. The death penalty has occurred for traffic of giant pandas.[47] Tiger smugglers also receive heavy penalties, with one of the Tibetans arrested in 2003 receiving the death penalty (later commuted to a prison sentence). Tiger smugglers can expect a combination of a lengthy prison sentence and heavy financial penalties. Sanctions in China are in general much more severe than those outside of China.[48]

Smugglers appear to have adopted two techniques to reduce this detection risk. The first is to reduce the size of their shipments. The volumes traded in shipments by smugglers outside of China are much larger than that within China. For instance, interceptions in Yunnan have involved: 11 tiger skins (1999); three skins and bones (1999); one tiger skin and bones (2000); 23 pieces of bone (2001); five skins (2002); two tiger skins (2005); and 175 pieces of bone (2005). Interceptions in Heilongjiang have involved one tiger bone (2004); six skeletons (2004); 1.75 kg of bone (2006); one skeleton (2006); one skin and 41 pieces of bone (2007). This can be contrasted with an interception in Nepal that had 32 tiger, 579 leopard and 665 otter skins in the same shipment.

The second technique is to specialize in tiger products. By operating in one market only, the customer base is relatively smaller and more insulated from other members of the public.[49] Of the 22 arrests in the Chinese data set, only three cases were multi-species. Only one case involved more than two species, and that was a Customs interception in Yunnan. This shipment included elephant, Indo-Chinese tiger, leopard, bear and red-panda parts. This specialization may also imply a shift in the connectedness of this market. Earlier in the supply chain, the procurement of tiger parts was shown to be strongly connected to other wildlife. The market for tiger parts, however, shows little connectedness to other species. This is despite leopard being one of the recognized substitutes for tiger bone in TCM.

Chinese law enforcement means that foreign-based smugglers face high risks if they try to market tiger products in China. Foreigners tend to be easily identifiable in China, and their movement is often tracked. Given the preponderance of arrests of Chinese nationals, this is consistent with a transfer to a Chinese organization occurring soon after the border-crossing. It would also be rational to use fewer intermediaries as this reduces the number of nodes an intercept could occur in. It also reduces coordination costs (fewer nodes require less negotiation with other middlemen). With fewer people involved in the smuggling there is less risk that informants will reveal the existence of the network. The reduction in intermediaries is signalled by the size of the arrested conspiracies in China. Only two of the 22 cases of seizures in China for real tiger parts involved more

47. Juan Carlos Vasquez. 'Compliance and Enforcement Mechanisms of CITES', in *The Trade in Wildlife: Regulation for Conservation*, ed. Sara Oldfield (London: Earthscan, 2003), 63–9.
48. Ibid., 68.
49. Chinese sources indicate that most arrests for trade in real tiger-parts came from tip-offs from the public.

than three offenders. One case was in 1999 (11 offenders in Yunnan) and the other was in 2007 (five offenders in Fu Dian). In contrast, seven of the 18 cases of seizures for fake tiger parts involved more than three offenders.

The second major transaction cost is associated with locating a customer and transporting the goods to them. The problem with transport costs may be reflected in the dominance of provinces that are near range states. Travel distance is a normal component of trade and can be expected to influence distribution decisions.

The biggest challenge for smugglers, however, is the distribution of tiger parts in China. Poachers in range states are a relatively small, geographically specific and easily corrupted segment of the population. Consumers of tiger parts, however, are geographically dispersed and may be motivated to tip off police to the presence of smugglers. This increases the coordination and evasion costs to complete a transaction. The challenges of distributing illegal products are not, however, unique to tiger smugglers. There are a number of options available to criminal organizations to distribute their products.

Trade in wildlife products such as elephant ivory in the 1980s took advantage of a legal distribution channel. Poached ivory was laundered into domestic markets in other countries. The legal market provided the least-cost way of distributing the product, solving the coordination problem for smugglers.[50] Customers bought the poached ivory using legal channels. They could not distinguish poached from legally sourced ivory. This made detection of smugglers by consumers practically impossible. It also lowered the evasion costs for smugglers.

Another option used in markets where laundering is not possible is to create a parallel market to distribute the product. Illegal narcotics like cocaine, for instance, may be sold at specific geographical loci. Customers can easily seek out these locations. The size and scope of these markets alongside the willingness of some drug traffickers to use violence to protect their market position makes suppression of these markets difficult. The market can have a sophisticated distribution structure with several intermediaries (wholesale and other middlemen) between the final seller and the customer.[51]

A third option is to 'sell to order'. The customer is organized before the product is smuggled. This has occurred in other wildlife markets. The NZ smuggler Freddie Angell first organized an Asian customer for tuatara (an extremely rare reptile), and then attempted to poach the animals.[52] 'Selling to order' has also been described for some Australian wildlife.[53] The common characteristics of this market are that it is a low-volume trade, dealing in high-value products. The low volume of this trade is likely to mean that demand is irregular.

It has been almost impossible to verify what distribution mechanism has been used to move tiger products within China. A transaction-cost economics approach would predict a mechanism that minimized coordination and evasion costs. This makes it unlikely that the legal TCM system is being used to sell tiger-bone products. A legal distribution network provides a convenient cover when the apprehension risk is low and the search costs for customers can be safely reduced. Nonetheless search costs are very high for customers, and smugglers are converting large bundles of multi-species products to a relatively small,

---

50. Brendan Moyle, 'Regulation, Conservation and Incentives', in *The Trade in Wildlife*, ed. Sarah Oldfield (London: Earthscan, 2003), 41–51.
51. Reuter and Kleiman, 'Risks and Prices'.
52. NZPA, 'Tuatara Theft Man Held in Custody', *The Press*, 4 September 1997, second edition.
53. Raymond Hoser, *Smuggled-2* (Doncaster, Kotabo Publications, 1996).

single-species product in China. This does not suggest that they are using a legal transmission system.

To date investigations like those undertaken by TRAFFIC have presumed that TCM retailers provide the mechanism to distribute tiger products. If consumers have prior knowledge of which shops sell the product, then this has the advantage of lowering the customer's search costs. Nonetheless it necessarily assumes that tiger products are being imported for speculative sales. There is good evidence that in some Western provinces this has been employed for tiger skins. The major problem with this approach is that making it easy for customers to find you also means that law enforcement agencies can do so as well. In eastern Chinese provinces there is less evidence of tiger skins for sale in shops and sales of skins are more akin to those of bone, in that these transactions do not have a fixed trading locus.

This method of buying tiger bone medicine thus imposes very high search costs on customers. It is also associated with two major risks for the participants. First, the potential customer will leave a trail of witnesses behind of either shop staff or other customers. For a product whose traffic can involve the death penalty, this creates a tip-off risk to authorities and inflates the expected sanction. There is also a risk for the shop. They have to hold stock of tiger bone on the expectation that they can sell it. This is not something that can be advertised, so they are in effect hoping for the coincidence of a customer arriving when they have the medicine in stock. If no customers arrive they are stuck with their investment in the products (financial risk). Finally, the store has to be confident that none of their staff will alert authorities. There are thus high coordination and evasion costs associated with the shops. Most of these costs can be reduced by not using TCM shops or markets. Another issue is that to sell traditional medicines a paper trail from manufacturer to retailer must be followed. It is of course not possible to *launder* poached tiger products at the moment in China because there is no legal trade that would make laundering feasible.

Hence, if there is no evidence that the legal market is being used to distribute bone (unlike skins in Tibet, Qinghai and Gansu) then an alternative distribution mechanism is likely. The penetrability of this network is likely to be very low given that the consumers will tend to be wealthy (thus can arrange private trading loci) and that trade in tiger products is probably a low frequency event. This alternative distribution network does not have to depend on import for speculative reasons.

A parallel illegal distribution system, such as one modelled on cocaine, suffers the defect of needing high setup costs. This may be economic if the volume of goods traded is sufficiently high that unit-distribution costs fall. For a low volume product the unit-distribution costs are likely to be too high. This seems to be confirmed by the small number of offenders arrested selling real tiger products. A more elaborate distribution system would require the involvement of more personnel.

The type of transactions that are being undertaken (irregular, low volume, low frequency and subject to harsh penalties if caught) imply that 'selling to order' is an appropriate organizational form for distribution. This lowers the evasion costs by committing the buyer and seller to the transaction before the goods are physically transferred. There is no readily observable evidence that a criminal act is being negotiated. The physical transfer is also easy to coordinate. A transfer at a discrete location, such as the buyer's residence, is also less risky than stocking TCM shops.

The business model used by smuggling networks may well leverage off the Chinese culture of *guanxi*. This is a system where relationships between people are developed using trust-enhancing mechanisms (such as gifts) and creates an effective insider–outsider system. Hence a smuggling cell within China based on *guanxi* ties would have low penetrability. If you are outside this *guanxi* trading relationship (as might be the case with law enforcement agents) then infiltration is going to be hindered. An existing *guanxi* network should also generate low transaction costs for marketing. For instance, such networks could buy tiger products to order and distribute to customers all insulated from scrutiny. Everything that was imported would have a pre-arranged seller. This system would also tend to make customers reluctant to reveal sources to Chinese authorities because of their personal relationship with the smugglers.

The use of a network of interconnected personal relationships to smuggle tiger products almost certainly precludes the participation of casual or poor smugglers. Such a point was practically confirmed at the TCM market in Xi'an. One trader candidly noted that they simply did not have the money to enter the tiger-part trade. Overcoming the Chinese monitoring and enforcement system requires both a high level of organization and a large capital investment (to procure the product). This, alongside the reputed high prices for bone, makes this a product that is probably restricted to the wealthier segments of Chinese society.

To summarize, the evidence on the organization of the black market in tiger products is as follows. First, poaching is done often with local cooperation by poachers who face low apprehension risk. Second, tiger-products are combined with other wildlife products, actually make up a minor physical component of the trade and are transported in bulk to the Chinese border. The low frequency of interdictions at the border shows that the risk of apprehension is very low.

Third, the Chinese black market shows strong geographical association with the closest range states. This implies that the transaction costs facing smugglers are now relatively high (otherwise they could penetrate other provinces with ease). It also probably reflects the endowment of existing trade routes and middlemen that existed prior to the ban.

There are important differences between the Chinese market for skins in the West, and the market for bones and skin in the East. The eastern provinces are characterized by small secretive conspiracies using non-specific trading loci. This reflects the now much higher risks of apprehension given the severe nature of Chinese sanctions. Tiger products are also likely to be a low-frequency trade, which further reduces the penetrability of the network. The most common means of detecting smugglers is either a chance interdiction or a tip-off from the public. Apprehension risk, like other illegal markets, appears to account for many of the organizational shifts that are being manifested in this market.

An overarching problem is that data on the black market is very poor. That has led to a number of extrapolations. An example of this is use of the India–Nepal–Tibet nexus as a model for the black market in other parts of China. This has been compounded by several instances of poor analysis. Procurement costs by poachers are often employed as an estimate of supply costs. EIA says 'A poacher in India could be paid $US1,500 for one tiger skin, whilst a trader in China may offer the same skin for as much as $US16,000 – a profit margin of over 900 percent'.[54] This inflates the profitability of poaching, and to be true assumes poachers have a costless and risk-free way of getting tiger products from reserves in Asia to Chinese consumers. Given that procurement costs make up a trivial element of other illegal products with most of the costs generated by the supply-chain, it is absurd to suggest that wildlife poachers are insulated from subsequent supply costs.

54. EIA, *Skinning the Cat*, 15.

Conclusion

It is possible to address the issues identified at the start of the paper. First, the arrest data strongly indicates that the trade is dominated by skins and bones. Other tiger parts make up an insignificant component of the trade. Second, the demand for bones is primarily driven by medicinal reasons. This medicinal demand reflects the long-standing TCM employment of tiger bones. The trade ban initiated in 1993 does not appear to have stigmatized the use of tiger parts in TCM. The high black-market prices for tigers are indicative that many consumers in China still have a high demand for these products.

The distribution of tiger parts within China remains poorly understood. The Chinese seizure data is not exhaustive but does indicate that there are regional differences. Tiger bone is more prominent in the east than the west. Tiger subspecies are generally found closest to their nearest range-state. Hence Indo-Chinese tiger parts are more common in Yunnan, Bengali in Tibet and Amur in Heilongjiang. This seizure data is not robust enough for statistical testing, however.

Smugglers appear to have a large set of options for crossing into China. Tiger parts have entered China via land, sea and air-routes. There is insufficient data to infer a preferred approach, albeit vehicles seem to be common through Nepal and Tibet. The geographical regularities in the trade point to the persistence of networks established before the ban, and the complicit involvement of border communities. The Tibetan community within China appears to provide a broad distribution network as far east as Gansu. This may mirror the way cocaine followed the migration of Colombians into the United States.[55]

Along the supply chain the criminal organization adapts the prevailing transaction costs they face. The distribution of tiger parts within China, however, remains the least understood. The logic of moving a low-volume, high-risk product would imply, however, the use of few intermediaries and discrete behaviour. This suggests that the criminal organizations within China have eschewed the use of the TCM retail system. The drug analogue here would be heroin, which also favours fewer intermediaries in response to the harsher penalties.[56]

In terms of developing anti-poaching policies, the prevailing problem is the lack of information. The ability to detect poachers in reserves is poorly developed. Successful poachers have been able to operate for lengthy periods without detection. This situation can be exacerbated by lack of or corrupt local law enforcement. A substantial commitment of resources to monitoring tiger populations and developing the support of local communities appears necessary to reduce poaching.

The benefits of increased interdiction, however, are less obvious. The border into China is very large and the criminal organizations involved have multiple entry methods and multiple entry points. There is considerable organizational scope for these conspiracies to switch entry strategies to evade detection.

There is a pressing need to develop better information about the nature of the conspiracies within China. Given that the traffic in tiger parts is already subject to very harsh punitive sanctions, increased criminal penalties are unlikely to have much impact. Increased effort at detecting the trade in tiger parts may be of value in the West. The reported sale of skins and low arrest frequency indicates that little effective deterrence has been achieved.

55. Reuter and Kleiman, 'Risks and Prices'.
56. Ibid., 292.

The original intention of the 1993 domestic ban was to reduce the demand for tiger parts. The price of tiger parts, however, has remained very high and this is consistent with a failure to stigmatize the trade. There is little basis to assume that the ban has been effective at reducing demand, albeit a reduction in the supply of tiger parts is likely. The high black-market price is consistent with a large supply effect on the market.

Education campaigns to reduce demand have been proposed. The difficulty here is in identifying the potential consumers. A blanket approach targetting the formal TCM sector may well have no effect. Existing black-market consumers may have little connection to this sector. It is also not clear what tactics will work to reduce demand. If the current consumers of tiger-products are not dissuaded by a US$50,000 price tag, a possible death sentence if caught and the knowledge that tigers are both endangered and threatened by this trade, what new information can an education campaign provide to reduce demand?

The use of tiger farms is a controversial proposal. The potential benefit is that it may cause some consumers to leave the black market and switch to the legally sourced bone. Farmed tiger-bone medicine eliminates the risk of criminal sanctions for consumers. The impact of such a policy shift will depend, however, on the distribution method employed and the types of medicines produced. For instance, limiting production to tiger-bone wine and distribution to some key TCM hospitals presents entirely different challenges to widening production and the distribution system. A restricted system would make monitoring easier and improve the barriers to laundered products.

This research, however, is not intended to identify the most effective strategies for reducing poaching. The intention is to identify what can be inferred about the organization of the black market. The reality is that conservation policy towards tigers remains poorly informed because knowledge of this black market is very incomplete. The cautionary message of this paper is that it appears to be organized along the supply chain to meet the critical transaction costs it faces. This makes it doubtful that the India–Nepalese–Tibetan nexus can be generalized to the entire black market within China, and it is also highly doubtful that the formal TCM sector provides the vehicle for the distribution of tiger parts in China. The challenges of finding information on small, secretive networks are, however, obvious. The effective deterrence of tiger poaching is going to require a better understanding of the Chinese black market.

Acknowledgements

I would like to acknowledge the Chinese State Forestry Administration for its support within China, and the Department of Commerce at Massey University for financial assistance with air-travel.

Exploring the organization of Russia Far East's illegal wildlife trade: two case studies of the illegal fur and illegal falcon trades

Tanya Wyatt[a]

[a]*University of Kent*

Introduction

Green crimes have been overlooked by criminologists and this is evident in the lack of research pertaining to the illegal wildlife trade, which experts estimate is worth between $10 and $20 billion[1] – a large variation due to the unknown shadow figure of illegal activity and the differing values used to estimate the value of wildlife and wildlife products.[2] Whereas this black market has and continues to receive focus from the conservation and biological aspects, there has been little study into the criminological aspects, such as the causes, profiles of the perpetrators, their motivations, and the political, social and cultural context influencing this crime.[3] This paper aims to fill part of the gap in this knowledge by using experts' opinions regarding two case studies – the illegal fur trade and the illegal falcon trade in Russia Far East – to explore how the illegal wildlife trade is carried out and its level of organization. From this information, the possible frameworks for these two distinctive black markets are developed. To begin, a brief overview of the illegal wildlife trade will be given. This will lead to the methodology section and then to the two case studies. Finally, the frameworks of the trades will be presented in the Discussion section.

---

1. National Zoo, *Lectures and Symposia*, http://nationalzoo.si.edu/ActivitiesAndEvents/Lectures/ (accessed 4 March 2008).
2. Dee Cook, Martin Roberts and Jason Lowther, *The International Wildlife Trade and Organised Crime: A Review of the Evidence and Role of the United Kingdom*, http://www.wwf.org.uk/filelibrary/pdf/organisedCrime.pdf (assessed 8 October 2005).
3. Greg Warchol, Linda Zupan and Willie Clack, 'Transnational Criminality: An Analysis of the Illegal Wildlife Market in South Africa', *International Criminal Justice Review* 13 (2003): 1–27.

Overview of the illegal wildlife trade

In order to describe the problem of wildlife trafficking, the specific terms used need to be defined. Wildlife is defined as any wild plant or animal, whether it is indigenous or exotic, and any derivative thereof.[4] Trade is defined as the collection, harvesting, possession, processing, acquiring or transporting of wildlife for the purpose of purchasing, importing, exporting, selling, bartering or exchanging.[5] Wildlife trafficking or the illegal wildlife trade is the specific name of the green crime that involves the illegal trade, smuggling, poaching, capture or collection of endangered species, protected wildlife (including animals or plants that are subject to harvest quotas and regulated by permits), derivatives or products thereof. The fur trade as defined in this research includes furbearing species such as the highly valued Russian sable, fox, beaver, squirrel etc., but, different from some trade definitions, also includes species that are categorized as 'skins' such as tiger, leopard and bear. In regards to the trade of falcons, the phrase 'raptor trade' is also used, as the market includes not only birds that are classified taxonomically as falcons, but also other birds of prey, such as hawks and eagles. These birds are captured for use in recreational hunting, known as either falconry or hawking.

Wildlife trafficking is a complex topic owing in part to the relationship between the legal market and the parallel illegal market. For endangered and threatened species, there can be international trade that is monitored and regulated through the Convention on the International Trade in Endangered Species of Wild Fauna and Flora (CITES). Species not listed in the appendices of CITES can be subject to national and regional monitoring and regulation and may also enter into trade. Russia is a party to CITES, so the international trade of endangered furbearing species is monitored by the CITES Secretariat, as are all falcon species since they are all endangered.[6] A complication with addressing wildlife trafficking is partly a causal one. Does legal trade provide the structure for the illicit trade? Or does banning trade altogether in certain species stimulate illegal trade? Or is it tied to the lack of enforcement of these crimes, as Moyle states: 'If the risk of being caught in violation of the regulations is not credible, then banning trade can promote wildlife decline'?[7] The issues raised by these questions will be analysed in the Discussion section for both markets.

As indicated in the Introduction, the aim of this paper is to explore the organization of the illegal wildlife trade and, since it appears to occur on a large scale, this introduces the possibility of the involvement of organized crime. Organized crime for this paper conformed to the United Nations definition: 'a structured group of three or more persons, existing for a period of time and acting in concert with the aim of committing one or more serious crimes or offences established in accordance with this Convention, in order to obtain, directly or indirectly, a financial or other material benefit'.[8] According to Interpol,

---

4. Markus Burgener, Nico Snyman and Maria Hauck, *Towards a Sustainable Wildlife Trade: An Analysis of Nature Conservation Legislation in South Africa with particular reference to the wildlife trade*, http://www.lib.uct.ac.za.criminology/sjrp (accessed 15 August 2004).
5. Ibid.
6. Convention on the International Trade of Endangered Species of Wild Flora and Fauna (CITES), *List of Contracting Parties*, http://www.cites.org/eng/disc/parties/alphabet.shtml (accessed 8 March 2006).
7. Brendan Moyle, 'Regulation, Conservation, and Incentives', in *The Trade in Wildlife: Regulation for Conservation*, ed. Sara Oldfield (London, Earthscan, 2003), 41–52.
8. United Nations, *United Nations Convention on Transnational Organized Crime*, http://www.uncjin.org/Documents/Conventions/dcatoc/final_documents_2/convention_eng.pdf (accessed 16 December 2008).

the International Criminal Police Organization, the illegal wildlife trade is tied to organized crime.[9] Poaching of endangered species and supplying them to manufacturers or the market requires some amount of organization.[10] As Ruggiero states, 'wildlife traffickers are opportunity perceivers'.[11] Cook, Roberts and Lowther relate that enforcers are convinced 'throughout the world that organized crime groups are increasingly entering the illegal wildlife trade as a low-risk and high-reward activity'.[12] Organized crime involved in the wildlife trade is said to be booming in part because of the possible exploitation of today's open borders.[13] This has particular relevance to Russia and the surrounding countries.[14] Research has found that the illegal wildlife trade is 'equally (or more) lucrative than [organized crime's] other criminal activities and considered less serious by enforcement agencies and the judiciary, hence less risky than other forms of crime, with lower penalties'.[15] Since criminology has not often engaged in a detailed examination of this topic, the exact structure of such operations is not known. In order to meet this research aim, the following methodology was employed.

Methodology

The dissertation from which this paper is derived used a multi-faceted approach to analyse a variety of aspects of the illegal trade in furs and falcons in Russia Far East. This paper presents the results from the semi-structured interviews with wildlife trade experts as to how they believed the illegal fur and falcon trades to be structured. More specifically, in-person interviews were conducted with one CITES official; international wildlife NGO officials including three employees of the Worldwide Fund for Nature (WWF) and one employee from the International Fund for Animal Welfare (IFAW); local NGO officials – one from Phoenix, and one from *Brok*; government officials in Russia including one employee of the Ministry of Hunting, one employee of the Ministry of Natural Resources and one prosecutor for crimes pertaining to biorseources; two United States government officials from the Fish and Wildlife Service (USFWS), one from the Moscow Embassy and one from the Vladivostok Embassy; one Russian hunting inspector; and two Russian academics from Far Eastern State University. This made a total of 17 in-person interviews. A further three people were contacted via email – one employee of the Russian animal rights organization Viva; one employee of the USFWS Russia Division; and one zoologist from the London Zoological Society, who was researching the Amur leopard in the field in the Far East. The CITES Senior Officer for Anti-Smuggling, Fraud and Organized Crime was interviewed by telephone. As this fieldwork was part of data collection for a doctoral thesis, the methods chosen were required to be low-risk, so the interviews were not conducted with people directly

9. Raymond E. Kendall, *Interpol Alert*, http://www.ourplanet.com/imgversn/105/kendall.html (accessed 26 November 2008).
10. Cook et al., *The International Wildlife Trade and Organised Crime*.
11. Vincenzo Ruggiero, *Organized and Corporate Crime in Europe: Offers that Can't Be Refused* (Dartmouth, Aldershot, 1996).
12. Cook et al., *The International Wildlife Trade and Organised Crime*, 14.
13. Juan Carlos Vasquez, 'Compliance and Enforcement Mechanisms of CITES', in *The Trade in Wildlife: Regulation for Conservation*, ed. Sarah Oldfield (London, Earthscan, 2003), 68.
14. Duncan Brack, 'Lessons from the Control of the Illegal Trade in Ozone-depleting Substances, Timber and Fisheries', in *The Trade in Wildlife: Regulation for Conservation*, ed. Sara Oldfield (London, Earthscan, 2003), 163–79.
15. Cook et al., *The International Wildlife Trade and Organised Crime*, 24.

involved in the illegal trade for the researcher's safety. This has resulted in a more secondary ethnographical study. The total sample of 21 people consisted of nine women and 12 men all with higher education degrees. The range of experience with illegal wildlife trade was from decades of experience – the employee of *Brok* who has been working in the field since the 1970s – to those just beginning to research the topic – the two academics, one of whom was a sociologist and the other the director of the organized crime research centre.

The questions that are pertinent to these case studies that were asked were:

1. Who is involved in the Russian illegal wildlife trade? Disorganized/organized or opportunist criminals?
2. Is illegal/legal wildlife trade isolated or combined with other crimes or illicit trades?
3. What is the mechanism of illegal/legal wildlife trade entry/exit into or from Russia?
4. Does this involve CITES permit forgery or another means of smuggling?

The answers that were elicited from these questions for each of the black markets are the main material that is presented in the following case study sections along with supplemental literature obtained in the Far East.

Illegal fur trade

The fur trade in Russia has been occurring for hundreds of years and historically is largely responsible for Russia's expansion into Siberia and the wealth of the Russian Empire at that time.[16] The Far East is still the centre of this activity and trapping is still a source of livelihood for many residents of this region. Fur harvesting is regulated through the Ministry of Hunting and Ministry of Natural Resources and endangered species, such as the Amur tiger and the Amur leopard, are protected through national legislation that complies with Russia's membership in CITES. Unlike the falcon trade, there is a legal, visible, large industry for fur that provides further regulation to the market and potentially further hurdles for the entrance of organized crime.

The first step in the operation is the capture of the furbearer. WWF Moscow report that poaching is done by people who do so in order to survive, and occurs on an individual basis.[17] The corresponding office in Vladivostok of WWF attributed poaching to the lack of other sources of income and the large amounts of money that can be made.[18] For instance, a tiger skin can be sold by a poacher for $5000. Staff at the US Embassy in Moscow and the Vladivostok NGO, *Brok*, believed that the amount of poaching and rule-breaking that was occurring was small and stemmed from poverty.[19] Poverty is more prevalent in the villages of Russia, and this corresponds to WWF Vladivostok's observation that the people engaged in poaching are inhabitants of villages, people who live in the taiga or the forest, and also official and amateur hunters.[20]

---

16. Raymond Fisher. *The History of the Russian Fur Trade 1550–1700* (Berkeley, CA: University of California Pubishers, 1943).
17. World Wide Fund for Nature (WWF) Moscow, interview with author, April 2007.
18. WWF Far East, interview with author, April 2007.
19. Deputy Counselor Officer of Environment, Science and Technology at the US Embassy in Moscow, interview with author, April 2007; Coordinator of the Russia Far East Forest Stewardship Council and Director of *Brok*, interview with author, April 2007.
20. WWF Far East, interview.

Those who illegally trade are apparently also those who legally trade. Sources indicate that often incidents of poaching involve professional hunters and trappers.[21] It challenges the claim that people poach out of poverty, but indicates relative deprivation as a more apt explanation in some cases. The staff of Phoenix gave four categories of poachers and illegal fur traders:

1. There are people that do not have money. They do not have the possibility to buy a license when they go to the forest.
2. In *Primorye*, there are 40,000 registered hunters, but there are less official licenses than that available. So there are people that can afford to buy a license, but there are not enough available. They are not poor people. They do not have the opportunity to hunt legally.
3. Another category of people is rich people for whom the fine for poaching is not that big. They are too lazy to go to the service center to get a license, and will simply pay the fine if they are caught.
4. And another category of poachers is those people who are not rich, but have some protected position or know someone. For example, a chief of police or a prosecutor knows that there will not be any sanctions against them because of their position in society. It is written in the Russian constitution that positions like that, the president etc, cannot be interfered with ... This is a problem because there are chiefs of police who engage in poaching.[22]

In the instance of legitimate trappers, the traps that they use do not always catch what the hunters want, so if something illegal is caught they sell it, sometimes by taking it to the Chinese border.[23] This is what Phoenix says can happen with tiger skins since they cannot be laundered through the legitmate fur industry like other common species.[24] According to one interviewee, illegal fur that enters China is collected by organized crime there.[25] It is feasible that this could occur for other species as well. A professional trapper told one source how he uses the same permits over and over again to take more than his licenced number of furbearers.[26] For instance, he will trap 20 squirrels, which is what his licence shows. If the inspector does not stop him and check his documents, then he will go every day and take as many squirrels up to 20 as he can, until the time when the inspector stops him and stamps the date and fills in the rest of the permit.[27] Also, this trapper hides pelts in the snow, as trapping occurs during the peak of winter when the pelts are at their fullest, showing the inspector only the proper number of skins that corresponds with the permit.[28]

These illegally obtained pelts can then become part of the legal trade during the second step in the trade of illegal fur, when they are bought by a middleman. This person supplies the fur industry, which seems to take all fur without asking questions about its origins. This is evident from the number of sable pelts each year at the Saint Petersburg fur auction

---

21. Far Eastern State University Professor, interview with author, April 2007; Phoenix, interview with author, April 2007; Hunting Inspector, interview with author, April 2007.
22. Phoenix, interview.
23. Ibid.
24. Ibid.
25. WWF Far East, interview.
26. Far Eastern State University Professor, interview.
27. Ibid.
28. WWF Far East, interview.

exceeding the number of animals that are allowed to be harvested.[29] Alternatively, the fur can also continue in the black market, as is suspected in Kamchatka, where the illegal pelts of arctic fox, sea otter and other marine mammals are then taken to Khabarovsk or Vladivostok to be smuggled out of Russia.[30] This is thought to occur in other seaside villages as well, which may even have a buyer living in the area.[31] According to sources, this portion of the smuggling is often conducted by militiamen or local administrators abusing their position.[32] There can be an additional buyer, who purchases the skins from several of the smaller regions and then smuggles them out of Russia.[33]

In the above scenarios, the initial hunting documents would be legal, but in other methods of smuggling it is the paperwork that has been forged to make an illegal animal appear to be legal. *Rosprirodnizor* stated that Customs in a few instances had called to verify that the documents of wildlife traders were authentic.[34] This was thought to be an infrequent way to smuggle, though, and staff believed that poachers mostly resort to hiding their products to transport them across the border.[35] The USFWS thought that smuggling occurs by every route possible – road, rail, river, marine and air.[36] For instance, it is known that the rivers in the Far East are used to transport contraband to China. Those obtaining fur in Kamchatka transport their goods by boat as well.[37] In the winter, when rivers and lakes are frozen, snowmobiles can be used to move contraband.[38] WWF Moscow reportted that trains often have hidden compartments, or vehicles have special places built into them to hide and smuggle wildlife and/or other contraband.[39] This can be a false bottom or compartments in the wheels.[40] Wildlife is also hidden on flights, but on planes and for other border crossings as well, smuggling is accomplished by the most common method of gaining access to transportation – that of the paid corridor.[41] In other words, bribes are used. Agencies differed in opinion with regard to whether they thought that wildlife trade was perpetrated in conjunction with other illicit trades. WWF Moscow thought that illegal wildlife trade was isolated, whereas the USFWS did not think that it was difficult to imagine wildlife trafficking being combined with drug smuggling or human trafficking.[42]

Furbearing animals are being taken in excess of governmental scientists' quotas, and endangered species that are protected under Russian federal law and international agreement are being poached. From the data collected from those working with wildlife issues, there is little indication that organized crime is involved at least in the illegal

---

29. Natalia Dronova and Alexander Shestakov, *Trapping a Living: Conservation and Socio-economic Aspects of the Fur Trade in the Russian Far East* (Moscow: WWF/TRAFFIC, 2005).
30. Sergey Lyapustin and Pavel Fomenko, *Borba s Kontrabandoy Obyektov Fauni i Flori na Dalnyem Vostokye Rossii* [The Fight with Smuggling of Fauna and Flora in Russia Far East] (Moscow: WWF, 2003), in Russian.
31. WWF Far East, interview.
32. Ibid.
33. Ibid.
34. Vladivostok Ministry of Natural Resources employee, interview with author, April 2007.
35. Ibid.
36. USFWS, interview via email with author, December 2006.
37. Lyapustin and Fomenko, *Borba s Kontrabandoy* [The Fight with Smuggling].
38. WWF Far East, interview.
39. WWF Moscow, interview.
40. WWF Far East, interview.
41. Ibid.
42. WWF Moscow, interview; USFWS, interview via email.

trading of species that are part of the licit fur market. There is speculation that, once some furs, such as tiger skins and other rare furs, cross the border into China, organized crime there plays a role in furthering the pelt in the market. This perspective is supported by other literature mentioned above. As will now be explored, the perpetration of the illegal falcon trade is organized differently.

Illegal falcon trade

As stated before, the trade in falcons is to fill the demand for birds used in the sport of falconry. All species are listed in the CITES appendices and therefore their trade is either restricted or banned. Historically, it is not known exactly where this activity was invented, but it is thought to have arisen in the Middle East or surrounding areas as an essential mode of hunting that enabled the people populating this harsh environment to survive.[43] Today, falconry is essential to very few people and has predominantly become a luxury activity of the rich.[44] CITES trade data indicate that the Middle East is a destination for falcons, but legal transactions are predominantly from captive-bred stocks. The majority of wild falcons that are legally taken from Russia are destined for Japan, though interestingly, as will be evident from the results of the interviews conducted, Japan is not mentioned by experts when discussing the illegal trade of raptors.

According to Russian ornithologists, the people responsible for the illegal falcon trade are specialists from Arab countries that have now endangered the populations of birds of prey in Russia.[45] The recorded instances of confiscations challenge this notion and offer a picture that shows a wider trend of Russians being involved in the illegal falcon trade from the beginning of the chain. Research by a former Russian Customs officer establishes a complex picture with a variety of people involved at different steps along the smuggling chain.[46] The first step in this operation, the capture of the bird of prey, appears to be perpatrated by Russians and some Middle Easterners.[47] This can be carried out by inhabitants of taiga settlements and villages, professional hunters, workers of hunting facilities and/or amateur hunters.[48] The Middle East Falcon Research Group cites that a minority of Syrian students are responsible for some of the poaching.[49] WWF Moscow and the International Fund for Animal Welfare (IFAW) claim that crime syndicates are involved in this trade, and this is facilitated through some Syrian and Lebanese students studying at Russian universities.[50] Research by WWF in Vladivostok supports that the capture of birds of prey is an organized operation.[51] In the mountains of Altai in southern Russia, reportedly, there are groups specializing in the capture of raptors.[52]

43. Lydia Ash, 'A Falconry Timeline', *The Modern Apprentice*, http://www.themodernapprentice.com/history.htm (accessed 28 August 2007).
44. Ibid.
45. Sergey Lyapustin, 'Kontrabanda Sokolov Dalnyevo Vostoka – Ugroza Suschyestvovaniyu Redkikh Ptits' [The Smuggling of Falcons of the Far East – A Threat to the Existence of Rare Birds], *Preservation of Bioresources* March (2006): 89–100, in Russian.
46. Ibid.
47. Ibid.
48. WWF Vladivostok, *Khischniye Ptitsiye* [Birds of Prey] (Vladivostok:WWF, 2006), in Russian.
49. Falco, 'The Newsletter of the Middle East Falcon Research Group', http://www.falcons.co.uk/mefrg/Falco/falcopdf/falco13.pdf (accessed 17 August 2007).
50. IFAW in Russia, interview with author, April 2007; WWF Moscow, interview.
51. WWF Vladivostok, *Khischniye Ptitsiye* [Birds of Prey].
52. Lyapustin, 'Kontrabanda Sokolov Dalnyevo Vostoka' [The Smuggling of Falcons of the Far East].

One such group consisted of four Syrians who had captured nearly 50 birds.[53] The leader was sentenced to $3\frac{1}{2}$ years in prison, and so were the Russian air transportation workers who assisted with the smuggling.[54] One media report claims that, after several arrests by Customs for the capture of falcons, the illegal trade became more professional in order to avoid inspectors.[55] The groups accomplished this through training, improving equipment and capturing falcons in more remote regions.[56] It is thought that they operate in small, closed groups of two or three people, and that they are filling orders that they have received from Moscow.[57]

After the capture of the live falcon, the bird is passed along the smuggling chain. Transportation in this process is key, and that is why the criminal network of smugglers is made up of drivers of cargo transport, personnel of the railways (mechanics, drivers, conductors), airline personnel (crew members, baggage handlers),[58] and tour firm employees.[59] In the capitals of the regions, there are specialists organizing such enterprises.[60] Russian Federal Customs officials believe that the very high profit of selling raptors attracts these international syndicates.[61]

The routes of the main smuggling operations are reported by WWF Far East in Vladivostok to be as follows – the birds leave from the northern far east airports on flights to the interior of Russia – Moscow, Novosibirsk, Yekaterinburg, Kazan and Ufa – and then on further flights to the Middle East.[62] The falcons from Kamchatka are sent by plane, and as quickly as possible because the birds fair badly in the bondage required for transportation.[63] Also, birds are smuggled on trains through Russia to the airports of Kazakhstan and Ukraine. According to WWF Far East, the following routes are used:

> Northern Kamchatka: Petropavlovsk-Kamchatka – Irkutsk – Baku – UAE/Saudi Arabia;
> Northern Kamchatka: Petropavlovsk-Kamchatka – Moscow – Baku/Yerevan – UAE;
> Northern Kamchatka: Petropavlovsk-Kamchatka – Yekaterinburg – Dubai (UAE);
> Northern Kamchatka: Petropavlovsk-Kamchatka – Novosibirsk/Moscow – Ukraine – UAE;
> Chukota: Anadir – Irkutsk – UAE;
> Magadan Oblast: Magadan – Moscow – Kazakhstan/Ukraine – UAE.[64]

Russian Federal Customs officials told the newspaper Versii that the destination for the falcons is Syria, and that they are taken first to Tajikistan.[65]

---

53. Ibid., 98.
54. Ibid., 98.
55. RIA – Siberia, 'From Siberia, Smugglers take Saker Falcons and Gyrfalcons', *Russian Agency for International Information and News*, http://ria-sibir.ru/viewnews/19836.html (accessed 10 August 2007).
56. Ibid.
57. WWF Far East, interview.
58. Ibid. WWF Moscow, interview.
59. WWF Vladivostok, *Khischniye Ptitsiye* [Birds of Prey].
60. Ibid.
61. Versii, 'Birds of Prey taken from Flight', *Versii*, http://www.versii.com/newss.php?pid=100249 (accessed 9 August 2007).
62. WWF Vladivostok, *Khischniye Ptitsiye* [Birds of Prey].
63. WWF Far East, interview.
64. WWF Vladivostok, *Khischniye Ptitsiye* [Birds of Prey].
65. Versii, 'Birds of Prey taken from Flight'.

Birds are wrapped in cloth that is taped closed, and then inserted into tubes.[66] Temperatures can reach 40°C and for birds from the far north these conditions are incredibly taxing.[67] Birds are also hidden in sports bags, under fruit and in diplomatic packages.[68] Their eyes can be sewn shut, supposedly to reduce nervousness, and once swaddled sometimes they can be packed into rigid suitcases with holes drilled in them.[69] Transport of the smuggled birds has a high mortality rate, with many dying from the stress and lack of food and water.[70] Integral to this operation is the payoffs of customs officials, other law enforcement agencies and border guards.[71] According to Phoenix, if guards cannot be bribed, there is always the chance that they will not look for live animals or ignore them if they find them.[72] This interviewee mentioned that customs agents just close their eyes because they do not know what to do, and have no way to keep illegal live animals.[73]

Interviews firmly support the literature that organized crime, as previously defined, is functioning in the illegal raptor trade. Experts thought that bird of prey smuggling was a highly organized operation involving many people. The network is transnational, running from Russia through various bordering states and most probably ending in a Middle Eastern country. The order of events from collection to buyer appears to be a simple chain. The buyer places an order for a falcon, and through the network a specially skilled collector captures the bird and passes it along the transportation route. The collector and each member of the chain only have contact with one other member, except for the organizer, who has contact with both the buyer and either the collector or a messenger, so the members do not know the other members of the criminal network. The literature and interviews did not indicate the predicted involvement of Russian organized crime. The two case studies present wildlife markets that appear to have similar characteristics that would draw organized crime, but this proves not to be the case and the reasons for this are now examined.

Discussion

From the interviews with people engaged with wildlife trade, possible frameworks were developed for these two case studies as to how the black markets of fur and falcons are organized. The result for the illegal fur trade was that this green crime is committed by individual people that are motivated not only by poverty (fur for personal use and financial reward), but also by wealthy people that take fur illegally, as a show of power, or because they are above the law due to their social status. Fur is not replaceable by another product and is an industry with legislation in place, although sometimes, as evident from the Saint Petersburg fur auction and the examples provided here, it is unregulated and unenforced. Smuggling is accomplished by simply hiding the illegally caught fur, forging permits

66. Lyapustin, 'Kontrabanda Sokolov Dalnyevo Vostoka' [The Smuggling of Falcons of the Far East].
67. Ibid.
68. Ibid.
69. Marina Kornilova, 'Falconry', *Novosibirsk Evening*, http://vn.ru/27.01.2007/crime/83716/ (accessed 13 August 2007).
70. Lyapustin, 'Kontrabanda Sokolov Dalnyevo Vostoka' [The Smuggling of Falcons of the Far East].
71. WWF Vladivostok, *Khischniye Ptitsiye* [Birds of Prey].
72. Phoenix, interview.
73. Ibid.

or misusing real permits. The fur is then sold to middlemen within the fur industry, where the illegal pelt then becomes part of the legal market. This scenario only applies to the species which can be laundered through the legal fur industry, however, such as sable, squirrel and fox. The rare and endangered skins of Amur tigers and leopards must be smuggled in a different way. In instances where the fur is smuggled out of Far East Russia, most likely to China, all modes of transport and hiding are used. Organized crime was not indicated as being involved in Russia in the laundering of illegally obtained pelts into the legitimate trade or in their trapping, but some fur smuggling does occur transnationally into China, where there is speculation by those interviewed and reports that organized crime might be involved. Further research is warranted to establish the structure of the organized crime that appears to be engaged in the smuggling of the fur of endangered species since it falls outside of the framework created here for those species that are regulated through the fur industry.

The illegal raptor trade proved to have a different structure. Falcons, too, are a commodity unable to be substituted for, and which also are affected by a lack of enforcement of the existing protective legislation. There are only two wildlife inspectors in the Far East, a region that is vast and remote, and they have little access to technology such as radios and computers.[74] The collectors might also act out of financial motivation, but a majority of the time this does not appear to be opportunistically, but at the behest of a buyer much further along the supply chain. The countries that are demanding the birds are in the Middle East, although CITES data indicates that the legal trade in wild raptors is fuelled by demand in Japan. As with the fur trade, a legal market can hide an illegal market, and therefore further exploration into falconry in Japan may be warranted. The illegal market in birds of prey is apparently run by Arab organized crime that seemingly has formed a simple chain network structure to facilitate the smuggling.

The two different structures raise the question as to why they are different. How does one wildlife commodity spur poor, opportunistic or high-status local individuals to illegally poach, and another wildlife commodity prompt a simple chain-structured network of international, organized crime? I speculate that the contrast stems from the nature of the wildlife product being traded, and in the existence or lack of a parallel legal trade, as was introduced in the Overview section. Lack of enforcement did not seem to create the difference, as both trades showed evidence that their protective legislation was not always enforced. The illegal fur trade is perpetrated by individuals already associated with the legal industry. Those poaching have the skills and equipment to trap the animals for the pelts. It seems simple for a trapper to take more than allowed, or to take something that is not allowed in the remote, mostly unchecked regions where hunting occurs. The poacher then can sell his pelts to someone within the industry who will not check too closely as to the origin of the fur, with the exception of the endangered species such as Amur tiger and leopard. Alternatively, the trapper can fairly easily take the fur across the long, unregulated border of the Far East if the opportunity arises. Either way, legitimate structures exist to further most pelts along the chain of suppliers, manufacturers etc., and what was taken illegally is lost within the legal fur market. For those exceptions, the smuggling requires further operations and appears to possibly have an organized element that must be studied further to establish its framework.

The illegal falcon trade has a different set of circumstances. Essentially, there is no legal industry through which illegally obtained birds can be laundered. This means that

74. Phoenix, interview.

each step of the process must be concealed. The effort to capture, smuggle and transport live falcons and then bribe people must be coordinated. This requires a great deal of organization, thus the niche is filled by organized crime. Other wildlife trades with similar dynamics will have to be examined in order to determine if these frameworks will stand. For instance, the illegal trade in timber could be compared with the illegal fur trade and more detailed examination of the black market in Amur tiger and Amur leopard skins could be compared with the illegal falcon trade. The frameworks established here hopefully contribute to further research into wildlife trafficking, which is necessary not only because of the threat it poses to national and human security, but also because of the danger it poses to the environment and wildlife, which have a value beyond their instrumental worth to humans.

Acknowledgements

I wish to thank the reviewers of *Global Crime* and Dr Martin Bouchard in particular for their comments and help in the writing of this article.

Index

Page numbers in *Italics* represent tables.
Page numbers in **Bold** represent figures.

For Product Safety Concerns and Information please contact our EU
representative GPSR@taylorandfrancis.com
Taylor & Francis Verlag GmbH, Kaufingerstraße 24, 80331 München, Germany

www.ingramcontent.com/pod-product-compliance
Lightning Source LLC
LaVergne TN
LVHW021109300926
849160LV00009B/664

* 9 7 8 0 4 1 5 6 3 3 9 7 0 *